The Oregon Literature Series

General Editor: George Venn
Managing Editor: Ulrich H. Hardt

Volume 3: Oregon Prose

A project of the Oregon Council of Teachers of English

The Oregon Literature Series

The World Begins Here: An Anthology of Oregon Short Fiction
        Glen A. Love

Many Faces: An Anthology of Oregon Autobiography
        Stephen Dow Beckham

Varieties of Hope: An Anthology of Oregon Prose
        Gordon B. Dodds

From Here We Speak: An Anthology of Oregon Poetry
        Primus St. John & Ingrid Wendt

The Stories We Tell: An Anthology of Oregon Folk Literature
        Suzi Jones & Jarold Ramsey

Talking on Paper: An Anthology of Oregon Letters & Diaries
        Shannon Applegate & Terence O'Donnell

Varieties of Hope
An Anthology of Oregon Prose

Gordon B. Dodds

Oregon State University Press
Corvallis, Oregon

Dedication

For Linda Dodds, reader and writer of Oregon prose, with much love

Cover art: "Light Changes" by Carol Riley, watercolor and pencil.
Photograph by Jim Stoffer
Cover design: John Bennett
Text design: Jo Alexander
Permissions: Susanne Shotola
Art photographer: Susan Seubert

The paper in this book meets the guidelines for permanence and durability of the Committee on Production Guidelines for Book Longevity of the Council on Library Resources and the minimum requirements of the American National Standard for Permanence of Paper for Printed Library Materials Z39.48-1984.

Library of Congress Cataloging-in-Publication Data

Varieties of hope : an anthology of Oregon prose / [edited by] Gordon B. Dodds.
    p. cm. -- (The Oregon literature series : v. 3)
    Includes bibliographic references and index..
    Summary: A collection of prose writings which present the hopes and expectations of many Oregonians from varied time periods and cultural backgrounds.
    ISBN 0-87071-373-6 (cloth : alk. paper). -- ISBN 0-87071-374-4 (paper : alk. paper)
    1. American prose literature—Oregon. 2. Oregon—Literary collections. [1. Oregon—Literary collections.] I. Dodds, Gordon B. (Gordon Barlow), 1932- . II. Series.
    PS571.O7V37   1993
    818'.08--dc20   93-11479
                                                 CIP
                                                   AC

Acknowledgments

Without steady collaboration by many individuals, agencies, and institutions, the *Oregon Literature Series* would never have appeared in print. We wish to recognize those who contributed support, time, and resources here—more or less in the order in which their contributions were received—and knowing even now that the real evidence of our gratitude lies open before all of them.

In 1986, the Executive Committee of the Oregon Council of Teachers of English (OCTE) began to discuss the idea of publishing a collection of Oregon literature. We wish to identify the members of that Executive Committee and thank them for their pioneering role: Lauri Crocker, Joe Fitzgibbon, Robert Hamm, Ulrich Hardt, Michelann Ortloff, and Ed Silling. Under then-OCTE President Ulrich Hardt, the Publications Committee was given the goal to further develop the idea of a state-based literary collection.

In 1988-89, the Executive Board of OCTE approved the pilot study by George Venn which became the *Oregon Literature Series*. We would like to recognize the members of that distinguished professional group of teachers by listing them here: Brian Borton, Sister Helena Brand, Suzanne Clark, Darlene Clarridge, Elaine Cockrell, Edna De Haven, Joe Fitzgibbon, Robert Boyt Foster, David Freitag, Debra Gaffney, Tim Gillespie, Irene Golden, Robert Hamm, Ulrich H. Hardt, Martha House, Ilene Kemper, Debbie LaCroix, Bill Mull, Thomas Nash, Debby Norman, Michelann Ortloff, Phyllis Reynolds, Eldene Ridinger, Mei-Ling Shiroishi, Andy Sommer, Daune Spritzer, Kim Stafford, Lana Stanley, Kathy Steward, Paul Suter, Nathaniel Teich, Linda Vanderford, George Venn, Michael Wendt, and Barbara Wolfe. Many members of that board gave many extra hours to reviewing the design, editorial guidelines, rationale, and budgets for that pilot project and other documents.

We would also like to acknowledge the following individuals from Oregon's literary and humanities community who reviewed the pilot proposal, made valuable suggestions, and gave their endorsement in 1988 to the idea of a collection of the best Oregon writing: Richard Lewis, Oregon Council for the Humanities; Brian Booth, Oregon Institute of Literary Arts; Peter Sears, Oregon Arts Commission; Jo Alexander, Oregon State University Press; Bruce Hamilton, Oregon Historical Society. OCTE President in 1988, Tim Gillespie, and Joe Fitzgibbon, OCTE President Elect, also reviewed the pilot proposal and made important contributions not only in these early stages but throughout the project.

When we presented the completed proposal for the *Oregon Literature Series* to the Editorial Board of Oregon State University Press in 1989, they broke with all precedent by signing a guaranteed publication contract and by agreeing to turn over editorial control of the content of the *Oregon Literature Series* to OCTE editors and appointees. We want to thank both press editors, Jeff Grass and Jo Alexander, and the members of that board who voted unanimously in favor of this project: Pat Brandt, Larry Boersma,

Richard Maxwell Brown, Bill Denison, Gordon Dodds, Mike Strelow, Dave Perry, Sandy Ridlington, and the late Marilyn Guin. Without their vote for collaboration and its implicit vote of confidence in us, we would have found it difficult to continue this project.

Our first financial support beyond OCTE was provided by a pilot grant from Eastern Oregon State College, School of Education. Specifically, we wish to thank Deans Jens Robinson, Gerald Young, and James Hottois for their willingness to grant a sabbatical and three years of part-time appointments to George Venn so that this project could be undertaken. At Portland State University, we want to thank Dean Robert Everhart, School of Education, for his steadfast support. He granted Ulrich Hardt a sabbatical to help launch the project, and he continued that support throughout the four years of the project. At Portland State University, we also want to acknowledge Interim Provost Robert Frank and Provost Michael Reardon for the faith they showed in the project by assigning graduate assistant Susanne Shotola to help us.

When we drafted our "Call for Editors" in 1989, we received helpful critiques from Kim Stafford, Edwin Bingham, Paul Suter, Sister Helena Brand, Edna DeHaven, Daune Spritzer, Lana Stanley, Michelann Ortloff, as well as other members of the OCTE Executive Board. When it was time to mail that "Call for Editors" to all Oregon libraries, newspapers, and other regional and national media, Lana Stanley assisted us. When it was time to select Volume Editors, these Publications Committee members assisted us: Robert Hamm, Marti House, Ilene Kemper, Debbie LaCroix, Mei-Ling Shiroishi, Michael Wendt, and Linda Vanderford. We'd like to thank them for the many hours they gave to evaluating the applications of 130 highly qualified individuals from Oregon and across the U.S. who applied for or were nominated for editorships.

When we needed to verify that these anthologies would, indeed, be both needed and used in the public schools, Portland State University School of Business Administration faculty member Bruce Stern gave us important assistance in designing a survey instrument which demonstrated a clear demand for the *Oregon Literature Series* in Oregon schools and homes. When we needed public relations expertise during editorial appointments, Pat Scott in the Portland State University Public Relations Office provided it.

When we needed legal advice, Leonard DuBoff and his firm of Warren, Allan, King, and O'Hara were more than helpful in contributing their contractual expertise.

As the project began to take a clear and definite shape in 1989, we received formal endorsements from these individuals whose confidence in the project made it possible to continue in spite of meager funding: Wes Doak, Oregon State Librarian, and Director, Center for the Book; Brian Booth, Director of Oregon Institute of Literary Arts; Kim Stafford, Director of the Northwest Writing Institute at Lewis and Clark College; Jennifer Hagloch, President of the Oregon Museums Association; Richard Lewis, Executive Director, Oregon Council for the Humanities; Joanne Cowling, President of the Eastern Oregon Library Association; Leslie Tuomi, Executive Director of the Oregon Arts Commission; Peter Sears, Oregon Arts Commission; Michael K. Gaston, President, Oregon Library Association; John Erickson, State Superintendent of Public

Instruction; Carolyn Meeker, Chair, Oregon Arts Commission; Carolyn Lott, Chair, National Council of Teachers of English (NCTE) Committee on Affiliates; Shirley Haley-James, president-elect of NCTE; William Stafford, Oregon's past poet laureate; and Terry Melton, Director of the Western States Arts Foundation.

Essential financial support after 1989 came first from a generous allocation from the OCTE Executive Board. Later, we received modest one-time contributions from the Oregon Center for the Book and the Jackson Foundation. We would also like to state that this project was made possible—in part—by two minor grants from the Oregon Arts Commission.

Our sustaining patrons in the final four years (1990-94) of the project have been five; each of them contributed amounts in five figures so that the *Oregon Literature Series* could be completed in a timely and professional manner:

(1) the OCTE Executive Board, who sustained and underwrote us when regional foundations failed us;

(2) the Oregon Council for the Humanities, an affiliate of the National Endowment for the Humanities, which made and honored an exemplary three-year commitment ably administered by Robert Keeler;

(3) the National Endowment for the Arts, Literature Program, which assisted us at a time when we had been sent begging by all but one of the private foundations in Oregon;

(4) Portland State University, which granted multi-year support for graduate assistant Susanne Shotola to help with the many details of the publication of this six-volume series;

(5) Oregon State University Press, where Jo Alexander and Jeff Grass contributed the vital tasks agreed to in 1989—designing, printing, and distributing these volumes. OSU Press set a national precedent by becoming the first university press in the United States to publish a multi-volume, comprehensive collection of a state's literature in the same state as the university press.

When we came to recommending graphics and cover designs for the *Oregon Literature Series* in 1992, we welcomed the generous and expert advice of three of Oregon's most knowledgeable art historians: Ron Crosier, Portland Public Schools; Gordon Gilkey, Curator, Portland Art Museum; and Nancy Lindburg, arts consultant and former staff member of the Oregon Arts Commission. Some of the works they recommended were selected by them from the slide inventory in Oregon's Percent for Art in Public Places Program. Other works were chosen from the Gordon and Vivian Gilkey Collection of Prints and Drawings at the Oregon Art Institute, and from the Institute's collection of photographs. Petroglyph images were provided by James L. Hansen from sites flooded by The Dalles dam. In addition to those three individuals, we were also fortunate to attract the services of John Bennett, book designer and publisher at Gardyloo Press in Corvallis, who collaborated on all features of the graphic design, and created covers for these volumes.

No literary project of this magnitude can be accomplished without skillful and reliable staff. The General and Managing Editors would like to express their profound appreciation to Susanne Shotola and Barbara Wiegele—both of Portland State University—for their patient, professional, and timely attention to thousands of pages of details during the past four years: keeping accurate records, handling all permissions and finances, doing all the copying, typing, and mailing. We thanked them during the project and here we want to thank them again. Thank you, too, to Gayle Stevenson, editorial assistant at OSU Press, for many hours of patient labor on this project.

Unfortunately, this naming of our benefactors will be incomplete. We cannot list here all of those writers, families, and institutions who waived permissions fees, those innumerable librarians, archivists, storytellers, and historians who have safeguarded many of these pieces of writing for more than 100 years, those many who sent us notes of encouragement, those members of the public press who considered this project worthy of coverage. What we can say, however, is that every contribution moved us one page closer to the volume you now hold in your hands. Those others who failed us when we needed them most—they may eat—well?—cake?

Finally, George Venn would like to thank his wife, Elizabeth, who has tolerated great financial sacrifice for four years and who has begun to wonder about this tough, miserly Oregon muse her husband seems to have been serving at the expense of his art and her budget. Also, Ulrich Hardt would like to thank his wife, Eleanor, for her insights and interest in this project as Social Studies Specialist for Portland Public Schools, and for being more patient than could have been expected and tolerant of being alone many evenings and weekends while he was occupied with editorial responsibilities.

Ulrich Hardt, Managing Editor   *George Venn, General Editor*
Portland State University   *Grande Ronde Valley, Oregon*
Portland and Stuttgart

September 1992

Editor's Acknowledgments

This edition of Oregon prose writing is the work of many devotees of its genres. Foremost among them is George Venn, the general editor of the *Oregon Literature Series*, whose impressive knowledge of Oregon writing furnished many of the selections, and whose enthusiasm and energy were unflagging sources of inspiration in the difficult days of the winnowing process. Ulrich Hardt, the managing editor of the series, contributed many useful suggestions about possible choices, and devised a valuable ranking system for them. Susanne Shotola, editorial assistant, helped in many ways: in preparing copy, in conducting bibliographical and biographical research, and in facilitating communication among the volume and series editors. She discharged the obligations of her demanding post with apparent effortlessness and evident cheerfulness. My fellow volume editors, Shannon Applegate, Stephen Dow Beckham, Suzi Jones, Glen Love, Terence O'Donnell, Jarold Ramsey, Primus St. John, and Ingrid Wendt, contributed much useful advice about distinguishing between the literary wheat and tares. They also, especially Shannon Applegate, brought many authors to my attention. The volume gained strength from the suggestions of its advisory board, Kay Atwood, Edwin R. Bingham, Patricia Brandt, Jeannine Douglas, Tim Gillespie, and Michael Strelow, men and women drawn from a variety of walks, but bound by their love of Oregon prose. Tim Gillespie, in particular, was helpful in diversifying the contents of the book. Brian G. Booth, out of his vast knowledge of the literature of his native state, suggested several writers whom I had overlooked. Others, too numerous to mention specifically, suggested possible contributors. Kelly Cannon and Patricia Erdenberger gave valuable assistance in research. The staff of the libraries of Multnomah County, the Oregon Historical Society, and Portland State University were courteous, resourceful, and tenacious in helping locate prospective selections. I am grateful to all of these students of Oregon literature for their assistance and am hopeful that this volume worthily reflects their interest and their effort.

Gordon B. Dodds

Contents

List of Art

General Introduction

T he idea for the *Oregon Literature Series*, six anthologies of the best Oregon writing, was first proposed to the Oregon Council of Teachers of English (OCTE) in 1988. At that time, OCTE decided to depart from the conventional state literary anthology—a monolithic tome put together by a few academic volunteers and generally intended for libraries and adult readers. Instead, OCTE decided to create six shorter, genre-based anthologies: prose, poetry, autobiography, folk literature, letters and diaries, and short fiction. OCTE would publish a public "Call for Editors," and the most qualified individuals would be hired for their expertise and treated professionally—honoraria, expenses, research assistance, travel, etc. The anthologies would be intended as classroom/reference texts for students and teachers, and as introductory readers for the general public. Books would be designed to be easily held, carried, and read.

Numerous arguments were raised against this innovative proposal—most of them signaling Oregon's 150-year status as a literary colony. *No one had ever done this before. Oregon's literature was non-existent. There wasn't much writing of merit. Most scholars and critics have ignored Oregon literature—even in the best histories of Western literature. There's no literary history of Oregon. It will take years to find this work. In Oregon, literature has the least financial support of all the major arts. We had no publisher. It might rain.*

Nevertheless, in 1989, Ulrich Hardt and I were appointed by OCTE to complete the *Oregon Literature Series.* The work began when we signed a publication contract with Oregon State University Press, our first and most important professional collaborator. Next, from a pool of 130 applicants, OCTE chose these editors to discover Oregon's literary heritage: Shannon Applegate, Stephen Dow Beckham, Gordon B. Dodds, Primus St. John, Suzi Jones, Glen A. Love, Terence O'Donnell, Jarold Ramsey, and Ingrid Wendt. Appointed in August 1990, those individuals began the search for Oregon writing that eventually spread beyond every corner of the state—from ranch houses to university archives, from oral storytellers in longhouses to Chinese miners in museums, from Desdemona Sands to Burns. Some editors traveled thousands of miles. Others corresponded with hundreds of authors. Most read thousands of pages. Poets, historians, folklorists, critics, scholars, teachers, and editors—they all benefited from and shared their research expertise. Even though honoraria were small, editors gave generously of their time. While the editors looked for Oregon writing, Ulrich Hardt and I sought out and received endorsements from many major cultural and arts organizations. Financial support was like rain in the time of drought, but we attracted a few wise, faithful, and generous patrons, as the Acknowledgments record.

Once the editors had discovered this vast, unstudied, and unknown body of writing, they assembled their manuscripts by using the following guidelines—guidelines that required them to choose writing—in its broadest sense—that might reveal the Oregon experience to both students and the public:

1. The volume must include a representative sample of the best Oregon writing from all periods, regions, occupations, genders, genres and sub-genres, ethnic, religious, political, and cultural backgrounds.

2. Oregon birth should not be used as a single criterion for inclusion. Oregon residence is important, but no arbitrary length of stay is required for a writer to be included.

3. Works about experience in Oregon are preferred, but editors are not limited to that criterion alone.

4. "Oregon" will be defined by its changing historical boundaries—Native American tribal territories, Spanish, Russian, British, U.S. Territory, statehood.

5. One or more translations and original from non-English languages should be included when appropriate to show that linguistic multiplicity has always been a part of Oregon.

6. Controversial subjects such as sexism and racism should not be avoided. Multiple versions of events, people, and places should be included when available.

7. Length of works must vary; limit the number of snippets when possible. Meet the need for diversity in reading, from complex to simple.

8. New, unknown, or unpublished work should be included.

9. Works will be edited for clarity but not necessarily for correctness. Editors may invent titles, delete text, and select text as appropriate and with appropriate notation.

Once assembled in draft, most of these manuscripts were two to three times longer than could be published by Oregon State University Press, therefore much fine writing had to be omitted, which all editors and our publisher regret. After being reduced to the requisite size, the manuscripts passed through two separate reviews: first, a different Advisory Board for each volume read and rated all selections; second, the Editorial Board composed of all fellow editors read, responded, and eventually voted to adopt the manuscript for publication. At all stages, both Ulrich Hardt and I worked closely with editors in many ways: readers, critics, fundraisers, administrators, arbitrators, secretaries, grant writers, researchers, coordinators, pollsters.

Now, we hope that these books will create for Oregon literature a legitimate place in Oregon schools and communities, where the best texts that celebrate, invent, evaluate, and illuminate the Oregon condition have been invisible for too long. Here, for the first time, students will have books that actually include writing by Oregonians; teachers can find original, whole, local, and authentic texts from all regions, periods, and peoples in the state; librarians will be able to recommend the best reading to their patrons; the new reader and the general reader can find answers to the question that has haunted this project like a colonial ghost: "Who are Oregon's writers, anyway?"

Let it be known that an Oregon literary canon is forming—rich, diverse, compelling. Here we give this sample of it to you. Let your love of reading and writing endure.

George Venn, General Editor
Grande Ronde Valley, Oregon
September 1992

The Varieties of Hope

Oregonians are all immigrants or descendants of immigrants. About 15,000 years ago, adventuresome if anonymous migrants crossed the land bridge from Siberia to become the first Oregon pioneers. Ever thereafter Oregon has remained a place of hope where men and women have sought secular redemption through casting off their burdens of misfortunes and mistakes by escaping into a new beginning. Yet all who have come to the new land have not shared the same hopes. Instead, Oregonians have possessed "varieties of hope."*

Hopes, indeed, are the subject of this book. It provides—through the medium of nonfiction prose—a selection of literature that illustrates how men and women of various cultures, occupations, and classes, from diverse geographic regions and different periods of time, have pursued their disparate goals in the land of opportunity. To organize biography, essay, history, and journalism about Oregon, the volume is arranged in seven thematic categories—from community to individualism—that recur throughout Oregon history and unify our common experiences. The major purpose of this volume, however, is to challenge readers to answer the questions: "What did men and women hope for in Oregon?" and "What happened to these hopes once they put down roots in their new homeland?"

If Oregonians' hopes have been infinitely varied, so are the roles and purposes of the prose authors who write of them. Readers of this volume will discover biographers, reporters, satirists, orators, advocates, interpreters, and promoters, each pursuing a different genre, each contributing to the clash of voices that mark democracy. After all, prose is the medium for discourse in a democracy. Indeed, prose is like democracy itself, which—as Plato wrote—"is a charming form of government, full of variety and disorder, and dispensing a sort of equality to equals and unequals alike." The purposes of these contributors to the common dialogue vary richly. Readers will see, for example, James DePreist advocating government aid for the arts, Frances Fuller Victor remembering the mountain man Joe Meek, Alice Day Pratt reporting on the Pendleton Roundup, H.L. Davis and James Stevens criticizing Oregon's literary taste, Chief Joseph defending his people, Barry Lopez teaching about Nature, and Ursula Le Guin describing the eruption of Mt. St. Helens.

From the first Siberian immigrants to the latest Californian seeking a job in the electronics industry, newcomers' hopes for a more fulfilling life have always been attainable only in company with others. While individualism contributed to the Oregon experience, no one walked the trails alone. So, at all times,

---

* This is a phrase taken from Kim Stafford's *December Meditation at Camp Polk Cemetery,* which appears in Section V of this anthology.

community helps define the scope of individual freedom. Thus, the first section of this volume contains selections illustrating the lives of Oregonians as they celebrate, work, and play. Authors deal with Portland's Rose Festival, the Pendleton Roundup, and the Portland Trailblazers, all community events and spectator galas. In another piece readers see and hear the Oregon fiddling community, whose play is their work while others dance. Oregonians at work are represented by writing about the earliest Euro-American occupations, the extractive industries of fur trade and lumbering and farming, and the newer professions such as health care in the nursing home. One writer describes her pleasure in living in Portland, the state's largest city, while a sympathetic federal bureaucrat criticizes the horrors of the involuntary community of the Indian reservation imposed upon the native peoples. In all of these community endeavors no one planned or wanted them to go wrong. Yet not all succeeded, and authors of these selections raise the questions of why some efforts bear fruit, while others wither. Is it something about the natural or social environment? The quality of leadership? The times? What determines whether a particular community's hopes are fulfilled or fail?

For most of its people most of the time, Oregon has been a peaceful place. First the Native Americans, then the peoples of Northern European stock, were the largely unchallenged majority. Nature was generous, history kind, and peace normal. Yet this calm is illusory, for not all Oregonians have resembled one another either in earlier eras or today. When the first territorial census was taken in 1850, 7.6 per cent of Oregon's citizens were foreign born. By 1900 this percentage was 15.9. In the first half century, substantial numbers of African Americans, Chinese and Japanese joined the Native-American and Caucasian peoples, although in 1900 the white population composed 95.4 per cent of the state's population. Almost 100 years later, the 1990 census records a population 92.8 per cent white, 4 per cent Hispanic, 2.4 per cent Asian, 1.6 per cent African American, and 1.4 per cent Native American. (The combined figure is more than 100 percent because Hispanic people may also choose to be included in other categories.) The foreign-born population is 4.9 per cent. Although probably every country in the world is represented in contemporary Oregon, the source of the majority of its people is ultimately Northern Europe: Germany, the Scandinavian countries, and the United Kingdom.

Today, as for generations, more people migrate to the United States than to all other countries of the world combined. Oregon has always been a part of that heritage of hope. Yet if expectations drove the newcomers to Oregon, conflict greeted them, for one of the great paradoxes of the land of opportunity is that each new wave of minority migrants, as well as the original inhabitants, confronted prejudice and discrimination in their chosen homeland. Some—discouraged, frustrated, alienated—fled homeward. Most stayed. A few accepted their lot passively, but almost all refused to be compliant victims.

Writers in the second part of this book, "Liberty and Justice for All: Oregon's Heritage of Conflict and Diversity," record the struggle by minority groups for economic, political and social opportunities. Here we see Native-American historians, reporters, critics, and advocates celebrating the original culture, calling for its renewal, listening to the white man's promises, and resisting their betrayal. Black American voices, eloquent, sorrowful, sarcastic, critics of hopes denied, advocates for hopes promised, speak of their people's achievements and their passion for justice. Japanese Americans chronicle the trials and accomplishments of the Issei and testify to their belief in the promises of America in spite of the flagrant discrimination they and their children were forced to endure. Readers may wish to speculate why those who have suffered so much for so long have the courage and tenacity to maintain their hopes as they go about their daily rounds.

Oregonians have faced conflict and contention in realms other than ethnicity and race. Three writers recount them in this book. One famous rebellion was a cultural one. Enraged by the complacency and commercialism of Oregon's literary establishment, James Stevens and H.L. Davis wrote a fiery and influential manifesto in 1927, *Status Rerum*, which satirized the leading poets, novelists, and teachers of creative writing in the state. A quarter of a century later, another pervasive controversy flared that caught up all literate citizens: urban and rural, majority and minority, conservative and progressive, not only in Oregon but across the United States. "McCarthyism," named for Senator Joseph R. McCarthy of Wisconsin, spread the fear that Soviet agents or domestic Communists were penetrating American governmental institutions, schools, universities, and religious denominations. To strike at this perceived threat, public and politicians rushed into law measures ranging from immigration restrictions to loyalty oaths. In "The Day We Passed the Oath Bill," Richard Neuberger, a journalist and legislator, describes the pressures brought upon him as an Oregon legislator to vote for a loyalty oath for teachers. As critics and reporters, all of these controversial writers cared deeply about social ills. But why did they bother writing about them? What could a writer do about social dislocations in a democracy? What hopes convinced them that their prose would be persuasive, could bring good of evil?

Oregonians have always been intimately connected with the natural environment. The native peoples found all of nature economically valuable and spiritually informed. Animals, waters, trees, plants, and birds gave them physical sustenance. Whether living on the Pacific Coast, or in the table lands of Southern Oregon, the Columbia River Valley, the Wallowas, or the semi-arid central and southeastern regions, the natural environment contributed fish and game, roots and berries and nuts. Nature, and the myths and legends that native storytellers invented, served non-material purposes as well, explaining creation, recording history, and inculcating values. The latercomers, Caucasians, African Americans,

Asian Americans, and Hispanics also bound themselves to nature and, in their myths and legends, celebrated, justified, and explained their relationship to the worldly environment. Fur traders, farmers, cattlemen, loggers, and fishermen regarded nature as a source of economic profit. The aboriginal peoples, and later painters, sportsmen, and tourists also found recreational, aesthetic and spiritual values in association with nature. In spite of hope that nature would provide wealth or peace or insight, none of these writers and storytellers could deny that the environment also had a frustrating, destructive, even terrifying side. Bad weather killed crops, floods washed away property and lives, volcanic eruptions destroyed life and order with their ash and lava.

Prose writers treat the natural environment in two successive sections, "Responding to Nature" and "All Creatures Great and Small." Although there is some overlap between the two, the first part contains writers who reflect on the natural world while the second includes writers who describe its inhabitants. Further, each of these writers has a different purpose and a different technique in presenting the world. Appropriately, the earliest written essay is an explanation of geology, Thomas Condon's description of his fossil discoveries in central Oregon that contributed to the great national debate over Charles Darwin's evolutionary theories. As a scientist, Condon sees the world as a place that rational, objective observers can make sense of. Anne Shannon Monroe's romantic response to the lake fronting her summer cottage is the work of an escapist seeking solace in the country from the abrasions of urban life. In Barry Lopez's sensitive suggestions about introducing children to the natural environment, he sees nature as a spiritual teacher. Ursula Le Guin deals with the destructiveness of nature, as a world to be respected if not feared, while William O. Douglas pleads for the preservation of a unique part of Oregon that he hopes will be saved for his children and his children's children. Douglas wants nature to be protected and admired, not used for gain.

Oregon's first great extractive industry was the fisheries, but men and women have also come from around the world to fish its waters for sport. As an anadromous fish that cyclically returns to its birthplace to spawn and die after years in the ocean, the salmon has captured the fancy of writers, scientists, and ordinary citizens as well as fishermen. No one has written more accurately or more colorfully about the salmon than Roderick Haig-Brown, who provides a fictional biography of an individual fish, "Spring the Salmon." Ben Hur Lampman describes the joyful reactions to the annual arrival of the eulachon ("the smelt") in the Sandy River. Yet many who deal with fish do so not under the open skies, but in canneries, a life that journalist Barbara Garson captures in "Tuna Fish," a chronicle of women workers. Joaquin Miller presents a delightful essay on bears, while Barbara Drake tells of city people introduced to the art of lambing. Although all the writers in the two sections about the natural environment share the belief that men and women are both a part of, and apart from, nature, they differ on the questions to be asked of nature. They also differ on the vital question of our time: can we hope to maintain a constructive rather than a destructive tension between humanity and the environment?

The Oregon Trail is one of the great epics of our national experience: the exodus from failures and frustrations on Middle Western farms to progress and fulfillment on the broad and fertile prairies of the Willamette Valley. The overlanders, more than most other people, personify the meaning of Oregon as a land of opportunity. The images of the covered wagon, the encircling Indians, and the pioneer family have seared themselves into the national consciousness. Separated by many generations, two members of the same family open the section "Opportunities in a New Land," by providing their perspectives on the great migration. Jesse Applegate, who crossed the trail in 1843, captures the sweat and dirt of a "Day With the Cow Column." His words are those of a eulogist attempting to impress upon a later generation the worthiness of a generation he called "men of destiny." His descendant Shannon Applegate also wants a later generation to remember by providing the less-known perspective of the female overlanders who were not struggling hopefully forward to reach new land, but looking sorrowfully backward at their old homes. Another who crossed the trail was Harvey Scott, the longtime editor of the *Oregonian*. In "Cure for Drones," Scott editorializes against the public high school as a useless institution that would create lazy and dependent students. His words are those of a critic who believes that his thoughts—although expressing disenchant- ment—will be so persuasive that society will address his concerns. Dorothy Johansen, a modern historian, depicts the Oregon migrants collectively, assess- ing their varied motives and comparing their aspirations with contemporary Californians heading for the gold fields. Kim Stafford concludes this section with a eulogy for a group of men and women some of whom did not find opportunity and success in the Oregon Country. "December Meditation at Camp Polk Cemetery" is his moving memorial to volunteer soldiers. Writers throughout this section raise the question of why Oregon met the hopes of only some who migrated to her.

Oregonians have been unsuccessful escapists. Most have come to the land of opportunity not only because of its attractive features, but also to flee crowding, disease, pollution, and violence elsewhere. Yet their new home has never provided relief from the pressures of the outside world. The Native Americans' life was disrupted repeatedly, first by the explorers who publicized their homeland for fur traders, missionaries, and farmers who brought encroachment on natural resources, disease, war, and ultimately, confinement on reservations. The maritime explorers and fur traders, who began this process of disruption, were all in the employ of the Spanish or British governments or New or Old England capitalists, men who brought the region into the orbit of international business. The maritime traders gave way to the beaver trappers, frontiersmen working for London, Montreal, or New York firms. Meriwether Lewis and William Clark, the first United States government explorers in the Oregon

Country, opened the region in time to the Christian missionaries and the pioneer farmers. Although Oregon enjoyed a long period of sustained and tranquil growth for about fifty years after statehood in 1859, the twentieth century, marked by the First World War, the Great Depression, another world war, the civil rights movement, and the Cold War gave Oregonians no place to hide from national and international pressures.

Several writers examine a few of these pressures from outside in a section entitled "Oregon and the World." It begins with a historical legend, the Chinook Indians' memory of their first glimpse of the European ships and their premonition of what they would bring. Frances Fuller Victor, in another historical piece, writes of the pioneers' desire for a formal government in her description of the journey of the colorful frontiersman Joe Meek to Washington, D.C., to request the President and Congress to create an Oregon Territory to protect life and property against those who were here first. Seventy-five years later, after the slaughter of the First World War, Americans vowed that their country should never again participate in war. In the 1930s, as the news from Europe and Asia became more ominous, Ronald Callvert's editorial, "My Country 'Tis of Thee," encapsulated Americans' illusion that they were safe from another cataclysm. But once in war, Americans demanded total commitment for the military effort. Those who refused to participate for philosophical or religious reasons were relegated to alternative service camps for conscientious objectors. Some of these dissenters were writers, men whose work profoundly affected America's cultural life after the war, as described in journalist David Johnson's "The Shadow of Camp Waldport."

The practically total support that the Second World War commanded was never gained in America's longest war, the Vietnam conflict. This war became increasingly unpopular as enormous casualties produced no tangible results. Dissent mounted to a cacophony of protest based on a variety of grounds. One of the objectors, Senator Wayne Morse, in his "Speech on the Tonkin Resolution," argued that American participation in the war violated international law. Concurrent with the war was the climax of something of far more enduring moment, the civil rights crusade. Journalist William Hilliard's retrospective essay, "King Pierced the Armor," captures the influence upon one Oregonian of its great leader, Martin Luther King, Jr. Symphony Director James DePreist's plea for continuing appropriations for the arts, "Missiles and Mozart," concludes this section with another dimension of the federal influences upon the state. Oregon's mythmakers, historians, journalists, orators, witnesses, and advocates all recognize the influence of the world upon their world. They respond with a twofold hope: to escape the world and to embrace the world, neither option fully satisfactory, neither completely possible.

Oregonians often see themselves as individualists. While our citizens tend to overemphasize this quality in their history, there *is* an individualistic element within the Oregon character. Writers in the final section of this anthology deal with a few of the men and women who have stood out in the state's political and cultural development. They include *ordinary people*, as the world defines the term, but who are indeed extraordinary: as family members, in the world of work, and in the teeth of community hostility or indifference. Here appear portraits of journalists, members of minority groups, writers, physicians, workers, and families. Chief Joseph, Abigail Scott Duniway, and Ken Kesey are among the household names, while others—far less known—demonstrate the courage or persistence or grace that stamp them as truly distinctive individuals. The writers who describe them are prose portraitists, seekers of what lies beneath the surface pictures of deeds and words, hopeful that they can limn the inner motivations of the dissenters, the unconquerable, the loyal minorities, the pathbreakers, the self-righteous, all who share the hope that their resources will change the world or change themselves.

Terence O'Donnell closes the book in an epilogue that served as the conclusion of his own history of the state, *That Balance So Rare*, a persuasive reminder that our generation—hurrying at an ever-increasing rate towards its own destiny—has links with its predecessors that can be broken only with great peril. Here is the writer as historian, confident that the past is prologue, hopeful that his words can inspire a democratic public to use its resources of intellect and soul to seek out the past, not in a judgmental manner but to gather its vicarious experiences for the common good.

The editors of the *Oregon Literature Series* hope the prose writers included in this book will stimulate their readers' sentiments and reflections about Oregon's history, about its natural worlds, about its contemporary life, and about its values. They anticipate, too, that readers will come to appreciate how Oregonians, men and women from many lands coming with many hopes— some realized, some untransacted—have created a distinctive community among the American commonwealths.

Gordon B. Dodds
Portland State University
May 1993

Prologue

H. L. Davis
1894-1960

The only Oregonian who has ever won the Pulitzer Prize for fiction was Harold Lenoir (H.L.) Davis. Davis was born in Douglas County, Oregon, lived with his family in several towns in western Oregon, and then moved with them to Antelope in 1906 and to The Dalles in 1908. He first came to national attention as a poet in 1919 when he won the Levinson Prize. With James Stevens he wrote a literary polemic, in 1927, *Status Rerum*, that attacked the quality of Oregon writers (see section II of this book). In 1928 he moved to Washington State, never to live permanently in Oregon again, although most of his later writings were about his native state. He began publishing fiction in 1929, and his first novel, *Honey in the Horn* (1935), set in the Oregon of 1906 to 1908, won the Pulitzer Prize in 1936. Davis's early fiction took a realistic (perhaps overly critical) look at Oregon, but his journalistic essays—published later—were more balanced. The following selection is an excerpt from his essay "Oregon," which appeared in his collection entitled *Kettle of Fire,* published in 1959. In it Davis describes a journey through several parts of the state and concludes with a lesson for all Oregonians from an encounter he has with one of its residents.

Oregon

There used to be an old sawmill and logging settlement back in the deep timber on the eastern fringe of the valley country, where my father taught school when I was not much over two years old. It was a small-scale sort of operation, with no prospects of expansion, because its local market was limited to a scattering of homesteaders and cattlemen around the neighborhood, and distance and bad roads made hauling its lumber out to the railroad impossible. Still, between the homesteaders and some half-breed fragments of an old Indian tribe back in the hills, there was enough to run a school on while it lasted. Afterward, the mill closed down, the homesteaders moved away, the Indians were rounded up and shipped north to the collective reservation at Siletz, and the school and settlement were abandoned for a good many years. Recently, after back-country logging had been put back on its feet by such new wrinkles as tractors, hard-surfaced roads, power chain-saws, truck transportation and a rising market for building material, a big lumber company bought up the old camp and the timber back of it, built a fence between it and the main road, and hired a watchman with experience in handling firearms to keep campers and hobos and log pirates out.

There was nothing about the old logging camp that I wanted particularly to see. I had lived in it when too young to remember it; the stories people used to tell about it afterward were associated with them, not with the place. It was the lumber company's watchman I went up there to call on. I had known him from years back, when I was on a Government survey in one of the national forests up in Northern Oregon, and he was guide and camp wrangler for a symphony-orchestra conductor from New York who liked trout fishing, or thought he did: a strutty, playful old gentleman who sang resonantly while fishing, and naturally never caught anything.

The watchman didn't have to work as a guide, being very well off from speculating in orchard lands around the Cascade foothills, but he liked the woods and would rather be working at something than sitting around doing nothing. He used to come over to our camp of an evening and tell stories about being sent out to track down people who had got themselves lost back in the deep timber. He held that anybody could get lost in the woods, there was nothing disgraceful about it, he had been lost in that very country half a dozen times himself, though he was accounted an authority on its geography and landmarks. Whether it turned out seriously or not depended on the kind of intelligence a man used after he got lost. A fool would never admit that he was lost; no matter how completely bushed he was, he always knew his location and directions exactly, and got himself worse lost trying to make them work out. The watchman said he had brought out lost hunting parties in almost a dying condition who were so positive he was taking them in the wrong direction that some of them had to be dragged to get them started. His stories were not only diverting but helpful. I have been lost in the woods a couple of times since then myself, and without them I would undoubtedly have done pretty much what he said the fools always did.

The hard-surfaced road back to the old logging camp had strung the twenty-mile stretch of adjoining country so full of small cottages and shacks and chicken-farm lean-tos that there was hardly any country left until I got within sight of the old logging-camp buildings and the lumber company's fence and padlocked gate. Beyond that, everything changed. There was a dirt road, sprinkled with dead fir needles, with a dusty spot showing where quail had wallowed. The big Douglas firs stood straight and tall and motionless up the sidehill, not crowded together as they are in the rainier mountains near the coast, but scattered out between clumps of hazel and vine maple and open patches of white-top grass and pink fireweed. There were no rusty car bodies or can dumps or barnyard manure piles in the creek. It rattled past clear and bright and untroubled, reaching back through thickets of red willow and gray alder and sweet bush to some old stump land overgrown with evergreen blackberry vines. There was a grouse clucking somewhere up the hill, in a sort of anxiously persistent tone that for some reason was restful to listen to. It was impossible to tell where it was coming from: sounds in timber country have a curious way of seeming to come from the air itself rather than from any tangible thing in it.

The old logging-camp buildings were all nailed up and deserted, except the one nearest the road. It had its windows unboarded, with a school election notice tacked to the door above a wooden-seated chair, and a tin tobacco box alongside containing a few rusty nails, a fire warden's badge, a carpenter's pencil, some loose cigarette papers, and a halfbox of .22 cartridges. The watchman was nowhere around. I left my car at the gate and climbed over it and walked up the road a few hundred yards to look around.

There were deer tracks in the road, a doe and two fawns, and big-foot rabbit tracks, and a blue grouse hooting in the firs somewhere, but it was not altogether as the Lord had left it. People had lived here once, up the dirt road for miles back into the hills. My mother used to tell about some of them: an old cattleman, enormously wealthy, who kept eight squaws, one at each of his line camps, and had children by all of them regularly, though he was then past seventy, and a town named after him which is still flourishing. And one of the young half-breeds who drew a knife on my father in school, and then tried to make up for it by bringing him presents—potted plants, ornamented mustache cups, dressed turkeys—all of which turned out to be stolen; and another half-breed, a youngster of about fifteen, who used to write poems, each stanza in a different-colored ink, and peddle them around the settlement at two bits a copy. People used to buy them and never read them. And another cattleman, middle-aged and quarrelsome, was supposed to have set himself up in business by murdering and robbing an old Chinese peddler, and had a mania for giving expensive wedding presents to every young married couple in the community, even those whose fathers he was sworn to shoot on sight. . . . There were more of them. It had been a big community once. There had probably been as many people in it as there were in the chicken-farm cottages down the creek, and they had stayed there at least as long. But they had marked it less, or maybe the marks they made were the kind that healed over more easily. A few were still visible: some old stumps grown over with vines, some half-burned fence posts showing through the fir needles, part of an old corduroy wood road running uphill into the salal, with rabbit fur scattered in it where a hawk had struck. The creek had taken out some of the old marks, seemingly. A tangle of whitened driftwood piled high above a cutbank showed that it had sometimes flooded. There were scuff marks across a strip of sand below the cutbank where some beavers had dragged sticks to use in building a dam.

They had their dam finished, and the cutbank was partly undermined where they had started a tunnel to their nest. It was nothing to be proud of, as far as workmanship went. I had always heard that beavers had a sort of obsession for work, and spent all their time at it because they enjoyed doing it, but the dam didn't show it. They hadn't cut down any trees for it at all, though there were dozens of alder and willow saplings within easy reach. They had merely made it a tangle of dry sticks from the driftwood, most of them no bigger than a lead pencil. The whole thing was so childish and flimsy that they had to weight it down with rocks to keep the creek from washing it away. It was some sort of commentary on modern times, probably, but a man gets tired of having the same thing proved over and over again. It was time for me to go back, anyway.

The company watchman was sitting in his chair by the door when I got back to the gate. There is always a certain trepidation about meeting somebody you haven't seen for twenty years, but he hadn't changed much. He had always been grayish and scrawny, and he was merely a little grayer and scrawnier. He apologized for being out when I came, and said he had been down arguing with some of the chicken farm people who kept trying to sneak through the company fence and dump garbage upstream in the creek. He didn't know why it meant so much to them to dump it upstream, and they hadn't been able to explain it very convincingly themselves. Their main argument seemed to be that it was a free country and the creek belonged to everybody, and the lumber company had no right to go around telling people what they could do and what they couldn't. It looked sometimes as if they couldn't stand to see anything in the country left as it had been before they got there. It preyed on their minds, or something.

"There's not much left for them to worry about," I said. "Not around here, anyway."

"It's no better up north," he said. "There's highways crisscrossed all through the mountains up there. A highway into the mountains lets people see what wild country looks like, if they can find room to drive between the log trucks. Nobody ever figures that the wild country might not want to see what people look like. It's like that old saloonkeeper up on the Columbia River that had himself buried in an Indian graveyard when he died, because he'd decided that Indians were better to associate with than white people."

I remembered the story. Everybody had been deeply impressed by his wish to associate with Indians after he died. Nobody had thought to find out how the Indians felt about associating with him. It turned out that they were not impressed by the prospect at all. After he had been buried in their tribal graveyard, they moved all their graves somewhere else and let him have it all to himself. Building a main highway into a wild country is like driving a red-hot poker into a tree and expecting the sap to start circulating in it. The living tissue of the tree draws back from it, and the sap goes on circulating around it; or else the tree dies.

"There's wild country left," the watchman said. "More than you'd think, from the way they've fixed things down the creek below here. It's not much different than it used to be, if you figure it right. You've got to figure it in time instead of mileage, that's all. It used to take a day for a man to drive up here from the railroad with a team and wagon. You probably drove it in less than an hour, and you're surprised that it's all built up. If you'll take a team and wagon and take out on some of these old corduroy wood roads into the hills for a day, the way you'd have done twenty years ago, you'll run into all the wild country you want. You may have to chop some logs out of the road and fight yellow jackets off the horses, but it'll be wild. The animals and everything else."

"Not all the animals," I said, and told him about the beaver and their scamped job of dam-building up the creek.

"They're Oklahoma beavers, I expect," he said. "Moved out from the Dust Bowl back in the hard times, more than likely. You've got to remember that they've been through a lot, and that it don't do any good to stand around and criticize. What they need is help. You ought to have chewed down a few trees for 'em, to get 'em started off on the right foot."

It was not the first tribute to the Oklahoma temperament I had heard, though most were less indirect. "Are they as bad as that?" I said.

"We're none of us perfect," he said mildly. "They're not exactly the kind of company I'd pick to be shipwrecked on a desert island with, but there's points about 'em. I had a crew of sixty of 'em fighting a little brush fire in some second-growth timber on Thief Creek last fall, and they were as conscientious as anybody could ask in a lot of ways. Paydays and mealtimes they never missed. They even fought fire off and on, till it got within about three-quarters of a mile of 'em. Then they dropped everything and legged it out of there at a gallop. Well, they have to learn. It takes time."

"It sounds as if it might take a lot of it," I said. "More than either of us will ever see, probably."

"I've seen 'em come in like this before," he said. "Some as bad, and some worse. They spread back into places like this and dumped garbage and slashed trees and strung fences and tore up grasslands and fixed everything around to suit themselves. Then they got old, and their kids grew up and moved away somewhere else and sent for 'em and a lot of 'em died out, and now they're all gone. They never last. They think they will, but they never do. They swarm in here with their car wrecks and bellyaches and litters of children, and they pile in to fix the whole country over, and it civilizes 'em in spite of themselves. Then they pick up and go somewhere else to show it off. I may live long enough to see it here yet. Hell, lots of people live to be over ninety nowadays. It'll happen, anyway."

It was looking past externals to an underlying purpose in the country, whether it was the right one or not. And it may have been the right one. Years before, when I was timekeeper for a Greek extra gang on the old Deschutes Railroad, the foreman of the outfit used almost the same terms in trying to explain about some squabble that had got stirred up among the men. The details were a little involved, and he finally brushed them aside and attacked the root of the problem.

"The trouble with these fellows is that they ain't been over here in this country long enough to know anything," he said.

He was Greek himself, from some small coastal village in the province of Corinth. He had left home when he was young, because of some parental difficulty: he had sneaked his father's muzzle-loading pistol out to see how it shot, and the load of slugs and scrap iron tore all the bark off two of the old man's best olive trees, so he ran away to keep from being skinned alive. "All these fellows know is how things are back in the old country. They think that's all they need to know, and it ain't anything. They ain't civilized back in the old country."

The idea that an expanse of Eastern Oregon sagebrush where horse-Indians still wandered around living in tepees and digging camass could represent a higher stage of civilization than the land that had cradled Sophocles and Plato was so startling that I laughed.

"Well, it's the truth," he said, "them people in the old country ain't civilized. They don't know what it is to be civilized till they've been over here a while. It takes a long time for some of 'em."

"You ought to be civilized by now, anyway," I said. "You've been over here a long time."

"If I was, I wouldn't be out in a place like this," he said. "I didn't say this country got people civilized. I said they found out what it was like to be civilized, that's all. That's as far as I've got."

It did work out to some kind of system. The older generation found out what civilization was; the younger absorbed it, and moved away somewhere else to show it off: Joaquin Miller from his parents' farm in the Willamette Valley to Canyon City, and to England, and to his final exhibitionistic years in California; Edwin Markham from Oregon City to California and to his end in New York; John Reed from Portland to New York and Mexico and to his tomb in Red Square in Moscow. . . . Civilization? At any rate, it was something.

I got a camera from the car to take some pictures of the old logging-camp buildings. It was not difficult to pick out the one we had lived in from the stories my mother had told about it. It was the one with the high front porch; she had told about two drunk half-breed Indians rolling and fighting under it one night on their way home from town, and how she lay in bed listening while one of them beat the other to death with a rock. She was alone in the house; my father was away at a teachers' conference in Roseburg, the county seat.

The watchman looked the camera over and said he had been intending to get one himself. He wanted to take some pictures of the country to send his son, who lived in Hollywood.

"San Fernando, I guess it is, but it's the same thing," he said. "He works in Hollywood. He's got one of these television shows, 'Know Your Neighbors,' or something like that; interviews with people, and things like that. He's doing well at it, but it don't leave him much time for anything else. He can't get away much. It'll be a big thing some of these days, but you have to stay with it. If you don't you lose out."

Erratum

We regret that page 9 was inadvertently omitted from this reprinting
and apologize for any inconvenience this may cause the reader.

The country north through the Willamette Valley is lovely in the spring, with long expanses of green meadowland and flocks of sheep and dairy herds and clumps of wild apple and plum and cherry flowering against the dark fir thickets along the streams. The towns have a certain New Englandish look about them, emphasizing a difference between their culture and that of the country around them that has existed from the earliest days. The townspeople came originally from New England, and were traders and small merchants and artisans. The settlers in the rural areas were mostly open-country cattle raisers from the Mississippi Valley—Missouri, Arkansas, Tennessee, Kentucky. The two cultures have never mixed, and there has been little sympathy or under-standing developed between them. Each is admittedly indispensable to the other: country people need towns, and towns have to live on the country, but there is not much enthusiasm in accepting the necessity.

A highway turns east from Salem across the Cascade Mountains by the Santiam Pass, following an old toll road built by cattlemen in the 1850s as a driveway by which to move their herds from the Willamette Valley to the open-country sagebrush and bunch-grass ranges of Eastern Oregon. It couldn't have looked like much of a move, as far as appearances went. The Willamette Valley grasslands are green, luxuriant, well-watered, and usually open for grazing throughout the entire year. East of the mountains the country is arid, color-less, baked dry in summer and whipped by blizzards in winter, its sparse clumps of whitish-green bunch grass not sodded, but spaced out two or three feet apart from each other with naked red earth showing between each clump, or sometimes hidden so close among the sagebrush roots that an outsider will wonder how cattle turned out on it are managing to keep alive, when they may have been put there to fatten for market. There is not much nutriment in grass that has had too easy a time of it; it will keep cattle alive, but not put weight on them. The bunch grass, which has had to fight for every inch of its growth, is far superior in nutritive value to any of the deep sod grasses west of the moun-tains. There might be some suspicion of a moral back of this, except that cattlemen are not interested in the moralistic aspects of the subject. Nor are their cattle.

Last April I drove east by the highway over the mountains through Santiam Pass. Deep snow all through the pass and in scattered drifts far down into the timber. Blue Lake down in a deep basin to the south, still and deserted; the snow roofs of the summer cabins looked peaceful and attractive. Not a living soul in any of them. Mount Washington towering back of the lake, its huge snowy peak striking into the blue sky like a spear. Snow in patches even below

the level where the fir timber changes to yellow pine; salal bushes in bloom among the pines, hanging full of little pink bells like heather, the shallow drifts of old snow under them splotched with pale yellow where their pollen had shed. No wild life in the fir timber, not even birds. A few magpies among the pines, and a tiny lilac-throated hummingbird working on the salal blossoms. Near where the pine thins out into scattering juniper, a little town called Sisters, where sheepmen used to load their pack trains for the camps in the mountains; remote, quiet and dusty, a movie theater showing some tired B-Western picture. A youngster of about sixteen at the gas station gave me some directions about roads, and then said, "What does television look like?" . . .

North through the Warm Springs Indian Reservation. Open juniper and grassland, the timbered Cascade Mountains off to the west, a few cattle and some scattering wheatfields. The agency was about the same as it was twenty years ago: the store and gas station probably new. Some young Indians in a car, apparently from Klamath or somewhere south, on their way to a spring salmon festival at Celilo on the Columbia River. I noticed that a couple of them had their hair marcelled, apparently to get rid of the Indian straightness. It didn't seem much of an improvement. Until recent years there were only dirt roads through the reservation, and it was even lonelier than it is now.

. . . North to the Columbia River at Celilo. It was late afternoon, and twenty years had not changed it much: the gigantic blue shadows reaching down from the gray-black cliffs over the white sand and dark water were still enough to make a man catch his breath and forget to let go of it. No picture can do what the place itself does; the pen-and-ink drawing that Theodore Winthrop made of it for his *The Canoe and the Saddle* in 1860 comes no farther from it than any of the modern photographs. They all miss the intensity of tones, and the scale—the cliffs a thousand feet high, the shadows half a mile deep and twenty miles long, the rapids thundering spray into the air higher than a man can see. The houses scattered in the rifts of cold sunlight have a helpless look, as if the whole thing stunned them. . . .

The salmon festival appeared to be all over with. Several dozen out-of-state cars were pulled up alongside the old Indian village (a huddle of unpainted board shacks along the river, dirt-floored and completely unsanitary, which seem now to have become merely a show piece; the Indians live in some large white corrugated-iron barracks on higher ground, which look very clean and thoroughly dull) and tourists were poking around asking questions of a few middle-aged Indians, with some squaws watching from an old Cadillac sedan. They had on their best clothes, and seemed prim and a little self-conscious. It couldn't have been much of a salmon festival. In the old days, the centerpiece of a salmon festival was always a wagonload of canned meat, and the ceremonies usually wound up in a big free-for-all fight. It was a little dangerous sometimes, but the guests did have something to talk about for the rest of the year.

The river seemed muddy, possibly because of blasting downstream for the foundations of a new hydroelectric dam at The Dalles. When finished, it will back the river up so there will no longer be any rapids, or any salmon fishing either. Probably it is as well. It can't be good for human beings to live as anachronisms, and a salmon festival that has to restrict itself to merely serving salmon is too meaningless to keep on with.

. . . South through the Sherman County wheatfields to Antelope. The wheat towns remain unchanged, at least: no new buildings, the old ones all still standing, though some seemed vacant. The great divisions of color in the wheatfields were beautiful: bright green winter wheat, black summer fallow, white stubble, running long curves and undulations across the ridges to the sky line and into the gray sagebrush to the south. A flock of sheep grazing along a little creek bed at the edge of the sagebrush, with the herder's camp wagon drawn up behind a clump of junipers; not much of a camp wagon, merely a small high-wheeled trailer with a stovepipe stuck through the roof.

The herder came out and stopped to talk for a minute: an elderly man, gray and stocky and taciturn. He complained of the long winter, which had been hard on the sheep, and offered to trade his high-powered rifle for my .22 pistol, because there was no longer anything around that a man could use a high-powered rifle on. He had herded sheep most of his life, he said, and didn't mind it. A man could get used to anything. It was easier nowadays, with cars and radios, than it had been. He had a radio in his camp wagon, and liked to listen to it, except the commercials, which made him want to buy things when he was miles from the nearest town and couldn't. His son was in college, he said, studying law, in Los Angeles.

Antelope had not changed in appearance since I lived there as a youngster. It was still a quiet, grayish little town with tall poplars lining the streets and a creek valley spread out below it. The only thing different was the people. They had been mostly Indians and Highland Scots: big lumbering men, some with the reddest hair I have ever seen, who talked English in a curious half-falsetto tone, when they could talk it at all. The only languages one commonly heard on the street were Gaelic and Chinook jargon. It had been a homesick experience, trying to get used to them at first. Now it was a homesick feeling not to find any of them left.

The newspapers had a follow-up story about the salmon festival at Celilo. There were a few touches of the old tradition in it, after all; according to the reports, some of the guests got drunk and got to fighting, and the venerable Celilo chief got poked in the jaw and was confined to his bed, feeling terrible. The stories gave his age as somewhere around eighty-two. It must have been all of twenty-five years ago that he appeared as a witness in a Federal-court hearing involving some old fishing-rights treaty, and gave his age as eighty-eight. Still, anybody is entitled to feel younger at a party than at a Federal-court hearing.

. . . South to Bend. The road follows the high country along the rim of the Deschutes River canyon, with a view of all the big snow peaks to the west: Mount Adams, Mount Jefferson, Mount Hood, Mount Washington, the Three Sisters, Broken Top. Sometimes, when the air is clear and the wind from the north, you can see Mount Shasta to the south. A man working in this country during the summer falls into the habit of counting these peaks from the north to south regularly every day, and watching to see how their snow lines are holding out against the heat.

In the irrigated lands north of Bend, there were ringnecked pheasants all along the road. They stay close to it, knowing that it is against the law to shoot from a public highway, but not knowing enough to keep out of the way of traffic. I counted eight that had been killed by cars, in ten miles.

The general notion about company towns is that they are ugly, spirit-destroying, and deliberately sordid and monotonous. Bend and Klamath Falls are both sawmill towns, dominated by big lumber companies. They are the two loveliest towns in Eastern Oregon, and perhaps in the entire West. Certainly there is nothing in California that can come anywhere near either of them.

. . . Southeast to Lakeview. The road from the Deschutes River into the Great Basin is through two great national forests, the Deschutes and the Fremont, with pine timber for miles on both sides of it. There are ice caves off to the north a few miles, probably originally blown into some body of molten lava by imprisoned steam, and not much to see. A cave is a hole in the ground, and ice is ice. The short dark-colored underbrush among the pines is used as summer grazing by the cattle herds east in the Great Basin, its foliage being highly esteemed for its meat-building properties. The stockmen call it "chamiso"; erroneously, since it bears no resemblance to the chamiso of Arizona and California, which is worthless as forage, is pale gray instead of dark, and grows only on ground open to the sun, never in woods.

This country has never been notably accurate in picking names for things. The little blue-flowered ground plant known here as "filaree" is not in the least like the afilerilla of the Southwest, and is not even the same botanical species. Nobody could possibly confuse the two, one being a flowering plant and the other a flowerless grass, so the misnaming must have been accomplished in the dark, or maybe it was mere cussedness. There are dozens of similar cases. The Douglas fir is not a fir, but a spruce; the Port Orford cedar is not cedar, but a sub-species of redwood; the sagebrush is not sage, but wormwood. Some local breeds of trout are really grilse, what the restaurants serve as filet of sole is either sea perch or flounder, and their lobster (which has no claws, merely antennae) is probably some kind of overgrown prawn.

. . . There are a few little towns scattered along this corner of the Great Basin: Silver Lake, Paisley, Valley Falls. They are old and a long way apart, with a subdued sort of charm about them—gray poplars lining the streets, old houses set back against the willows along the creek, lilacs and bleeding heart and white iris coming into bloom behind the gray picket fences. The little creeks hurry past bright and swift and eager, though there is nothing much for them to hurry to. Since the waters of the Great Basin have no outlet to the ocean, the only end its creeks can look forward to is stagnation in some of the alkali lakes down in the desert.

One of the towns had a small roadside lunchstand run by an elderly couple who had owned a cattle ranch in one of the valleys back in the old wagon-freighting days. The old gentleman came out and visited while I had lunch. He was bright, alert, and quiet-spoken. Nobody would have guessed him to be much over fifty, though he must have been considerably past that to have been running a cattle ranch so far back. He spoke of some of the old wagon-freighters, and said he had lost his ranch in the Depression, and had been in the country so long he couldn't bring himself to strike out for a new one. There was no chance of starting over again where he was; all the small ranches had been wiped out in the bad times, and the country had fallen into the hands of four or five big cattle syndicates, which ran it to suit themselves. They had everything bought up—homesteads, small ranches, Government land leases—and they hung onto it. A small outfit would not stand a dog's chance trying to buck them. They were the main reason that the town was dead. With the syndicates sitting on everything, there was nothing for new people to come in for.

"They must bring in some business themselves," I said. "You can't run cattle outfits that size without a payroll."

"It don't amount to much," he said. "Not the way they run things, with cross fences and branding chutes and trucks and tractors and everything done by machinery. When they hire a cowboy, they don't ask him if he can stay on a horse or handle a rope. What they want to know is whether he can repair a truck and dig postholes. In the old days, any of those outfits would have kept seventy or eighty men on regular. Now they get by with a dozen apiece; fifteen, maybe. They pay 'em well, I hear. More than they're worth, to my notion. Most of 'em couldn't work for me for nothing. Assembly-line mechanics, that's all there is to 'em."

We talked about men we had both known. One had started a bootlegging business in a small sheep town up north, and when things began to slow up and the businessmen began to close down and move out, he decided to take over all their businesses and run them himself, to keep the place going. Now, in addition to his bar, he ran the drugstore, the grocery, a hay and feed business and the barbershop, besides handling a small line of dry goods, notions, plumbing supplies and fuel. He also repaired shoes, sold hunting and fishing licenses, ran a branch of the county library, and was agent for a laundry and dry cleaner in one of the bigger towns.

"I hope he stands it, handling all that," I said. "He must be old by now."

"A man will stand a lot to hang on in a place he's got used to," the restaurant man said. "Anyway, he's not old. He can't be much over sixty."

. . . All the Great Basin is high country. The altitude of the flatlands around Picture Rock Pass is over 4,000 feet, and the mountains are twice that. In the short timber northeast of Picture Rock Pass are mule deer; to the southeast, around Hart Mountain, there are antelope. In between, lying under the huge hundred-mile length of mountain scarp known as the Abert Rim, is a chain of big alkali lakes—Silver Lake, Summer Lake, Abert Lake, Goose Lake. Some are over thirty miles long. During cycles of scant rainfall, they are dry beds of white alkali, as they were during the 1930s, and in 1858 when Lieutenant Philip H. Sheridan camped in the area on some obscure Indian campaign. When the cycle turns, they run full of water again, as they are beginning to do now. The water is too alkaline for any use except as scenery, and Abert Lake has a pronounced odor, but it is pleasanter to live with than the dust clouds, and the uselessness seems a small thing when the great flocks of wild ducks and geese and black-headed trumpeter swans begin to come down on it in their northward migration every spring.

There is something wild and freakish and exaggerated about this entire lake region in the spring. The colors are unimaginably vivid: deep blues, ferocious greens, blinding whites. Mallard ducks bob serenely on mud puddles a few feet from the road, indifferent to everybody. Sheep and wild geese are scattered out in a grass meadow together, cropping the grass side by side in a spirit of complete tolerance. Horses and cattle stand knee-deep in a roadside marsh, their heads submerged to the eyes, pasturing the growth of grass underneath the water. A tractor plowing a field moves through a cloud of white Mormon sea gulls, little sharp-winged creatures, no bigger than pigeons and as tame, following the fresh-turned furrow in search of worms. A flock of white snow geese turning in the high sunlight after the earth has gone into shadow looks like an explosion of silver.

The black-headed swans trumpeting sound like a thousand French taxi horns all going at once. If you happen to be close when they come down, the gigantic wings sinking past into the shadows will scare the life out of you. It is no wonder that the Indians of this country spent so much of their time starting new religions.

. . . Frenchglen, Steens Mountain. Nobody hears much about the Steens Mountain. It is near the southeastern corner of the state, a 10,000-foot wall separating the Great Basin on the west from the tributaries of the Snake River on the east. There is a wild-game refuge in a creek valley along the western rim, with antelope and pheasants and flocks of wild ducks and geese scattered all through it.

. . . The little lake high up in the mountains looked about as it did when we used to ride up over an old wagon road in the late summer to fish for speckled trout. It was small, not over a quarter of a mile long, and not shown on most maps at all. The thickets of dwarf cottonwood around it had not grown or dwindled, the water was rough and dark and piercingly cold, and the remains of old snowdrifts in the gullies back of it still had the curiously regular shapes that looked, at a little distance, like spires and towers and gables in a white town. There was no town anywhere near; the closest was over a hundred miles away. It looked as quiet as it always had at sundown—the dark water, the ghostly cottonwoods, the scrub willows along the bank, a few scrawny flowers spotting the coarse grass. About dark, a wind came up, and it began to rain and kept it up all night. By morning it had eased up a little, but the wind was stronger and it was spitting sleet. Being snowed in, in such a place, was not a tempting prospect. I loaded the soggy camp rig into the car, turned it around gingerly in the mud, and headed out.

There was a sheep camp in the cottonwoods at the head of the lake where the road turned down the mountain. The camp tender was striking camp to pull out, the tent hanging limp on the ridgepole and flapping cumbrously when the wind struck it, the pack mules standing humped against the grains of sleet and gouts of foam from the lake that kept pelting them. The sheep were already on the way out; they were jammed so close together down the road that it was impossible to get the car into it. I stopped, and the herder called his dog and went ahead to clear a lane through them.

It was slow work trying to crowd them off into the cottonwood thicket and there was open ground beyond, so I waved to him to drive them on through to where they would have room to spread out. He nodded, and came back to stir up the tail-enders. It was not a big herd; three hundred, maybe, mostly old ewes, hardly enough for two full-grown men to be spending their time on. He got the tail-enders started, and stood back and dropped the cottonwood branch he had been urging them along with. I expected him to say something, but he looked away, watching the dog round up a few stragglers. He was about forty, heavy-boned and slow-looking and bashful, as if he was trying to avoid being spoken to. It struck me what the reason might be, and I took a chance on it.

"*De Vascondaga, verdad?*" I said.

That was it. He had been trying to dodge around admitting that he didn't know English. A good many Basque sheepherders in that country didn't.

"*Sí, Vizcaya,*" he said. "*Aldeano de Zarauz.*"

Vizcaya was one of the Basque provinces. Vascondaga was the collective name for all of them. He was from the country adjoining some town named Zarauz.

"*Hace mucho?*" I said.

"*Dos anos,*" he said. "*Mas o menos.*"

He was not being exactly cooperative. I would have given a good deal to be able to sling a sentence or two of Euskera at him, just to see him jump, but wishing did no good. Spanish was the best I could manage. I tried a change of subject.

"It is slow moving a camp with pack mules," I said.

"We work with what we have," he said.

There didn't seem much left to say on that. I tried the weather.

"Que tiempo malo," I said.

"Hay cosas peores," he said. "There are worse things." He was loosening up a little.

He had something specific in mind, I thought. If he had been over here only two years—"You saw the Civil War in Spain?"

He nodded, and took a deep breath. "Nobody sees all of a war. I saw people shot. I saw our house burned. My father was shot. I didn't see that, but I saw enough."

"You are *desterrado?"* I said. It was a polite expression the Spaniards used for a political refugee. It meant something like exile.

"A little," he said. Then he took it back. "No. I am not *desterrado.* This is my country, here. It is the only one I need."

His handful of lumbering old ewes plodded down the open slope in the wind. The mules flinched and humped uneasily as a blast rattled sleet against them. Some torn leaves from the cottonwoods skimmed past.

"Some people would call it bleak," I said. "Weather as cold as this."

"Nobody can know what is good until he has seen what is bad," he said. "Some people don't know. I do."

He went to help the camp tender with the packs. I drove out of the cottonwoods and through the sheep and on down the mountain. It was Oregon, all right: the place where stories begin that end somewhere else. It has no history of its own, only endings of histories from other places; it has no complete lives, only beginnings. There are worse things.

Suggested Further Reading

Bryant, Paul T. *H. L. Davis.* Boston: Twayne Publishers, 1978.

Davis, H. L. *Beulah Land.* New York: William Morrow & Co., 1949.

———. *Honey in the Horn.* New York: Harper & Brothers, 1935.

———. *Kettle of Fire.* New York: William Morrow & Co., 1959.

———. *Team Bells Woke Me and Other Stories.* New York: William Morrow & Co., 1953.

SECTION I
Oregon Communities:
Celebrating, Working, Playing Together

Alfred Meacham
1826-1882

Alfred Meacham was a white man who was a friend of
the Indian. Born in Indiana, Meacham was appointed
superintendent of Indian Affairs for Oregon by
President Ulysses S. Grant in 1869. He visited the
Warm Springs Reservation in 1870 and wrote of the
appalling conditions he found there in his book,
Wigwam and War-Path (1875), an excerpt from which
follows. Meacham was so angry about the unjust
treatment of the Native Americans, and so candid in
describing it in his book, that he was dismissed in 1871
following incessant complaints from those whose
misdeeds he exposed. However, he continued to
support Indian rights after leaving Oregon until the
close of his life. Meacham headed the Modoc Indian
peace commission in 1873, and was shot and knifed
during a session of the council with the Indians. After
leaving Oregon he worked on behalf of the Native
Americans by lecturing, founding a newspaper (*Council
Fires*), and serving as a commissioner to the Indian
Territory.

A Dangerous Place for Sinners

Leaving The Dalles early one morning in February, 1870, with Dr. W. C. McKay as guide, I set out on my first visit to Warm Springs Agency. Our route was over high grassy plains, undulating, and sometimes broken by deep cañons, occasionally wide enough to furnish extensive farm lands. Tyghe Valley is traversed by two rivers that flow eastward from the foot of the Cascade Mountains. It was, originally, a very paradise for Indians. It is a paradise still; but not for them. "White men wanted it"; hence our present visit to Warm Springs.

In 1855 the several Indian tribes occupying the country east of the Cascade Mountains, as far up as John Day's, south of the Columbia River, and north of the Blue Mountains, met in Treaty Council those who had been selected as the representatives of the Government.

The Indians confederated, settling all their difficulties as between different tribes, and also with the Government. They went into this council to avoid further hostilities. From Dr. W. C. McKay I learned that a body of troops were present; that the Indians insisted on Tyghe Valley as a home; that the Government refused, and that the council continued for several days; that, finally, under threats and intimidations, the Indians agreed to accept a home on what is now Warm Springs Reservation, the Government agreeing to do certain things by way of furnishing mills, shops, schools, farms, etc.

At this time certain members of the Tenino band were in possession of, and had made improvements of value near The Dalles. Under special agreements in treaty council these improvements were to be paid for by the Government.

Nineteen years have passed, and John Mission and Billy Chinook have not yet received one dollar for the aforesaid improvements. These men were converts to Christianity under the ministration of Father Waller and others, who were sent out by the Methodist Church as missionaries. These Indians are still faithful to the vows then taken.

Here is a good subject for some humane, sentimental boaster of national justice to meditate upon.

Had these men broken their compact with the Government, they would have been punished; and, had they been like other Indians who have figured in history, they would have been at last rewarded; not because the Government is prompt to do them justice, but because they would have *compelled* justice to

come to them, though filtered by blood through the bones of innocent settlers and sweetened by tears and groans of widows and orphans.

Strong language this, I admit; but history supports the declaration. For nineteen years have these two humble red-skinned men waited patiently for remuneration; for nineteen years have they waited in vain. Poor fellows, I pity you! Had you a vote to give, your claim might have been paid years ago. Then some ambitious politician, anxious to secure your suffrage, would have importuned the department at Washington to do you justice; and the department, anxious for influence in Congress, would have recommended payment, and some member would have found it to his interest to "log-roll" it through. But you are unfortunate; you cannot vote. You are no trouble; you are peaceable and faithful, and you *dare* not now make any noise about your claim. You are dependent on a Government that has so much more important business to look out for, you are unknown.

Rebel once against your masters, and millions would be expended to punish you. A few thousands would make you rich, and would redeem the honor of the other "high contracting power." But you will not be made glad now in your old age, because you are but "Injuns," and the good ones of your people "are all under ground." So say your white brethren, who now own what was once your country. Be patient still. The God, of whom you learned from the lips of the honored dead, will yet compel a nation of conquerors to drink the bitter dregs of repentance, and though you may never handle one dollar of the money due you, your children may. And somewhere in the future your race may come upon the plane where manhood is honored without the question of ancestry being raised.

Climbing a steep bluff, going south from Tyghe Valley, we look out on an extensive plain, bordered by mountain ranges, facing us from the further side. Forty miles brings us, by slow and ever-increasing easy grades, to the summit of the plain, where the road leads down a mountain so steep that two common-sized horses cannot even manage a light carriage without rough-locking the wheels. From the starting-point into the chasm below, a small stream, looking like a bright ribbon that was crumpled and ruffled, may be seen. Down, down we go. Down, still down, until, standing on the bank of Warm Springs River, we behold the ribbon transformed into a rapid rushing current of snow-water, whose very clearness deceives us in respect to its depth. We drive into it at a rocky ford, and we are soon startled with the quick breathing of our team, while the water seems to rise over their backs, and we, standing on the seat, knee deep, encourage our horses to reach the other shore.

For nineteen years has the business of this agency been transacted through this current. We are on the other side, vowing that "Uncle Sam" *must* and *shall* have this stream bridged. So vowed our predecessors, and so our successors, too, would have vowed had they ever passed that way. A few miles from the crossing and near our road we see steam ascending, as if some subterranean monster was cooking his supper and had upset his kettle on the fires where it is supposed wicked people go. The nearer we came to the caldron the more we were convinced that our conjectures were correct, and stronger was our resolve to keep away from such places. Brimstone in moderate quantities scattered along the banks of this stream adds to our anxiety to reach a meeting-house, where we may feel safe.

This spring gives name to the Reservation, though twelve miles from the agency; to reach which, we climb up, up, up once more to another high sterile plain, devoid of everything like vegetation save sage bush. Mile after mile we travel, until suddenly the team halts on a brink, and we, to ascertain the cause, alight. Looking down, away down below glimmer a dozen lights. Tying all the wheels of our vehicle together and walking behind our team for safety, we go down into this fearful opening in the surface of the earth, and find Warm Springs Agency at the bottom of the chasm.

The country comprising this Indian Reservation is desolate in the extreme; the only available farming lands being found in the narrow cañons hemmed in by high bluffs. The soil is alkaline and subject to extreme drought.

Warm Springs Agency I have and ever will declare to be unfit for civilized Indians to occupy. Since they were compelled to take up their abode thereon, not one season in three, on an average, has been propitious for raising farm products. When a people hitherto accustomed to ramble unrestrained, are confined on a Reservation that has not the necessary resources to sustain them, they should be permitted the privilege of going outside for subsistence.

Shame on a powerful people who would deny them this privilege; yet it is done. While these Indians on Warm Springs have had many hindering causes why they should not progress, they have nevertheless made decided advancement in the march from savage to civilized life.

Suggested Further Reading

Meacham, Alfred. *Wigwam and War-Path: or, the Royal Chief in Chains.* Boston: J.P. Dale and Co., 1875.

————. *Wi-ne-ma (the Woman Chief) and Her People.* Hartford: American Publishing Co., 1876.

Confederated Tribes of the Warm Springs Reservation. *The People of Warm Springs.* Warm Springs, OR: Confederated Tribes, 1984.

Eva Emery Dye
1855-1947

One of Oregon's most popular writers in the early part of this century was Eva
Emery Dye. Born in Illinois, she was educated at Oberlin College. Moving to
Oregon City with her attorney husband, who was opening a practice there, she
became infatuated with the history of exploration and the fur trade in the Old
Oregon Country. She also was an enthusiastic colleague of Abigail Scott Duniway in
the woman suffrage movement. Dye's works were written in a romantic style that
found favor with both young and adult Oregonians for her emphasis upon the
courage and skill of her heroes and heroines. Her books include *Stories of Oregon*, a
children's book; an account of the Lewis and Clark expedition; *McDonald of
Oregon*, about a former Hudson's Bay Company employee who was the first English
teacher in Japan; and *McLoughlin and Old Oregon* (1900). The following excerpt
from this last book describes the departure of a Hudson's Bay Company party for
the beaver-trapping region of northern California.

The Brigade to California

D r. McLoughlin had much to do in gathering up the threads of routine. "Where is our Spanish brigade?" he asked.

"Ready equipped at Scappoose Point," answered Michel La Framboise. "We start tomorrow."

There was always bustle when a brigade set out. At daylight two hundred horses were pawing at Scappoose Point just across the western end of Wapato. Tom McKay had a ranch there, rich in sleek horses and cattle, and oceans of grass. A string of boats came down from the fort with a jolly picnic party to give the trappers a send-off. The cottonwoods were yellow on Wapato, sprinkling with gold the old council ground of the Multnomahs. October russet dotted the Scappoose hills. The Cascade Mountains lay in banks of crimson against the sunrise. The ladies from the fort leaped to their saddles tinkling with tiny bells. The gentlemen rode at their sides, gay as Charles's cavaliers, with lovelocks round their faces.

As usual, Dr. McLoughlin took the lead on his Bucephalus. Madame rode Le Bleu, a dappled white and sky blue, that in her day had galloped seventy-two miles in eight hours, to carry the tobacco, the *sine qua non* of an Indian trade. David mounted Le Gris de Galeaux like a Cossack. Rae and Eloise followed on Guenillon and the snowy Blond, all favorite horses at Fort Vancouver. Ermatinger with his Bardolphian nose cut a laughable figure on Le petit Rouge by the side of his fair bride Catherine on Gardepie.

After the gentry came La Framboise at the head of his long array of French trappers in scarlet belts and Canadian caps, with their picturesque Indian families, the plumes of men and women dancing and waving in the wind, brilliant as a hawking party in the days of mediaeval song.

Michel La Framboise had been a famous voyageur, one of the picked few sent out by John Jacob Astor. He could flip his canoe over the choppy waves where no one else would dare to go. Now, every autumn after the harvest was over, he led the horse brigade to the Spanish country.

The trappers always travelled with their families; the mother bestrode the family horse, with its high-pommelled Mexican saddle; the children jogged along on their Cayuse ponies and slept until night, when down they slid, full of glee, gathering flowers, shooting their little arrows, and listening to tales of grizzly bears and Blackfeet.

La Framboise was proud of his half-breed wife, Angelique, his Grande Dame, in her bloomers of beaded blue broadcloth; Angelique was proud of the pretty white pappoose that dangled from her pommel, asleep in its little *miau* of beads and ribbon. Close behind came the children, with elfin locks and flashing eyes, with one hand whipping their horses to make the bells go "zing-zing-zing," with the other hugging tight the buckskin dollies with blue bead eyes and complexions chalked to the whiteness of the charming missionary women.

The Indian boys brought up the rear, lashing their unruly packhorses heavily laden with camp equipage and Indian goods. All were in fine feather; the capering steeds, the crisp air, the scintillant sun, the tuneful meadow lark, harmonized completely with the bursts of song and gay and lively laughter.

The Willamette was carpeted with green from the early autumn rain. Scarlet-flaming thickets of vine maple glowed along the watercourses. Every hill-slope was a bank of burning ash. The cavaliers were armed to the teeth; from every belt depended a leathern firebag with pipe, tobacco, knife, and flint and steel. There were hunters in that brigade, rough as the grizzlies they hunted; hunters keen as the deer, suspicious as the elk; hunters that read like a book the language of tracks. Leaning over their horses' necks, they could discern the delicate tread of the silver fox, the pointed print of the mink, and the otter's heavy trail. With whip-stock in hand La Framboise points—"A bear passed last week," "An elk yesterday," "A deer this morning." In a moment a deer tosses its antlers, sniffs the wind, then bounds with slender, nervous limbs into the thickest shade.

A brisk morning ride over the Scappoose hills and down into the Tualitan plains was followed by a picnic dinner around a gypsy fire, then McLoughlin dismissed the trappers into the Indian country.

The parting cavalcades looked at each other from their curveting steeds. "Beware on the Umpqua," called the doctor. "If the new men get the fever give them plenty of broth and quinine." Again he turned with a parting word and gesture: "Look out for the Rogue-Rivers; they'll steal the very beaver out of your traps."

With gay farewells the fort people galloped back to the crossing at Wapato. The California brigade followed along the winding trail to the south. La Framboise always touched at La Bonte's, a solitary garden spot in miles and miles of prairie. "How much land do you own, mon frère La Bonté?"

"Begin in the morning," the old trapper was wont to say—"begin in the morning on a Cayuse horse. Go west till the sun is very high, then go south till it is around toward the west, and then back to the river; that is my manor."

And, too, there was always a stop at Champoeg,—every man at Champoeg was "mon frère" or "mon cousin" to La Framboise. Beside his wide hearth for many and many a year La Chapelle loved to sit and tell of the days when he, too, was *bourgeois,* and Madame his wife was the grandest dame that ever bestrode a pony. And for the thousandth time the good dame brought out the dresses stiff with beads that were worn in that gay time when the Monsieur led the hunt to the headwaters of the Willamette.

The head waters of the Willamette was a royal beaver republic. There the little colonies cut down whole forests, built up wonderful dams and bridges, scooped out lakes, and piled up islands. With their long sharp teeth they cut up the timber and shaped their houses, plastering them neatly with their broad, flat tails. They had rooms in their houses and dininghalls and neat doorways, these deft little builders, more cunning than the fox, more industrious than the bee, more patient than the spider, more skillful than the Indian. "The beaver can talk," says the Indian. "We have heard them talk. We have seen them sit in council on the lazy ones. We have seen the old chief beat them and drive them off."

Two hundred miles south of the Columbia, La Framboise descended from a high ridge of mountains down to a little plantation on the banks of the Umpqua, the fortalice of old Fort Umpqua. Carronades peeped from the donjon tower. Tom McKay built it after that disaster to the American trappers—sometimes they called it Fort McKay. Here a solitary white man ruled the Umpqua. Jules Gagnier was a Frenchman, the son of an honorable and wealthy family in Montreal. In vain they made efforts to reclaim him from his wanderings and his Indian wife. Hither, twice every year, La Framboise came, twenty miles off his trail, to bring Gagnier Indian goods and to carry away his beaver. Here, summer and winter, year in and year out, the jolly, genial Frenchman traded with his red friends and cultivated his little patch of garden. Such were the first white men who broke the way for pioneers on the northwest coast.

La Framboise's brigade wound along gorges and canyons, through the Rogue River Valley with its orchards of sunlit manzanita and hillsides of gnarled madrono and chinquapin, into the Switzerland of America, where Mt. McLoughlin on the summit of the Cascades was the most conspicuous landmark on the southern trail. One more pull—over the Siskiyous—and they have crossed the Spanish border. As a rule the brigades started early, to avoid the snows of Shasta, where once they lost the whole of their furs and three hundred horses. All day long, for days and days, the triple peaks of Shasta watched them winding down the Sacramento. La Framboise set his traps. Sutter's men began to look with unfriendly eye upon the intruders from the Columbia, but the Hudson's Bay Company had a permit from the Spanish Governor Alvarado.

Suggested Further Reading

Dye, Eva Emery. *The Conquest: The True Story of Lewis and Clark*. Garden City, NY: Doubleday, 1902.

———. *McLoughlin and Old Oregon: A Chronicle*. Chicago: A.C. McClurg, 1900.

———. *The Soul of America: An Oregon Iliad*. New York: Press of the Pioneers, 1934.

———. *Stories of Oregon*. San Francisco: The Whitaker & Ray Co., 1900.

Swanson, Kimberly. "Eva Emery Dye and the Romance of Oregon History." *Pacific Historian* 29 (1985): 59-68.

Alice Day Pratt
1872-1963

The Pendleton Roundup, first organized in 1909, is one of Oregon's oldest civic festivals and the second-oldest rodeo in the West.

Alice Day Pratt was born in Minnesota and lived as a child in a remote cabin in South Dakota. In 1911, this self-described "old maid" schoolteacher, who was then almost forty years old, filed on 160 acres of land in Central Oregon's Crooked River Valley, near the tiny community of Post, 30 miles southeast of Prineville. Pratt helped to support her homestead through her earnings as a schoolteacher, and raised chickens, dairy cows, wheat, and rye. She became a popular writer, especially through her stories and articles about her homesteading experiences. This account of the Pendleton Roundup is an excerpt from *A Homesteader's Portfolio* (1922), which tells of her eighteen years as a homesteader.

The Pendleton Roundup

The dingy streets of Pendleton, on this final and great day of the show, were filled with a seething and motley multitude. There had been a street parade and its elements passed hither and yon on various errands, mingling with guests from a dozen states who had honored the event with their presence. Dashing western gentlemen—officers of the day—sheriffs and mayors and private citizens, galloped this way and that, making arrangements for the afternoon. Young buckaroos in outlandish chaps—black and white, crimson, mustard-colored and green—paraded with due importance, three or four abreast. Here and there a group elicited loud applause from the bystanders. Women of all grades, from pretty ladies in handsome riding costume to savage-looking squaws bare-headed and blanketed, made common holiday. Scores of spectators crowded about a harness-maker's window in which were displayed the gold-and-silver-inlaid saddle and the jeweled bridle—prizes to be awarded the champion of the buckaroos and of the equestriennes. Evidently there was no nooning on this festive day. Lunches were hastily snatched from booths on the street, and the crowd melted from the thoroughfare to reappear in the great outdoor amphitheater, which, by one o'clock, was packed to the last seat on the bleachers.

Five hundred horses chafed at the gates; one hundred wild-eyed young steers tossed their horns in the enclosures; the band played intermittently and the feet of the expectant crowd beat time upon the benches. In the arena, the water wagons prepared the ground, and that ubiquitous black-eyed horseman of the official declaration—the goal of numberless feminine eyes—the marshal of the Roundup—sped his deputies hither and yon. Above all hung that indescribable, diamond-dust western sky, swept by fleeces of cloud soft as the down on the breast of a swan. Near at hand, low, rock-rimmed hills enclosed this new-world drama from all the world without.

The trumpet blast, the instant parting of the great gates, the forward leap of the leaders of the grand parade, and in they come—gallant gentlemen and dainty misses of the western metropolis, browned ranch maids and buckaroos, male and female champions of the ranges, sullen squaws in rainbow garb and resplendent savages in paint and feathers. Varied as the hues of their habiliments are the riders, yet exhibiting without exception that one gift in common—the careless command of the horse and saddle. While the audience roars itself hoarse for its favorites, they ride below in proud and smiling nonchalance. The broad felt hat is raised to this hail and to that. The gauntleted hand flies up in joyous salute to neighbors and home folks on the benches. One guesses how many days of ranch-house drudgery have been lightened for that smiling maiden by the thought of this day when, with new riding suit and saddle, she will ride with the youth of her choice in the Roundup at Pendleton, or, during how many solitary nights on the plains that champion has pictured the face that shall witness his triumph in the Pendleton arena.

On the benches, alert and keen-eyed western citizens, professional men late from eastern universities, grizzled ranchers and homesteaders, and many a king of wheat and of cattle claim their share in the grace and new-world chivalry, the dauntless courage and conquest of Nature represented there below. Little wrinkled grandmothers scramble to their feet and cackle congratulations to Buddy or Sissy for whom they once played cock horse back there in the old ranch kitchen. Sunburned ranch mothers claim proprietary interest in "Buck" and "Hank," who have herded their husbands' steers. A continuous round of applause accompanies each of half a dozen champions as he makes the circuit. Hat in hand and smiling, rides Buffalo Vernon, king of the rangers, indomitable tamer of the cayuse and the steer. A slender woman—Mrs. Dell Blanchett—spares one hand from the management of her careering horse to answer a thousand plaudits. The Indians, proud and stoical, greet the uproar of the spectators with hideously striped and stony visages.

The parade disposed of, the program leads up gently from less violent feats of horsemanship to the grand climax—the bucking scene. The slender son of a ranger has trained three little grays to act in response to his touch and voice with the precision of a mechanical toy. Neck to neck, with even, unbroken gait, they trot, gallop, and leap the hurdle, while the young master stands lightly with a moccasined foot on either outside horse, the third running beneath the arch of his limbs. There is a cowboy race abounding in right-about turns and breakneck maneuvers, that call for the sure-footedness of a cat and the agility of an ape. There is a girls' relay race—three times round, change horses each time and saddle your own—in which an agile slip of a girl, with a bunch of curls tied in her neck, is about to win in the final round. Suddenly her horse bolts, crashes into the fence, falls and flings his rider headlong into the pen of steers. The hush of horror is broken only by a deafening strain of applause, when, up, mounted, and passing her mates with a backward smile, she reaches the goal an easy length ahead. Next, he who can run down his steer, rope, throw, and hog-tie him in the minimum number of seconds, comes in for his reward. Buffalo Vernon must show how, unaided save by his own native

strength, he can fling himself from his horse upon the neck of a racing steer, conquer, bring him to earth, and hold him there with his teeth, raising both hands to the crowd above the prostrate captive.

The bronco-busters' contest today is the grand climax not only of the day's program but of the three days' show, the most desperate horses having been reserved, and the successful contestants of the preceding days being elected to ride them. Each candidate is provided with an untried horse, and both brute and human, as if conscious of their responsibility to the expectant throng, rise magnificently to the occasion. There is one new and final feature. There remains an unconquered bronco—a horse unsuccessfully attempted on the two preceding days. It happens that Joe Raley alone among the contesting buckaroos has not yet essayed to ride him, and now there are cries from the spectators of "Raley! Raley! Let the youngster try him. Let Raley ride him." Raley comes forward from the group of contestants and removes his hat, bowing to the crowd.

And now at length *he* stands—the observed of all observers—in the center of the arena—the Outlaw, the rebel, the man-hating, untamable cayuse! He is held at halter's length by a man on horseback. He stands stiffened, braced, with all four feet apart, his head drawn back. He is approached only on horseback. Two horsemen ride up quietly one on either side. Gently and with infinite deliberation they draw the blind over his eyes. From now on he is motionless, save for a trembling that possesses him wholly—a seemingly cold, stark terror of man and his ways. A man on the ground passes the saddle—high-backed, two-cinched, equipped with bucking rolls—to the horseman on the left. The horseman transfers it by imperceptible degrees to the back of the Outlaw. The man on the ground, reaching beneath the ridden horse, places the straps in the cinch rings and passes them to the horseman, who draws them up, inch by inch, inch by inch, to a viselike tightness. He then gives the signal to the waiting buckaroo. Now Joe Raley steps forward between the Outlaw and the ridden horse on the left. With a quick movement he places his foot in the stirrup and swings himself to the saddle, his right foot dropping as if by instinct into its place. The horsemen on either side, having removed the halter, back quickly away, drawing off the blind. The Outlaw is left without bridle or halter. The rider raises both hands to the benches in token of good faith. He must not "touch leather" during the trial. He pulls off his hat and strikes the horse upon the shoulder.

The Outlaw, the vision of the vast human herd being suddenly laid bare before him, sits back upon his haunches as if confronting a specter. Then he rises slowly upon all fours and then on two feet, pawing madly in the air. The blow of the hat upon his shoulder startles him and he makes a great leap forward, and another, and another, striving to plunge from under the terror that bestrides him. He takes an instant's counsel with himself. He cannot run from under the terror. He must dislodge him. Gathering himself together he leaps almost directly upward, coming down with stiffened limbs, humped back and all four feet together. Again and again, higher and higher he leaps. The force of his impact with the earth is terrible. The spectators lean forward breathless. Raley sees them through a blinding mist, every faculty of his being concentrated upon the one task of sticking to his steed. His young face is a furrowed mask of deadly determination. He gathers every last resource to meet some new emergency. What is it? The horse is shaking himself till his bones rattle in their sockets. Then, as if beside himself, he runs sideways, bursts through the slight inner railing that encloses the field, smashes up against the wall of the grandstand, and stands with head hanging, resource exhausted, confessedly beaten.

The marshal gives the signal. Time is up. The buckaroo has won! He leaps to the ground and bows to the wildly cheering crowd. And so, with the awarding of the prizes, the inlaid saddle to Joe Raley, youngest of the buckaroos, the jeweled bridle to the little lady with the bunch of curls, the chaps, the spurs, the lasso and the rest, so it closes—the great show, a show unsurpassed as an exhibit of native strength and physical prowess, not without brutality—a brutality that will pass away in the coming years before the finer chivalry that evolves the gentle man.

Suggested Further Reading

Pratt, Alice Day. *A Homesteader's Portfolio.* New York: Macmillan Co., 1922. Reprinted by Oregon State University Press, Corvallis, with introduction by Molly Gloss, 1993.

Kesey, Ken. "The Blue-Ribbon American Beauty Rose of Rodeo," *Oregon Magazine*, September 1986, pp. 22-28.

Stewart Holbrook
1893-1964

The lumber industry has long been the economic underpinning of Oregon. Its people, its folklore, and its written literature have been colorful and substantial. Certainly the most famous—and probably the most beloved—historian of Pacific Northwest logging (and many other topics) was Stewart H. Holbrook. A transplanted New Englander, Holbrook came to the Pacific Northwest in 1920. After working as a timekeeper in a lumber camp, he began a career as a freelance writer, then worked as a staff member of *Lumber News*, an organ of the lumber industry, and later became a contributing writer to the (Portland) *Oregonian*. Over his entire career he wrote scores of articles and more than thirty books, one of which was *Holy Old Mackinaw* (1946), from which this selection is drawn. Many of his books dealt with national as well as regional history.

The Passing of a Race

The loggers never looked backward—eastward. Had they done so, the more reflective among them might have seen what was happening— that as fast as they abandoned their old works a horde of farmers, traders, and city slickers moved in to grub stumps, plat town sites, and make highways out of the grass-grown logging roads. It was the loggers' ancient enemy, Civilization, following hard on their tails, and they wanted none of it.

There was always timber, plenty of timber—just over the next hump. The first hump was Bangor. The boys duffed in and cut so much white pine that Maine's founding fathers put a replica of *pinus strobus* on their state flag. They gave New England a close shave—once over for pine, once for spruce—then swept on into York State and Pennsylvania, pausing a brief moment at Glens Falls and Williamsport to whack hell out of what timber was left. York's and Penn's woods went down before the onslaught like so much wheat in a storm, and the boys piled into Michigan, making sawdust forty feet deep on which to build Saginaw. They went West and North in Michigan, clearing the upper peninsula last of all before they moved into Wisconsin to fill the rivers full of round-stuff and make bedlams out of Ashland, Wausau, and Chippewa Falls.

Michigan and Wisconsin lasted a goodly time, as time was reckoned by loggers, but it had an end. When it came the boys stopped only long enough to file the teeth of their saws, then swarmed into Minnesota like locusts. Like locusts, too, they took everything in their path. They cut the white men's forest. They drove most of the remaining red men from the reservations, often married their squaws, then cut the reservation timber. The Twin Cities reared up from the piles of chips and sawdust they made. But daylight got into the Minnesota swamp powerful sudden, and this time the boys faced a long jump before they could hide in more timber.

Most of them took an extra gallon of drinking liquor, to lighten the ghastly trip across those plains where there weren't even stumps to look at, and struck out for the Pacific Northwest and California; many of them moved direct to British Columbia. The others went to the Deep South, from whence they would have to move again, and move West, too, for the virgin timber beyond the Great Plains would outlast all else.

They came down the Columbia River into Oregon and Washington with a monstrous clanking of peaveys and immediately sailed into bigger and thicker timber than any of them had ever known. And now, although probably not one of them realized it, the loggers were in their last stronghold, their backs to the sea. There was no hump to go over from here. Civilization had caught up with them at last and civilization would lay the true species of logger lower than any stump they ever cut.

Horse-logging and bullwhacking were the lumberjacks' manner of work for two hundred and fifty years. It was a primitive method, and because it exactly suited the race of primitive men who used it, it survived for many years after steam-driven machinery was common everywhere except in the woods.

But steam finally drove the "hay burners"—the horses and oxen—out of the timber and with them went the colorful teamsters and bullwhackers. With it steam brought a bewildering amount and variety of machinery and an industrial routine and discipline that tended to make proletarians out of a race of men who had belonged to no order or class but their own. Steam did away with the cant-dog men. It drove the white-water men from the rivers—to be jammed on Garry's Rocks no more. In 1938 gasoline-driven machinery bids fair to drive the fallers and buckers—the very last of the manual laborers—out of their lair in the swamp.

The old-time log bunkhouses, as related, disappeared and in their place arose barrack-like structures; then the barracks were made into neat bunkhouses where every man has an army cot to himself and a locker in which to put his store clothes. Once started on improvements the boss loggers went wild. They stocked white sheets and pillow slips and added a bedmaker to the payroll. Lamps and lanterns gave way to electricity. Many of the companies threw out the grand old privies—some of them truly monumental jobs—and installed flush closets. A camp without a showerbath became a curiosity many years ago.

At about this time the girl waitresses put in an appearance. They made loggers restless, but they married loggers quickly and this fact gave some canny timber baron a bold and provocative idea: It might be possible to hire loggers who would stay married more than one night. It was tried and it worked beautifully. With the missus right in camp, the logger had no need to visit the fleshpots of the cities. Labor turnover was reduced, production speeded. The logging operators were quick to build houses in camp for married men.

Such doings naturally resulted in children. Today there is no large camp in the West that does not have its school and schoolmarm. That is, except in camps which are not camps at all, such as that of a large redwood operation where there are no camp buildings of any kind; everybody drives his car to and from his home in one of five towns within a radius of thirty miles of "camp."

The highways, in fact, have done as much or more than the women to reduce the logger to proletarian status. When the hard-dirt or paved road got within shouting distance of camp, the first shout loggers heard was that of automobile salesmen. You'll find a garage in almost any camp today, large or small. Unmarried loggers who, in older and more moral days, never saw a gaslight between late December and July Fourth, run to town on Saturday night and sleep it off Sunday afternoon. The highways are doing other things to the camps. Just as steam drove out the bulls, paved highways are driving out the steam locomotives. Trucks are doing the hauling to sawmills these days; gasoline-driven tractors are laying the fires in the donkey engines.

Comforts, marriage, and children, machine logging and highways—from this point onward it is easy to trace the complete disintegration of the tough and hairy species that was formed on the grim wooded shore of Maine three hundred years ago.

The Western loggers began subscribing to daily newspapers and to correspondence courses in everything from Personality to Saxophone Playing. Instead of spending all their money for booze and other necessities, some of them began carting radios into camp, where they still bleat nightly to the disgust of the few remnants of veritable *Pithecanthropus erectus* who had rather stove log about the time so-and-so loaded too high with the cross haul and came down Seney Hill like yaller hell and busted runners, with the snub line broken and no hay on the road. . . .

Loggers changed their tobacco habits. Thirty years ago a man who came into camp smoking a cigarette was usually eyed coldly, allowed to eat his supper, then sent packing down the trail. "A man who will smoke one of them pimp sticks," old Jigger Jones said soberly, "won't stop at nothin'." Jigger and his contemporaries considered a cigarette smoker to be worthless as a logger, and a degenerate as well. Today's logging-camp stores sell more cigarettes than smoking and chewing tobacco combined.

Suggested Further Reading

Booth, Brian, editor. *Wildmen, Wobblies & Whistle Punks: Stewart Holbrook's Lowbrow Northwest*. Corvallis, OR: Oregon State University Press, 1992.

Holbrook, Stewart. *The Columbia*. New York: Rinehart & Co., 1956. Reprinted by Comstock Editions, Sausalito, CA, 1990.

———. *The Far Corner, A Personal View of the Pacific Northwest*. New York: Macmillan Co., 1952. Reprinted by Comstock Editions, Sausalito, CA, 1987.

———. *Holy Old Mackinaw: A Natural History of the American Lumberjack*. New York: Macmillan Co., 1946. Reprinted by Comstock Editions, Sausalito, CA, 1979.

Linda Danielson
1941-

Linda Danielson was born in Colorado and has lived in Oregon since 1968. She teaches Native American literature, folklore, and writing at Lane Community College in Eugene, Oregon. In 1975-77 she directed the Oregon Old-Time Fiddling Project, upon which this essay is based. During the project she interviewed and recorded the music of thirty fiddlers in Lane, Douglas, and Jackson counties. Danielson has done fieldwork in traditional music for both archives and folk festivals; in addition, she has designed traditional music adaptations for theater and played fiddle for numerous Eugene-area bands. The following selection was first published in *Oregon Folklore* (1977) by Suzi Jones.

Fiddling

"**S**oldier's Joy," "Turkey in the Straw," "The Girl I Left behind Me," "Git Outa the Way Federals," "The Last of Callahan," "Redwing," "Peek-a-Boo Waltz"—these and countless other old tunes still pour from the fingers and bows of Oregon fiddlers. Some of the tunes were popular on the radio in the 1920s and 30s; others can be traced back to the fiddlers' ancestors of Civil War days; and still others must have come over with colonists as far back as the 1700s.

The fiddlers are quick to tell you that their music is not violin music—make no mistake, it is fiddle music. (One fiddler says that you can tell which is which because a violin is carried in a case, and a fiddle in a gunny sack. He's kidding now, but a generation ago it was often true.) It depends on how you play the instrument. Violin music is played according to written score, with a firm conception of details dictated by that score. In other words, there is a right way to play the tune. Fiddle music is generally learned by ear, played by memory and improvisation, and tunes vary quite a lot from one fiddler to another. You could listen to a whole group of fiddlers play off their versions of "Ragtime Annie," and you'd hear that they were playing the same tune, yet each fiddler would have his own way with the tune—his own set of details: there are many right ways to fiddle the tune.

On almost any Sunday afternoon fiddlers gather to play old tunes at public jam sessions somewhere in Oregon. When summer starts, you can find them at county fairs, ready to provide an afternoon's entertainment, or at occasional fiddling contests in such places as Forest Grove, Pendleton, Canyonville, and Drain. Fiddling is still a lively art here in Oregon. True, there aren't as many fiddlers as there once were, and the average age of fiddlers goes up at the time. But some children and young people are becoming interested and learning the old art. An educated guess is that there are four hundred fiddlers scattered around the state. So fiddling certainly hasn't died out here—in fact, besides New England, the South Atlantic states and the Ozarks, Texas and the Pacific Northwest are probably the hottest spots in the country for fiddling.

It's hard to tell why this should be so, but maybe the reasons go something like this: most of the people who play the fiddle and live in Oregon came here from somewhere else (a quick spot check among area fiddlers shows the score running about twenty-six non-natives to four native Oregonians). When people emigrate, the culture and the memory of the old home sometimes becomes extra-important—and maybe that's why some people cling to the old ways. Then, too, in lots of places fiddling was until very recently the only available dance music—just as it was for past generations. It really hasn't been that long since Oregon was frontier, and in the 1960s at least fiddlers were still playing square dances in school houses and grange halls in isolated parts of eastern Oregon. Besides, fiddling is just plain good music—it's fun to play, to hear, and to dance to.

There was a time when it seemed like fiddling was about to be forgotten, though, right after World War II, in the wake of the Big Band sound and Rock 'n' Roll. Then in about 1960 people began to notice fiddling again, perhaps under the influence of the folk music revival. Contests brought fiddlers together; many an ex-fiddler went home after going to a contest "just to listen" and hauled out the old fiddle case. Bows were rehaired, broken strings replaced, and the ex-fiddlers started playing again.

In 1965 the Oregon Old-Time Fiddlers Association was founded by a dozen people on a Sunday afternoon in Waldport, and it's been growing ever since. Oregon fiddling has been changing too. It used to be that fiddlers played mostly for dancing—now, more often the fiddlers' audience is there to listen. At the old-time dances fiddlers had to play hard and loud to be heard, with no amplification—so sometimes the sound was harsh. Now fiddlers strive for a sweeter sound since they have the help of amplification to make themselves heard. In times and places when many folks lived on land their parents or grandparents had farmed, each region had its distinctive fiddling style and characteristic stock of tunes. Now, most Oregon fiddlers actually started playing somewhere else and then moved here, bringing with them developed styles from other parts of the country. Too, fiddlers travel to distant contests, tape record each other's playing, and buy records of fiddlers from the other end of the country. Their playing becomes technically better, more sophisticated, more cosmopolitan.

In fact, many young people who are taking up fiddling don't even learn from the local old-timers anymore. Many of them prefer to learn the style of their favorite fiddler from some other part of the country. These days that is often Texas. Texas has produced a particularly elaborate and sophisticated, sweet, bluesy style of fiddling that is currently a good bet for winning the regional and national contests. So there is a kind of generation gap among the fiddlers. On one side are the older fiddlers who learned from grandfathers, mothers, or neighbors, then never passed the art on to their children (who were listening to Glen Miller, and later to Elvis Presley). On the other are the crop of new young fiddlers, mostly under thirty, who learn their fiddling from a variety of sources and regions. They are generating new, homogenized blends

of fiddling that have ties to Texas fancy contest style, western swing, jazz, bluegrass, and Canadian prime-time television show-style fiddling.

Because most older fiddlers are emigrants to Oregon, it appears that we don't really have an Oregon style of fiddling. That's true, but we do have a characteristic cluster of styles, brought from homes in other states by those older fiddlers. Probably the greatest number of Oregon fiddlers come from the upper plains states: North Dakota, South Dakota, Minnesota, Nebraska. Another group comes from the Arkansas-Missouri-Oklahoma region. Still others come from Canada and from nearby states—Washington and Idaho. Most of the tunes are from the British Isles—English, Scottish, or Irish. But the North Plains also give us a stock of tunes from Scandinavia, Bohemia, and Germany. The fiddlers of British background often prefer to play hoedowns—the fast moving square dance tunes, with lots of action and rhythm from the bow. By contrast, the European-descended fiddlers play a smoother, sweeter style, and prefer the polkas, waltzes, and schottisches. These ethnic, regional, and individual styles never completely blend, but the movers and travelers who are now Oregon fiddlers do grow to appreciate each other's diversity, and pick up a tune here and there from each other.

Postscript 1992. Since this essay was written fifteen years ago, many of those older fiddlers who brought developed styles and repertories from other places have stopped fiddling or died. With them have gone unique tunes and distinctive stylistic features. Meanwhile, the rest of us have gotten older. Now Oregon, and perhaps the whole Pacific Northwest, seems to be developing a kind of common denominator style. Today we play fewer hoedowns as a rule, and more of the older popular songs. More of Oregon's currently active fiddlers have learned to play here, both young people and retirement-age beginners, so we sound more like each other, although a two-caste system does seem to be developing as contest and "strictly old-time" fiddlers seem more and more distinct from each other. Nowadays, most of Oregon's champion fiddlers are young people who play the nationally influential Texas style. Fewer small contests can be found today than in 1977, but many grange halls are opening their facilities to Association members, who once again are playing for dances in rural communities. The traditional art of fiddling is simply finding new ways to fit into contemporary Oregon life.

Suggested Further Reading

Danielson, Linda. "Oregon Fiddling: The Missouri Connection." *Missouri Folklore Journal* (forthcoming).

Williams, Vivian. *169 Brand New Old Time Fiddle Tunes.* Volume 3. Seattle: Voyager Publications, 1990.

George Venn
1943-

George Venn was born in Washington State. He has
studied in the United States, and in Ecuador, England,
and Spain. Since 1970, Venn has been a member of the
Department of English at Eastern Oregon State
College. He is General Editor of the *Oregon Literature
Series*. He is the recipient of a Pushcart Prize for poetry
(1981) and an Oregon Book Award (1988). His writing
has appeared in *Folklore India, Western American
Literature, Montana, the Magazine of Western History,
Poetry Northwest*, and many other publications. He has
received grants from the Sierra Club, the Oregon
Council for the Humanities, and the Oregon Arts
Commission. His genres include essay, fiction, and
poetry. "Barn," from his *Marking the Magic Circle*
(1987), is his reflection upon the connotations of that
word.

Barn

"How much hay will this one hold?" I asked and swung open the old doors. Inside, I could hear the shapes begin to move, the silence yawn.

Call it close place of barley, summer's house, call it stable. Remember the swallow, owl, mouse living inside the word larger than the neatness of furnished rooms. Name the tack room harness—hames, collars, tugs, bridgen, whiffletrees, bridles, bells. Note the granary, its sacks of oats bulging, its old bins and smell of mice. Touch the chewed wood of the manger, the dung-splashed stanchion. Remember the shake roof, its acres of cobwebs draped gray and shaking thick with dust, its chinks of light. Remember the dead flies against the splotched milky glass, the bedding three feet thick and reeking of ammonia. Name the gutter, scoop, cupola, bag balm, hayhook, pitchfork. The words come over the threshold like cattle called "Comeboss, comeboss" ringing their bells through the deep mud trail in the alder woods while other words hide silent in the straw.

Outbuilding. Away from the house. Inside, the barn's gray rain-polished boards let in long slats of yellow light where we played wild yelling bootless Kings of the Mountain in the loose hay. I saw the hay dust boiling up toward the rain tapping the cedar shakes above the loft. In that Platonic cave, rich with the odor of cut clover, we climbed the high solid bones of rafters and beams, rode the braced timbers like horses of joy. Somewhere, the quick squeak of mice—a nest of pink thumbs squirming. When the dog barked, we looked out through the unbattened cracks, our hair full of seed, our rioting stilled.

Grandpa and Grandma coming through the pasture swinging the milkpail between them like a silver moon. Suddenly, we were spies whispering over our wooden guns. Sucking her splayed hooves out of muck, the Jersey cow swayed in like a steaming orange-white giant, her hooves thudding the planks, her udder swollen with milk. We watched through the knotholes as Grandpa swung down the three-legged stool, Grandma dumped feed in the manger and called the cow who came forward. Latching the stanchion shut, Grandma talked to the cow until the first milk pinged into the pail, the white foam gradually building on the surface and the ping changing to one-two-one-two low pulsing spurts. Out of nowhere the wild barncats crawled, waiting by the pail until Grandpa aimed a teat of milk, squirting over their faces, the cats licking so fast, so hungry, pawing the sweet air for more, then slinking away. Upstairs, we laughed and heard the cow low. Nothing seemed to be too much in the barn except that sudden hoof in the milk bucket, that sudden swat of a wet tail in the face.

How we learned to say "close the door; were you born in a barn?" I don't know. How we learned to tease the kid throwing snowballs with "you couldn't hit the broad side of a barn" I don't remember, but the kid always threw harder and missed more. And the chubby girl I loved who was "broad as a barn" and the hot-to-trot girl who "lit out of here like a heifer out of the barn" who probably took too many tumbles in the hay? Where have these come from? Early, somewhere, even before kindergarten, I learned to see the open zipper on my brother's jeans, his flannel shirt stuck out and a flash of white underwear and even now the phrase bolts: "Your barn door's open." There was subtle pleasure in saying a thing that way. For emphasis, we might add "Cows are getting out." Everybody knew what it meant, but something was still spared the unzipped kid; something became laughter that could have been cooped up and unhappy. Once, I said that to an old carpenter at work. He looked down, took hold of his fly, and as he slowly zipped it up, he winked at me and said "No old horse gonna get outta that barn anyway." He laughed as he said that and I laughed too.

"Now up on the home place, at least we had a good barn," Uncle Leonard would say as he lit the match with his thumbnail and sucked the flame down into his pipe. "My father built that barn by hand the third year we moved out from town. I split the shakes after school. That's the only thing I don't like about this place." He paused, blew a mouthful of smoke toward the ceiling, then said: "just a bunch a rundown sheds." I drank coffee and listened. I could tell he didn't even like to say *shed;* it meant an inferior structure—small, weak, inadequate. I guessed then that the high basilica of his father's Dutch barn— the center bay with loose hay mowed to the rafters (under the Jackson fork) and two side alleys for feeding stock—those spaces he carried inside him like a sanctuary.

The first year we built the new barn, swallows with gabled tails swarmed to its fir boards and tacked their mud apartments to the joint between the rafters and the plate under the eaves. In and out all summer they swooped, banked, glided, dived, and mosquitoes disappeared in their wedge-shaped beaks. Resting on wires between the house and barn, twittering constant in the late evening, the slate sheen of their wings would flash any light. For hours, they carried my eyes and ears in and out of their nests, where four or five smaller peeping wedges would plug the mud tunnel entrance. In September after the first frost, they would gather by the lake in thousands and, seeing them there, I would feel as though the barn were flying away, as though they were taking it south with them. Then, I would try to make up a song.

In the lower stall one September, I noticed a barn swallow apparently hanging in mid-air. Walking closer, I saw the thin irridescent gleam of fishline. Woven tight into the mud-daubed nest, one dangling loop of leader had caught the swallow's wing and it fluttered there until it died. I left it there—one swallow making a fall.

The cats who came from nowhere and stayed all winter, the mice by the thousands they chased; the barrel of skunks my cousin jumped into one day playing hide and seek; the owls perched in the loft, their heart-shaped faces white as ghosts; the rats who packed all the apples, tinfoil, and nails into their nest; the nights in England I slept out of the rain in English barns; the men who have slept as strangers in our barn; the North Wind robin I memorized early who flew to the barn to keep herself warm and hid her head under her wing: who are we all together here like refugees in a line? Is this barn the wood shape of hope? Nothing so tightly built or locked that some other unknown life can't get in, sleep warm and dry a night or a year and, somehow wake and go on?

"Never play with matches in the barn," Grandma said. "Rats will light them with their teeth." "If someone wants to sleep in the barn, always ask them if they smoke. If they say yes, don't let them sleep in the barn—no matter what." I saw her do that once. The men promised they wouldn't smoke, but she turned them away to the road again after supper. "We don't want to see the barn burn down," she said. "What would we do then?"

Old Jesse told me once how all the farmers sat in their barns rainy days and just watched out the door. They couldn't stay in the house; the wife would nag them to death. They leaned over a stall and watched the horses snort through the hay. When they raised a barn for neighbors, and all the men and women around worked together for a day, they'd dance that night on the threshing floor in the center and fiddles would winnow and flail until midnight or later. "A bunch of men could build a big barn like that an' they didn't have no architect," he said. "But these here schools, now, they have to pay a bundle just for a damn architect, but when you go inside them schools, what do you find half the time: a big space in the middle and alleys down both sides—just like a barn."

"Out behind the barn" was the locale of emergencies. If two men had a quarrel, they settled it there. If a boy got in trouble, he took his lickin' there. Old Jesse asked me why I was trying to turn back the pages of time, and I said what did it matter if that time was seen solid and clear. Maybe we should live in barns like the Dutch just to keep us loose and imagining more than the human city, I said. I wondered out loud where all the fighting and smoking and screwing around was happening now. Probably down some back alley or in the back seat of a car, old Jesse said. Even the wild oats gone to town. Give me the squeak of the latch on the stable door, I told him. That's just enough time to get on your clothes and hide in the hay somewhere while your mother calls your name and you can keep on kissing. "George, you come in the house now, wherever you are," that big voice would say.

One summer a swarm of wild bees hung thick, gold, trembling near the ridge-pole, slowly surging back and forth over each other—a dangling cluster. Gradually, they began to draw out white slabs of new comb. We left them alone, except for the rocks boys will throw on dares before they run from the stinging sure to come. Those bees stayed up there three years. "It's a good thing they're not in the attic," Grandma said. They left one spring in a great swirling swarm, just as they had come. We never could climb high enough to reach that honey in the peak.

His little finger clamped against his right palm told a story. In Wisconsin in the barn one summer, that finger caught in a hay pulley, didn't heal right, never went to town to have it set by a doctor. Grandpa called it his hook and, pulling fingers, he would always match his bent hook against any man's straight one. He said he always won, except the last time he went back to Wisconsin and some husky cousin pulled that little finger straight—the wound opening again. He doused it with mercurochrome and refused to see a doctor. Back west in Washington, he let it heal to his hook and never pulled fingers again.

And how many men found hanging by their own ropes in the barn? And how many girls, how many women, giving birth still to their children in the mother hay? And how many men falling from the timbers, crushed under the weight of grain, kicked by horses in the stalls? And how many calves butchered and hung high to cure, and how many lambs and pigs—all these gone to veal, mutton, bacon? This is the house of blood, breaking water, birth, afterbirth, despair, mistake, meat, death. Yet the newborn calf wobbles slick and wet and does not hesitate to drink.

The green leatherbound diary doesn't show his crippled walk, his arthritic hands on the pitchfork loading the wheelbarrow in the dark barn. These were his record of four days in 1949:

Sunday, June 12: To Sunday S. and Church, Oliver Aus here, got sheep. Mrs. Mayo and boys here, had lunch on lawn. Robert Mc. here in evening.
Monday, June 13: Sharon and Shirley wheeled 90 loads manure. Alice washed dishes. Bible study in eve.
Tuesday, June 14: Cleaned out sheep barn all day. Sharon and Shirley wheeled 100 loads manure. Alice washed dishes. Robert Mc. got hurt in woods.
Wednesday, June 15: Nice day 68-38. Hard wind in afternoon. Sharon and Shirley wheeled 68 loads manure. We finished in forenoon. To Bible study in afternoon. Barn ready for hay now.

These are the names of Alder neighbors and friends to him. I am called "boys," one of those eating on the lawn. Later, I would wheel the barrow for him too, a nickel a load, and count with Uncle Charlie the number of times I rolled down the planks and out the door to the steaming pile.

In my dream, there is a girl leading me by the hand to her barn. Inside, her high swing hangs from the beams by two thick ropes. The seat is wide enough for both of us and we begin to sway and pump our legs easy and rise slowly holding onto each other and the ropes. Swinging higher and higher over the hay, the pits of our stomachs beginning to glow, our faces tighten as we get ready to bail out and fall forever to loose hay loose hay, the swing above us gradually slowly waving over us like a dark pendulous jewel.

Eli and I worked together that summer outside Cheney filling the barn with bales. I drove the truck that pulled the wheel loader while Eli balanced on the bed and stacked the load. At the barn, I backed into the dark huge doors and stopped. While I climbed to the top of the stack, Eli started the mechanical stacker and set the bales on and they climbed to me waiting high in the peak sweating like a horse up there close to the metal roof pinging everywhere and baking my head in an oven, the sweat stinging every scratch it could find. Below, Eli stood in place—calm, old, red-faced, white-haired—drinking water. Watching him from the high stack, I knew suddenly why the work divided this way. I was young and smart—I thought—but Eli worked in the cool and stood in one place. We piled that hay for four weeks right to the rafters and out the door, me on the hot stack in the barn, and driving, Eli riding the cool truck deck and smiling. At night, before we slept in the sweltering bunkhouse, coyotes and black-spangled sky everywhere, Eli told me all about riding trains and sleeping in barns and under bridges all over the country. At a rescue mission, he had to sing an hour for just a doughnut and coffee. I couldn't stay awake to hear all his stories—the kid, the summer hayhand, who pretended not to be a student at all.

⸻

Will these fit somewhere? The joke Jesse told about the farmer who went crazy in a round barn looking for a corner to piss in; and Uncle Leonard saying as he smoked how, if the barn was larger than the house, you knew the man was boss, even as we sat in his small house surrounded by sheds; and the farmer who went to Portland where he saw the high hotel and asked, "How much hay will it hold?"

⸻

The troupe director said actors have been barnstorming since Shakespeare or before; the poet told me to watch for a barn converted into a house near 20th Place; the doctor invited me to play a little barn basketball; the secondhand store owner has his barn filled to the peak with furniture; the magician had his barn packed with books; the evangelist held his revival meetings in a barn outside Seattle; the curator stands in his converted museum; the grocery called the Red Barn stays open later than Safeway: these are some of the possible interiors, the shapes a huge container can contain. These are just a brief beginning.

⸻

I think of the ark, the barn Noah built to hold the animals and family two by two, the barn as ship creating the world again. Across the wide stubble, such barns appear to be huge wood ships moored to the fencerows—the rainbow of old wood that men built as covenant with the animals, neighbors, children, gods. Strong enough to hold some huge possibilities through the temporary chaos of flood or winter, then wise enough to let the sheltered all go out again to recreate the world, such structures seem to always be getting built in spite of scoff, despair, doubt. In winter storms, they seem to float.

⸻

Is this the modern fear that fixes old barn boards and beams in the houses of cities, that makes the barnboard market great? The ark—that covenant of husbandry, magnanimity, community, regeneration, memory, family—all being lost little by little as we watch the dream of barns disappear in the nightmare of urban boxes thick with only pets? Do we want those barns back, say, one barn for every three blocks, a barn for every school to prevent complete illiteracy, the gable or the gambrel roof that puts the hand of the ancient in every day?

⟶

"And did you close the doors?" he asked me.

"I left just a crack—enough for the cat to get in," I said. It was dark then, and we went toward the house. Behind me, I felt the barn settle, articulate with weight. We had filled it again. Everything seemed to hold together now by what we didn't say.

Suggested Further Reading

Venn, George. *Marking the Magic Circle: Poetry, Fiction, and Essays.* Corvallis: Oregon State University Press, 1987.

———. *Off the Main Road: Poems by George Venn.* Portland: Prescott Street Press, 1978.

———. *Sunday Afternoon: Grande Ronde.* Portland: Prescott Street Press, 1975.

Sallie Tisdale
1957-

Sallie Tisdale was born in California, although she writes, "I'm very much a child of rough mountains, flat rivers, valleys scattered with cattle and sheep, rain, manzanita, blue-belly lizards, but I'm never quite at home. Everything is *story*; writers are an amoral bunch, and those who love a writer need a thick skin, because sooner or later, everything gets written." A registered nurse, Tisdale has written books about her work in nursing homes in *Harvest Moon* (1987, excerpt below) and in hospitals; about salt; and about her life in the Pacific Northwest. She has won several literary awards for these works. She has also published in magazines such as *Esquire, Harper's,* and the *New Yorker*.

Harvest Moon

H arvest Moon Care Center is a nursing home for one hundred people, located in a residential neighborhood in a medium-sized West Coast city. The architecture is undistinguished, the landscaping ordinary and not quite finished. The walls inside are broad and painted in cheap, dull colors, decorated with amateurish oil paintings of fruit bowls and flower vases. In these characteristics Harvest Moon is like most of the thousands of nursing homes in the United States. In some respects, though, Harvest Moon is different, even unique. It is owned by a large fraternal organization with a long-standing interest in caring for the elderly, and has a good reputation in the community. People sometimes wait months for a vacancy here. In a market turning toward for-profit corporate control at an almost frantic pace, Harvest Moon remains decidedly nonprofit, surviving partly on donations and second-hand equipment, and run by a board of directors determined not to sink in an increasingly cutthroat market.

Cathy Bosley, a plump blond woman in her late twenties who works as the activity assistant, heads briskly down the hall a half hour later. It is almost eleven and time for the weekly Trivial Pursuit game she conducts with a passion. As she passes Phoebe White's room she sees an aide helping Phoebe into a wheelchair; Phoebe, too, has a passion for the game, when she remembers. Cathy stops at the central hallway beside a small woman in a wheelchair.

"Are you coming to Trivial Pursuit?" Cathy asks, leaning down, hugging her arms possessively around the woman's shoulders. She speaks in a loud, cheery voice. Verna Livingston looks up at her from a few inches away with a sour face.

"All right, all right, I'll go," she finally answers. "You go first, then I'll go. All right, all right." She starts to turn the chair toward the dining room where the game is played. "I don't have anything else to do."

The dining room borders the double front doors, which in turn open to a crowded parking lot bordered with a hedge. Visitors enter the front hallway beneath a windblown American flag, pass a receptionist at a desk, and face the smokers' table in the dining room a few yards away, before they turn. Near this table a small quiet group gathers.

A sullen man in a white uniform positions the many wheelchairs in place at the table. When Phoebe White arrives she beams happily as she is parked beside Max Kleiner, a whitehaired, lump-faced man with jug ears that pitch wildly out from his head. Since a stroke several years ago he has been unable to walk. Max talks in a stream of diphthongs and phonemes repeated in happy verbosity. Now he sits at the table laughing continually, head turning rapidly from face to face, following the movements of each person in the room.

"Wee-wee-wee, bay-bay-bay!" he cries. "Woo-woo, wee-wee-wee." Each phrase is uttered with maximum expression, the sounds of an infant discovering his toes, sounds of delight and invention, lewd in their insinuation of sensual promise. Max Kleiner's fat vowels are so close to actual words that listeners strain to understand until, with reflection, they finally turn to something else.

Phoebe turns to Max now and her face brightens with memory.

"That's him! That's the man! They had me married to him this morning!" she cries to the table, pointing to Max with a long finger. Then she turns to Verna Livingston beside her. "I'm Bernice's sister. She owns this place."

The sullen young man announces that the players should separate the tiles in front of them into piles, and leaves the room.

"Why separate them?" asks Phoebe.

Verna answers, still sour. "I don't know. I don't know why."

"It doesn't make sense."

"No, it doesn't make sense."

"What's the point?"

"I don't know the point," says Verna, and reaches for a mound of tiles, beginning to stack them. Max reaches, too, but the aide has placed the tiles out of his grasp. He plays with his hands.

"If they're going to give us tea, I have a cookie," announces Verna. She holds up a pink napkin she has kept hidden in her lap. "Here's my cookie. I have one cookie and it's cracked."

Cathy Bosley, meanwhile, has pulled a stack of cards out of the Trivial Pursuit box and is ready to begin. The game requires only that Cathy read the question to the group. Whoever knows the answer calls it out. The first correct answer wins the speaker a tile, and when one person has collected three tiles, they are gathered back and the game begins again.

"Who was the 1960 *Sports Illustrated* Sportsman of the Year?" Cathy asks, speaking in a loud, ringingly cheerful voice. She glances around the table, then repeats the question.

"Bobby Orr." The voice belongs to Maude Davis, a ninety-three-year-old woman who rarely attends activities, preferring in her irritation the solitude of slow prowls and her room.

"That's right! Goodness, that's correct!" cries Cathy, shaking her head. She hands Maude a tile and Maude retreats into silence.

"Buddy, are they going to give us tea?" says Verna loudly. "I have a cookie."

"No," replies a husky, dark-haired young man down the table.

"Well, I guess I won't get to have my cookie, then."

"Who was Sherlock Holmes's smarter brother?" calls out Cathy. No one answers. Two nurse's aides walk in and head for the vending machines in the corner. Smoke drifts to the table from the three patients sharing a newspaper and smoking break nearby. Overhead four electric fans turn in lazy imitation of the slow pace below. Cathy repeats the question.

"Um, um, eighteen, um, eighteen seventy-nine!" says a woman hunched down in her seat.

Phoebe suddenly grabs Max's hand and smiles hugely; Max starts babbling with excitement. "Whoo-whoo!" he cries like a train whistle. "Whoo-whoo, ha-ha-ha, whoo-whee!"

Phoebe laughs happily. "Ouch! Ouch!" she giggles.

And this is how the days go, in dreamy conversations of unclear intent, jokes without punchlines, sorrows without end. The patients who retain their wits often avoid these gatherings, the odd meetings in the hallways, the chaotic winds of damaged cerebrums as much as possible. But they are here, too, and sometimes here to stay.

Here there is a constant going on, and a constant staying the same. Phoebe and Max and Verna lead lives of sameness disturbed by tiny and constant stimulations of brain and body. When I am in their midst it seems a world in continual refinement, even renewal. It is as though each member were almost, but not wholly, complete, and sought through the repeated, inactive days a final harmony, a topping off. Someday it will be my turn—to be old, to be sick, to feel my own dying surround me in a cloud of soft certainty. Perhaps someday I'll rock myself to sleep like Anna, singing old songs creakily in the dark, and the young face that passes briefly over mine like a revenant will pay no heed, bear no mind to the meaning of the words. It won't be that young girl's fault; she'll be too young to know.

A hum of activity underlies the passiveness—it is velocity without motion. It is, after all, a community of human beings going about their complicated and inexplicable business. But the climax is never reached. A Greek chorus murmurs in the background, and now and again individuals step forward, as though on cue, and deliver brief and poignant lines. These are the questions no one else thinks to frame.

Suggested Further Reading

Tisdale, Sallie. *Harvest Moon: Portrait of a Nursing Home.* New York: Henry Holt & Co., 1987.
———. *The Sorcerer's Apprentice: Tales of the Modern Hospital.* New York: McGraw-Hill, 1986.
———. *Stepping Westward: The Long Search for Home in the Pacific Northwest.* New York: Henry Holt & Co., 1991.

Deborah Fairley
1951-

Deborah Fairley was born in Nebraska and grew up a few miles from the ruts left by emigrants traveling west on the Oregon Trail. After graduating from the University of Nebraska and working as a reporter for the *Omaha World-Herald*, she followed the trail to Oregon and settled in Portland. She has since been a television producer, assistant editor of *Oregon Magazine*, and—since 1990—program director of Pioneer Courthouse Square. The following selection is excerpted from her essay on the history of Portland's Rose Festival, one of the oldest community celebrations in the state. The complete essay appeared originally in *Oregon Magazine* (1988).

Glory Days

Ever leaf through your grandmother's high-school yearbook? Remember how hard it was to connect the mild-mannered matron you knew with the cheeky young flapper in the pictures?

Portland's Rose Festival is kind of like that.

The Rose City's *grande dame* has been around so long that few people still remember the spunky, spirited youngster she once was. Sometimes even she has a hard time remembering those days. Ask her about her youth, and she dismisses the era with a few brief stories of quaint goings-on. Perhaps, after decades of headlines proclaiming "This Year's Rose Festival to Be Biggest, Best Ever," the old girl has started believing her own clippings; eighty years of ever-more-spectacular festivals would seem to indicate that those early events were modest indeed. In fact, the lady's official history refers to "small beginnings eighty years ago."

Small beginnings? Pardon us, ma'am, but those early years weren't exactly chopped liver.

Yes, festival attendance figures were smaller then—but so was the population. Many events actually drew more people, per capita, than they do today. And in some ways, the festival's aim was much broader. The queen, for example, was selected by a vote of the entire city—in some years, by the entire *state*. Ballots were printed every day for two weeks in all three Portland newspapers, a circumstance that not only encouraged civic involvement, but must have caused circulations to skyrocket.

The final day of the festival was at one point both a city and a state holiday. Grand-opening ceremonies for major projects such as the St. Johns Bridge and the Columbia River Highway were timed to coincide with the festival. Railroad lines lowered their rates and conducted national publicity campaigns to encourage attendance. Two hundred miles of roses were planted alongside city streets and sidewalks. Festival pageants featured 2,000-voice choirs or, in one case, a crowd of 8,000 children. These people thought BIG.

Early festivals were, nevertheless, grass-roots affairs. Floats were decorated, not with roses from commercial hothouses, but with cuttings from thousands of backyards. Residents who weren't able to deliver blossoms in person could bundle them onto any streetcar, and the floral supplies would be dropped off free of charge. Homes and businesses were festooned with roses, as were the private carriages, automobiles and motorcycles citizens drove in the parades.

Within a few years of the first festival, the Rose Society estimated that 2 million roses were being used in the grand floral parade, as many as 60,000 blooms per float.

There was an exuberance and across-the-board involvement to those early festivals. If today's festival is a well-oiled machine, yesterday's evokes the image of an excited young Mickey Rooney grabbing Judy Garland by the shoulders and blurting out, "I've got it! We'll put on a play! We can use the old barn! *Everybody* will come!"

It was an era of dreamers and unabashed boosters. Portlanders, like other Americans, were convinced of the inevitability of progress; it was just a matter of time until their city became, as one fanciful map already labeled it, "New York on the Willamette." If the rest of the country hadn't caught on yet, why, Portland would put on a show and get everybody to come. Once here, visitors would be inevitably smitten by the city's charms.

It had worked once before, during the 1905 Lewis and Clark Exposition. Not only had that extremely successful event drawn international exhibitors and attention, but it also had gained the city thousands of new residents. When the exposition closed and that gratifying national spotlight faded, the city fathers grew restive. They proposed another attention-getting event, a festival built around the Portland Rose Society's annual rose show. The society, the oldest rose group in the country, had sponsored the shows for nearly twenty years; by 1904, the exibition was a fiesta complete with a parade.

And so in 1907, the first official Rose Festival was unveiled—but it was not a humble beginning. "Humble," in fact, may be the last word that should be used to describe those early days. With hyperbole that today would make the brashest promoter blush—and ambitious plans that almost justified the over-blown rhetoric—Portland orchestrated its return to national prominence.

"Portland welcomes the world during the Festival season when the 'Rose City' becomes the Summer Capital of America and the paradise of tourists," proclaimed one early festival publication. "Rex Oregonus, the merry king of the Festival . . . presents for the delectation of the vast concourse of spectators what is probably the most glittering, gorgeous, dazzlingly spectacular and beautiful pageant ever seen in the Western World."

Most of the events now familiar to today's festival-goers were present right from the beginning. The 1907 children's parade attracted 2,000 participants, who, said observers, performed drill maneuvers that would have brought credit to polished military units. At the racetrack, an overflow crowd cheered Barney Oldfield, the greatest automobile racer of his day, as he set a new world record for the mile—a smoking sixty-eight miles per hour. The floral parade, two and a half miles long, attracted nearly 100,000 spectators that inaugural year. Afterwards, an estimated 25,000 people swarmed into the huge log Forestry Building on the Exposition Grounds to see the rose show. There weren't enough streetcars to accommodate everyone, so the crowds clambered onto trolley fenders and roofs or clung to the guardrails. At the show, they compared 200 varieties of roses and visited the oriental tea garden or a half dozen other refreshment stands. By 4 p.m. the crowds were so dense that a cordon of police was compelled to intervene.

Other first-year entertainments included visits from U.S. Navy ships; fireworks; a boat parade on the river; athletic events; and a "spectacular" night run of the fire department through darkened streets to Multnomah Field. Once at the field, spectators were treated to another novelty—a baseball game played under electric lights.

Within days of that first festival's close, supporters agreed that the event was a success beyond their wildest expectations. They also decided that its possibilities scarcely had been touched. "Given months rather than weeks in which to perfect plans and enlist public interest and support," organizers declared, "the carnivals of the future can be made second to none that have ever been held in the world's greatest centers of flowers and beauty." In other words, just wait till next year.

This year's Rose Festival undoubtedly will be proclaimed the biggest and best ever. Portland's *grande dame* wouldn't acknowledge anything less. And she does put on a quite a show—but then, she always did. Small beginnings, indeed.

Suggested Further Reading

Fairley, Deborah. "Glory Days," *Oregon Magazine* (May-June 1988): 34-36.

Katherine Dunn
1945-

Katherine Dunn was born in Kansas. Until the age of thirteen she traveled with her family, who were migrant agricultural workers in the Pacific Northwest. She attended Portland State University and Reed College and published her first novel, *Attic*, in 1970 and her second, *Truck*, the next year. Her novel *Geek Love* was one of five finalists for the 1989 National Book Award. Dunn has published short fiction, essays on boxing, and an array of journalistic articles including a column, "The Slice," that appeared in (Portland) *Willamette Week* from 1984 to 1990. The essay below appeared in *Pacific Northwest* (1989).

Why I Live in Portland

I don't always love Portland, but I am attached to it by an umbilical cord of piano wire. In crankier moments I think of this city as the dank armpit of the nation. Other times, I am stunned by its beauty, delighted by its multifarious possibilities and fascinated by its mysteries.

One of the city's charms is that so many Portlanders seem to have been spawned in other parts and drawn here under strange circumstances. Bewildered by the seductive power of the place, I have acquired a habit of asking new acquaintances how they happened to land in this town—how they got hooked.

"I was sailing around the world alone in a 28-foot ketch," one man told me, "when I decided to put in here to patch my bottom, replace my Mozart tapes that had washed overboard along with the cat in a storm off Cape Fear, and visit an old school chum."

I've heard gutsy tales of thousand-mile leaps into the unknown, triggered by a three-line ad in the classifieds, and of sweethearts followed home across the continent. There are hideous sagas of flights from war to a green refuge. There are shy confessions of small-town kids, like myself, drawn toward the seductive glow of the biggest town on the horizon. But the punch line of all the stories is the same: "I liked it here, so I stayed."

The character of the place is stamped by generations of people with tales like these to tell. We're about as far west as it gets, a natural magnet for the energy of those itchy-footed dreamers too cantankerous to fall for the more conventional delights of California or Seattle.

Our relationships with towns are as passionate, engrossing and fickle as our human connections. For me, the romance began when I was a bookish, goggle-eyed teen in a small hamlet 20 miles up the road. Portland was the town I ran away to, a mecca of sinister excitements. Borrowing my dad's car keys on a Saturday night could take me on a cruise of life's mysteries. With my heart thumping like a burglar's, I'd plunge in, greedy to see for myself all the terrifying things that to a country kid spelled c-i-t-y: crime, grime, danger and art, the glories of the underworld.

Portland gave me what I was looking for. That spike-heeled, purple-lipped woman might actually be a hooker. This crumpled form in the doorway must be a drunk. I flattened my nose on the windows of tattoo shops and pawnbrokers, spied on the entrances to steam baths and porno bookstores. I squandered my berry-picking money cynically on psychic readers and fortunetellers who analyzed everything from cards and palms to tea leaves and coffee bubbles. Jazz riffs seeping out of a basement bistro and the click of balls from the open door of a pool hall were theme music for dark adventure to a freckled kid who had read a few too many detective novels.

By the time I moved into town to enter one of our half-dozen colleges, I'd discovered the art museum and the downtown library. I had classmates from all over the country. I've always been afflicted by restless curiosity, and this avalanche of news about other worlds inflamed my youthful Marco Polo gland. Portland suddenly seemed cramped and musty and boring. I had to leave or suffocate in the safeness of what I'd once thought such a risky town.

I was gone for a decade, rambling the planet. Then, with a child to raise and a living to get, I decided to settle down for a bit. My itchy feet were tired. My son wanted to go to school. I could have chosen any place, but I came back to Portland. There were old friends here and attractions I'd scarcely noticed in the old days. Good schools, for example, and clean air and cheap rent.

Our weather has its critics, but it isn't out to get you. Even in January I won't freeze to death between my front door and the grocery store. Having wintered once in Vermont, where I encountered the lunacy of 60 degrees below zero, I find Portland's mild climate soothing. During my exile in the wider world I was breakfast for the crow-sized mosquitoes of Nova Scotia. I hurled suitcases at the 10-inch cockroaches of the Yucatan, only to have them swagger away, undented. I fought scorpions with a can opener in Belize, battled the red ants of Greece with kerosene and heard the rattle of diamondbacks in Nevada. There were earthquakes in Spain, bombs in Ireland and Parisians in France. An occasional opossum on the back porch in Portland is a relatively friendly sight.

I came back because Portland is an easy place to live. But my son is grown now, and I stay on because this place is lush and wonderful and each day reveals another rich secret behind a seemingly bland door. I keep running into those same former New Yorkers and Californians who complained about the lack of "real" bagels, "real" pizza, "real" nightlife and sunshine while we were all college students in the late 1960s. Twenty years later they are back, or, more often, still here. They are eloquent converts to this gentle region and have guaranteed the quality of the local pizza and bagels.

Many people like Portland's easy access to the wild for hiking, skiing, fishing and so on. I'm glad it's out there, but I spent too much of my youth in farming to have much enthusiasm left for camping out, trekking up hills that don't cooperate or eating food that fights back. My contribution to the wilderness is to stay away from it. I love the outdoors—outdoor cafés, window shopping, concerts in Pioneer Square and neighborhood festivals—but where the side-

walk ends, so do I. For me the city itself is Oz with mist softening the edges and the long angles of the sunlight washing every brick with gold.

I had no way of knowing before I returned that Portland is also a prime scribblers' country. After a day of glaring into the green screen of my computer terminal, there are a hundred cafés or bars where I might run into some poet, reporter, novelist or playwright who will startle me with fresh notions, give me tips on the craft, introduce me to out-of-the-way books and authors or provide riotous entertainment in the gossip and tall-tale departments. On the other hand, after eight years of scouting I still haven't located a bookie willing to take my 50-cent bets on boxing matches.

The fact that this is what's called an "informal" town is considerable consolation for the bookie shortage. It means the restaurant won't turn a man away for lack of a jacket or tie and you're just as comfortable at the symphony whether you're wearing jeans or silk. We're tolerant of sartorial eccentricity but death on air pollution. Smoking and strong perfume get more complaints than toxic waste or radiation.

Sometimes I wonder about our priorities. We get a gorgeous new fountain on the riverfront just as the park department's budget for children's programs gets slashed. And the town splits up in strange pockets. Last summer, for example, North Portland was besieged by gang wars and drive-by shootings and the southeast was frenzied over drugs and burglary. Meanwhile, activists on the west side picketed, protested and prayed to save an oak tree. The tree still thrives, but so do the gangs and burglars.

Despite our growing big-city troubles, there is a small-town feel to the neighborhoods. The shopkeepers soon know you well enough to cash your checks—or not, as the case may be. And if your kid is spending his lunch money on candy bars, the checker at the supermarket will let you know. But Portlanders are a restrained and courteous people as a whole. If you decide to wear a tank top on a hot day, nobody will comment on your dragon tattoos. We are far too polite to admit we're staring.

For me, being in Portland is like living in an endless novel. Characters from old scenarios reappear in new guises. The fierce young artist I met in college is one example. In those days he was struggling to escape poverty on the wings of his paintbrush. Twenty years later, he is a respected visionary with grants and commissions, but he still isn't immune to pain. His murals grace public monuments, but his children are innocent victims of gang violence. In this city no story ends, even in death. The children and grandchildren and second cousins of every tale go on connecting and reconnecting in intricate patterns.

These cycles must play themselves out in every city. But the mysteries of Portland feel accessible, as though given time and energy I could track down every convoluted saga and touch the enormous hidden heart that powers the whole shebang. That illusion is addictive. It makes every day dawn with a certainty that anything at all could happen right here in the Rose City. It's beautiful, and it isn't always pleasant, but for me it's home.

Suggested Further Reading

Bolle, Sonja. "Katherine Dunn," *Publisher's Weekly* (10 March 1989): 66-67.
Dunn, Katherine. *Attic*. New York: Harper & Row, 1970.
———. *Geek Love*. New York: Alfred A. Knopf, 1989.
———. *Truck*. New York: Harper & Row, 1971.
———. "Why I Live in Portland," *Pacific Northwest* (January 1989): 44, 47.

Karen Karbo
1957-

Karen Karbo was born in Michigan. She has written two novels. *Trespassers Welcome Here* (1989), for which she received the 1989 General Electric Younger Writer Award for Fiction, was also nominated for a Pulitzer Prize. *The Diamond Lane* (1991), a Literary Guild Selection, was nominated for the 1992 Oregon Book Award. Her short stories have appeared in the *Village Voice Literary Supplement*, the *Massachusetts Review*, *Quarterly West*, and *ZYZZVA*. Her nonfiction has appeared in *Esquire*, the *New York Times*, the *Village Voice*, and the *Seattle Times*. In 1989 she was awarded a fellowship in fiction from the Oregon Institute of Literary Arts. In 1992 she received a National Endowment for the Arts grant for fiction. The following essay appeared in the *Sunday Oregonian*'s *Northwest Magazine* (1991).

Blazers on My Mind

Mid-November, Blazers 8-0. Never been to a professional basketball game. Decide it might be a hoot. Drop by the G.I. Joe's ticket outlet. Stand in line behind smelly teen humming "Cracklin' Rosie" along with the Muzak. Line quite long. Everyone ahead of us also thinks seeing ball game might be a hoot. Overhear ticket seller breaking bad news: Few tickets left. Thinks she means for upcoming game. Turns out she means for rest of season. Smelly teen purchases pair of tickets for last two seats together. In nosebleed section, two rows from the top. Blazers vs. high school-caliber Minnesota Timberwolves.

Go home, mildly annoyed. Before becoming Blazer maniac last spring, spent entire adult life looking down nose at professional sports, especially baseball (guys stand around, nothing happens). Finally caving in to appeal of professional basketball. Irrational feeling universe should reward me for new-found normalcy in the form of a pair of tickets. Too much to ask? Apparently.

Telephone friend who still looks down nose at professional sports. Confess attempt to purchase tickets. Confess burning desire to see game. Confess surprise that everyone else in Portland has identical burning desire. Friend reports that when Blazer season ticket holders die, they pass their tickets on to their children. Don't believe her. Check phone book to see if I have any relatives in Portland I don't know about.

Next a.m. take bull by horns. Call Blazer ticket office. Have developed silly notion that Blazer games are accessible to anyone with pluck. (Will find out soon they are available to anyone with bucks.) Silly notion fostered by media. Blazer doings reported on nightly news as regularly as the weather. Game highlights feature points scored by Clyde, Buck. No last names necessary. Newscasters and fans alike talk about "our" team, "our" guys. "We" win or "we" lose.

After discouraging number of rings Blazer ticket line answered by exhausted-sounding front-office minion. Explain my dilemma: new Blazer fan, no luck at G.I. Joe's, no luck with friends, all intellectuals who think professional sports is opiate of people. Blazer minion very nice, although tone of voice tells me a good laugh will be had at my expense the instant I hang up. She suggests trying Ticket Exchange in Classifieds.

Realizing dedicated Blazer fan must plan ahead, ask about possibility of season tickets for next year. She says 3,000 people currently on waiting list. She says prices range from about $800 to $3,300 a pair per season. That's this year, she says.

Two tickets advertised in Sunday Classifieds for Jan. 3 Lakers game. Husband warns me they will cost an arm, leg. Serious discussion ensues. How much to spend. We are both freelancers; he makes films, I write. Advances for my novels come in every 18 months like clockwork. Not rich, in other words. Still, willing to go $50 each. Tickets will be my Christmas/birthday present for next two years.

Make phone call. Nice, sheepish season ticket holder practicing good capitalism. Has pair of tickets in nosebleed section, just behind end zone. Asking price: $200. Each. $400, for those of you too astonished to do the math.

Point out to sheepish capitalist her tickets are in nosebleed section. She says yes, but in middle of nosebleed section, just behind end zone. Admits she and enterprising hubby are trying to sell a few sets of tickets this year so they can afford season tickets next year. Sorry, I say, starving artists. So are we, she says. Not likely.

Call licensed ticket brokers, also advertised in Classifieds. $85 for ticket with face value of $39.50, $45 for $10.50 ticket. No tickets at all for Lakers, Suns.

Resign myself to settling for television. OK. Not so bad, really. Close shots of sweaty, earnest faces. Instant replay. Comfort of own home. No parking problems. Television? All right.

Not all right. Friends with Paragon Cable can pay per view, call 15 minutes before game, say "hit me," get charged $14.95 on next month's billing. Those of us with TCI not so lucky. Blazer Cable package is whopping $159.95. No other choice. Again, reluctance to dip into savings account, Christmas coming, quarterly tax payments, general principle of the thing. Beginning to suspect Blazer basketball is as elite as opera. More elite than opera. Opera you can get tickets for.

Blazers 10-0. Go to Best Bet in Beaverton for communal viewing experience at reasonable $7 per person. Beer $2.75. In the Stadium Club lounge, where we find an empty booth, there are 18 televisions. Also, giant screen TV flanked by two smaller TVs, opposite rows of plastic chairs. Very Orwellian. Husband and I arrange ourselves so I'm watching one TV over his shoulder and he's watching another one over mine. Unnerving, but endurable. Fifteen minutes before tip-off an important personage comes round with a remote control and taps up the sound on all 18 TVs. Our first Blazer Cable game. BC runs commercials just like network. Here, we enjoy them at ear-splitting volume.

Stadium Club starts to fill up after the half. A crowd of Vietnamese arrives, eats hot dogs, chain smokes. Three elegant Persians in tasseled loafers glide in, too refined to whoop and holler at the giant screen TV. Good time marred by concern for intensity of electromagnetic waves emanating from 18 TVs in one room. Go home. Check moles.

Blazers 11-0. Step up quest for tickets. Begin entering drawings at bars, restaurants, quick-lube shops. At dry cleaners notice canister by register labeled "Win Free Blazer Tickets!" Canister stuffed with pink cleaning receipts. Owner draws winning pink slip when spirit moves him, i.e., whenever he doesn't want his tickets, one of the counter girls confides. Begin taking my sweaters in one at a time. Accumulate 4-5 pink slips per week. Stuff in canister. Clear my calendar for March 24, night of Blazer-Hornet game.

Look forward to Phoenix-Portland game for days, scheduled for TNT. National airing, no danger of being blacked out by provincial TCI Cable. Tip-off is 5 p.m. to accommodate East Coast. Make popcorn, unplug phone. Two minutes before 5, in middle of advertisement for Clint Eastwood video library, signal is suddenly scrambled, then somber white-on-black Woody Allen style announcement appears: "Due to NBA Regulations we are required to black-out tonight's Portland Trailblazer Game. . . ."

Feel cheated, furious at management, players, Ted Turner for not standing up to NBA. Eat popcorn, feel better.

Turn on KATU to check score around 5:45, imagine I can sneak a soundbite-sized peek of game highlights thus far. News is News, I reason: Trail Blazers are News even when they're desultorily shooting baskets at Jewish Community Center.

KATU sports reporter and Archie Andrews look-alike Jerry Murphy valiantly and pointlessly coming to us live from Coliseum. Only fans visible in background. They stand up. They sit down. More mysterious regulations forbid showing field goals, fouls or rebounds made by "our" team. Grisly car wrecks are shown on the news. Mothers wailing over the bodies of their gun-downed children, detailed diagrams of presidential polyps. Nothing sacred. Except Blazer basketball.

Stop thinking of the Blazers as our guys. Start thinking of them as something copyrighted.

Resign myself to settling for radio. Teeny bit humiliated. Used to envision self as hip 'n' happening thirtysomething, up and coming literary luminary. Huddled around transistor radio with husband, dogs, feel as though I'm awaiting news of Allied invasion of Normandy. Have not turned into parents, as once feared, but grandparents.

Situation made no better by utter inability to understand irrepressible Bill Schonely play-by-play patter: "Bryant Ainge Bryant Ainge stop unload iron glass iron NO! T.P. climbs the ladder for the rebound wheels and deals from back court throws it up doesn't get the roll . . . !" Plunged into slough of despondency. Realize French 1 teacher was right: Have no facility for foreign languages.

Blazers 11-1. Take sweaters, shirts to dry cleaners every day, tuck pink slip in canister. Must have two dozen in there. Try to look through slit in top. When counter girl isn't looking pick up canister and shake it. One day dry cleaners calls to tell me, I imagine, that we have won tickets to the Blazer-Magic game. No, she says, but we were able to get that stain out of your pink shirt.

Blazers 12-1. Slightly mollified by Blazer-Sonics game, televised for unwashed masses by KOIN-TV. Unfortunately missed first three quarters of game, participating in Miller Lite Fan Vote. Each quarter one telephone call is intercepted; caller wins pair of free tickets. Question being put to a vote: If you were the general manager of the Sonics, would you trade Dale Ellis? Finally discover use for redial button on telephone: Vote four times to trade him, three times to keep him. Call is not intercepted. Who is Dale Ellis, anyway?

Blazers 16-1. Ice Capades comes to Coliseum. Consider seeing Ice Capades on last night, then hiding in ladies' room until next Blazer game. Problem: sitting through the Ice Capades.

A friend in the know suggests hanging out in front of Coliseum before game, seeing if we can scalp some tickets. Worry that I'm a little rusty. Last tickets I bought from scalper were for Eagles/Jackson Browne concert at Anaheim Stadium the year I got my driver's license.

We go. Bone-cracking cold. No scalpers; only fellow rubes unaware of large sign saying "NOTICE: resale of tickets to events at municipal facilities is prohibited. Persons without tickets for the event in progress are not allowed on Coliseum premises."

We are approached six times by people wondering do we have tickets to sell.

For a laugh I wander over to box office. Trio of friendly bicycle cops say sometimes extra tickets are turned in by players before game time. Fatherly, empathetic ticket seller says, "Only had four tickets today, honey. And those went three hours ago."

Cop trio advises us against scalping. Feel like high school sophomore being advised to Just Say No. Trio says scalped tickets are often from home burglaries. You slip scalper $200 for a pair of tickets, then go inside to find the original ticket holders sitting in "your" seats.

Hungry. Cold. Head back to car, push against sea of freshly scrubbed fans headed for game. Main scalping action turns out to be just across the street. Accosted by three would-be linebackers, guys you'd never want to meet in a clean, well-lit alley, much less a dark one. One is close enough to get a good look at my ear drum. "Behind the bench, $60 each," he hisses.

Inexperienced, yes. Dumb, no. Brought along handy dandy wallet-size Far West Federal Bank Trail Blazer schedule with map of the Coliseum. Dig it out of pocket, peer at it in the dark. Where behind the bench? I ask.

By then he has sold the tickets to someone else.

Blazers 17-1. To my chagrin, have grown fond of KEX Blazer broadcasts. Decide I like low-tech radio listening experience. Like hearing *thok* of ball as it plunges through the net, also grunts of players and occasional profanity. Finally getting hang of Schonely talk. Realize he is not sportscaster, but beat poet manqué.

"Duck Buck Duck Buck Duck
Throws it up Buck!
Duck!
Nothing but cord! Duck
Back to back buckets!
EERRIPPP City!"

Consider suggesting him for Portland Arts and Lectures series.

Still, my dry cleaners has not come through. Decide to take matters into my own hands. Next time I drop off a sweater, I say, I'm here to pick up my Blazer tickets. Counter girl finds pair of tickets behind counter, asks, "Two tickets for Johnson?" All I have to say is yes! Realize if I filch these tickets I'll never be able to come back here again. Problem: They have all my sweaters.

No, I say. Just kidding.

During the Blazer-Bulls game, also televised by KOIN, become more aggressive in voting during Miller Lite Beer Fan Vote. Question: Which one of these teams (Pistons or Bulls) will make it to this year's Eastern NBA Conference Championship? Despite curious phrasing, voted for Detroit nine times, the Bulls seven. Phone call not intercepted.

Blazers 19-1. Consider cashing in United Airlines Mileage Plus Miles to fly to Sacramento, buy tickets to Kings-Blazer game at Arco Arena. Watch game, fly home. Problem: Not worth dying in plane crash for Blazer-Kings game. Maybe playoffs.

My hair dresser says it wasn't always this way. She had season tickets for 10 years. Three years ago she couldn't sell her tickets at face value, couldn't even con friends into being her guest. She turned her tickets back in to Blazer front office. Now everyone tells her she blew it, tells her they would have happily bought her season tickets. Now they would, but not then. Women brought their knitting, then.

Consider enrolling in elementary school. Trail Blazers and Avia give away free tickets to reward scholastic excellence. Ideally, I would become scholar of the month, Clyde or Buck would visit my class, set me on his knee, hand over tickets. Room mothers would take Polaroids. Problem: Bad at long division.

Blazers 20-2. No hope of tickets in sight. Cleanest sweaters in Portland, though. Consider becoming Winter Hawks fan. Problem: the Winter Hawks.

Suggested Further Reading

Karbo, Karen. "Blazers on My Mind," *Sunday Oregonian Northwest Magazine,* January 13, 1991.

———. *The Diamond Lane.* New York: G. P. Putnam's Sons, 1991.

———. *Trespassers Welcome Here.* New York: G. P. Putnam's Sons, 1989.

SECTION II
Liberty and Justice for All:
Oregon's Heritage of Conflict and Diversity

Santiam Kalapuya Indians

During the decade of the 1850s, all over the Pacific
Northwest, the Indians were forced to sign treaties with
representatives of the government of the United States.
Under these treaties, the Native Americans agreed to go
on reservations in exchange for money and services.
They were to become Americans: Christians, farmers,
and literate in the English language. The following
speech is how members of the Santiam Kalapuya Indians
of the Willamette Valley remembered the promises of
the United States agent Joel Palmer in 1855. The
original text is in *Kalapuya Texts* (1945).

The Indians Hear a Treaty Speech

The Americans (troops) arrived. They spoke as follows: "Qa'yaqats! (chief's name) Now we will give you quantities of money, (and) all sorts of things. So then you will not be poor. All your tribespeople will be just like Americans. You will be given everything—(property such as) cattle, horses, wagons, blankets, breeches, hats, coats, overcoats, quantities of flour, sugar, coffee. You will be given food for five years. The Americans will watch over you. They will make your fences. They will plough your land. They will fence your land. They will make your houses. They will build a hammer house (blacksmith shop). A man will come who knows how to make all sorts of things (a blacksmith). He will fix your wagon for you if it should break. He will make the handle of your ground breaker (your plow). He will just fix it (at cost). The great headman (the government of the United States—symbolized in the President) will pay for it. Whatever you may desire, he will make it.

"A trading house (a store) will be built. You may obtain (there) whatever you wish. An iron house (a blacksmith shop) will be erected, to repair what has gotten spoiled. Whatever sort of iron thing you may want, you will not have to pay for it. There will be erected a paper (book) house (i.e., a school building). Your children will speak (read from) the paper (book). That is the way they will do like Americans. Twenty acres (will be given to) each person (Indian), and as long as you remain on the place, then it will be your own place. The great headman (the United States and its President) will give it to you to be your own place. After twenty years the (last) payment for your place will cease, and then no one will (be necessary to) watch over you. You will take care of your own heart (you will then be no longer a government ward). That is how you will be (then) just like an American. . . ."

Suggested Further Reading

Beckham, Stephen Dow. *The Indians of Western Oregon: This Land Was Theirs.* Coos Bay, OR: Arago Books, 1977.

Jacobs, Melville, editor. *Kalapuya Texts*, Volume II. University of Washington Publications in Anthropology. Seattle: University of Washington Press, 1945.

O'Donnell, Terence. *An Arrow in the Earth: General Joel Palmer and the Indians of Oregon.* Portland: Oregon Historical Society, 1991.

Ramsey, Jarold, editor and compiler. *Coyote Was Going There: Indian Literature of the Oregon Country.* Seattle and London: University of Washington Press, 1977.

Chief Joseph
ca. 1840-1904

Chief Joseph (Hin-ma-toe-yah-laht-khit) is the best-known figure in the history of the Pacific Northwest. His life, and the experiences of his Nez Perce people, is one of the great epics of the region. Christian missionaries came to settle and proselytize among the Nez Perce in 1836. In 1855, the United States government, anticipating settler pressure on Nez Perce lands, made a treaty with the tribe that gave them a reservation of 10,000 square miles in Washington, Idaho, and Oregon. In 1863 the reservation was reduced through a new treaty because of the advent of gold miners in the Indian country. Some of the Nez Perce never agreed to this second treaty. One group, led by Chief Joseph, living in the Wallowa River Valley in northeastern Oregon, refused to go on the reservation. Finally, under pressure of the United States army led by General O.O. Howard, responding to white settlers who wanted the Wallowa Valley, Joseph's band agreed to go to the reservation in 1877. Shortly before his people reached the reservation, a violent incident occurred, war broke out, and Joseph and the other non-treaty Indians began their famous flight toward refuge in Canada. This selection is an excerpt from a longer speech by Chief Joseph and appeared in the *North American Review* (1879).

An Indian's View of Indian Affairs

Soon after this my father sent for me. I saw he was dying. I took his hand in mine. He said: "My son, my body is returning to my mother earth, and my spirit is going very soon to see the Great Spirit Chief. When I am gone, think of your country. You are the chief of these people. They look to you to guide them. Always remember that your father never sold his country. You must stop your ears whenever you are asked to sign a treaty selling your home. A few years more, and white men will be all around you. They have their eyes on this land. My son, never forget my dying words. This country holds your father's body. Never sell the bones of your father and your mother." I pressed my father's hand and told him I would protect his grave with my life. My father smiled and passed away to the spirit-land.

I buried him in that beautiful valley of winding waters. I love that land more than all the rest of the world. A man who would not love his father's grave is worse than a wild animal.

For a short time we lived quietly. But this could not last. White men had found gold in the mountains around the land of winding water. They stole a great many horses from us, and we could not get them back because we were Indians. The white men told lies for each other. They drove off a great many of our cattle. Some white men branded our young cattle so they could claim them. We had no friend who would plead our cause before the law councils. It seemed to me that some of the white men in Wallowa were doing these things on purpose to get up a war. They knew that we were not strong enough to fight them. I labored hard to avoid trouble and bloodshed. We gave up some of our country to the white men, thinking then we could have peace. We were mistaken. The white man would not let us alone. We could have avenged our wrongs many times, but we did not. Whenever the Government has asked us to help them against other Indians, we have never refused. When the white men were few and we were strong we could have killed them all off, but the Nez Perces wished to live at peace.

If we have not done so, we have not been to blame. I believe that the old treaty has never been correctly reported. If we ever owned the land we own it still, for we never sold it. In the treaty councils the commissioners have claimed that our country had been sold to the Government. Suppose a white man should come to me and say, "Joseph, I like your horses, and I want to buy them." I say to him, "No, my horses suit me, I will not sell them." Then he goes to my neighbor, and says to him: "Joseph has some good horses. I want to buy them, but he refuses to sell." My neighbor answers, "Pay me the money, and I will sell you Joseph's horses." The white man returns to me, and says, "Joseph, I have bought your horses, and you must let me have them." If we sold our lands to the Government, this is the way they were bought.

On account of the treaty made by the other bands of the Nez Perces, the white men claimed my lands. We were troubled greatly by white men crowding over the line. Some of these were good men, and we lived on peaceful terms with them, but they were not all good.

Nearly every year the agent came over from Lapwai and ordered us on the reservation. We always replied that we were satisfied to live in Wallowa. We were careful to refuse the presents or annuities which he offered.

Through all the years since the white men came to Wallowa we have been threatened and taunted by them and the treaty Nez Perces. They have given us no rest. We have had a few good friends among white men, and they have always advised my people to bear these taunts without fighting. Our young men were quick-tempered, and I have had great trouble in keeping them from doing rash things. I have carried a heavy load on my back ever since I was a boy. I learned then that we were but few, while the white men were many, and that we could not hold our own with them. We were like deer. They were like grizzly bears. We had a small country. Their country was large. We were contented to let things remain as the Great Spirit Chief made them. They were not; and would change the rivers and mountains if they did not suit them.

Year after year we have been threatened, but no war was made upon my people until General Howard came to our country two years ago and told us that he was the white war-chief of all that country. He said: "I have a great many soldiers at my back. I am going to bring them up here, and then I will talk to you again. I will not let white men laugh at me the next time I come. The country belongs to the Government, and I intend to make you go upon the reservation."

I remonstrated with him against bringing more soldiers to the Nez Perces country. He had one house full of troops all the time at Fort Lapwai.

The next spring the agent at Umatilla agency sent an Indian runner to tell me to meet General Howard at Walla Walla. I could not go myself, but I sent my brother and five other head men to meet him, and they had a long talk.

General Howard said: "You have talked straight, and it is all right. You can stay in Wallowa." He insisted that my brother and his company should go with him to Fort Lapwai. When the party arrived there General Howard sent out runners and called all the Indians in to a grand council. I was in that council. I said to General Howard, "We are ready to listen." He answered that he would not talk then, but would hold a council next day, when he would talk plainly. I said to General Howard: "I am ready to talk today. I have been in a great many councils, but I am no wiser. We are all sprung from a woman, although we are unlike in many things. We cannot be made over again. You are as you were made, and as you were made you can remain. We are just as we were made by the Great Spirit, and you cannot change us; then why should children of one mother and one father quarrel—why should one try to cheat the other? I do not believe that the Great Spirit Chief gave one kind of men the right to tell another kind of men what they must do."

General Howard replied: "You deny my authority, do you? You want to dictate to me, do you?"

Then one of my chiefs—Too-hool-hool-suit—rose in the council and said to General Howard: "The Great Spirit Chief made the world as it is, and as he wanted it, and he made a part of it for us to live upon. I do not see where you get authority to say that we shall not live where he has placed us."

General Howard lost his temper and said: "Shut up! I don't want to hear any more of such talk. The law says you shall go upon the reservation to live, and I want you to do so, but you persist in disobeying the law (meaning the treaty). If you do not move, I will take the matter into my own hand, and make you suffer for your disobedience."

Too-hool-hool-suit answered: "Who are you, that you ask us to talk, and then tell me I shan't talk? Are you the Great Spirit? Did you make the world? Did you make the sun? Did you make the rivers to run for us to drink? Did you make the grass to grow? Did you make all these things, that you talk to us as though we were boys? If you did, then you have the right to talk as you do."

General Howard replied, "You are an impudent fellow, and I will put you in the guard-house," and then ordered a soldier to arrest him.

Too-hool-hool-suit made no resistance. He asked General Howard: "Is that your order? I don't care. I have expressed my heart to you. I have nothing to take back. I have spoken for my country. You can arrest me, but you cannot change me or make me take back what I have said."

The soldiers came forward and seized my friend and took him to the guard-house. My men whispered among themselves whether they should let this thing be done. I counseled them to submit. I knew if we resisted that all the white men present, including General Howard, would be killed in a moment, and we would be blamed. If I had said nothing, General Howard would never have given another unjust order against my men. I saw the danger, and, while they dragged Too-hool-hool-suit to prison, I arose and said: "*I am going to talk now*. I don't care whether you arrest me or not." I turned to my people and said: "The arrest of Too-hool-hool-suit was wrong, but we will not resent the insult. We were invited to this council to express our hearts, and we have done so." Too-hool-hool-suit was prisoner for five days before he was released.

The council broke up for that day. On the next morning, General Howard came to my lodge, and invited me to go with him and White-Bird and Looking-Glass, to look for land for my people. As we rode along we came to some good land that was already occupied by Indians and white people. General Howard, pointing to this land, said: "If you will come on to the reservation, I will give you these lands and move these people off."

I replied: "No. It would be wrong to disturb these people. I have no right to take their homes. I have never taken what did not belong to me. I will not now."

We rode all day upon the reservation, and found no good land unoccupied. I have been informed by men who do not lie that General Howard sent a letter that night, telling the soldiers at Walla Walla to go to Wallowa Valley, and to drive us out upon our return home.

In the council the next day, General Howard informed me, in a haughty spirit, that he would give my people *thirty days* to go back home, collect all their stock, and move on to the reservation, saying, "If you are not here in that time, I shall consider you want to fight, and will send my soldiers to drive you on."

I said: "War can be avoided, and it ought to be avoided. I want no war. My people have always been the friends of the white man. Why are you in such a hurry? I cannot get ready to move in thirty days. Our stock is scattered, and the Snake River is very high. Let us wait until fall, then the river will be low. We want time to hunt up our stock and gather supplies for winter."

General Howard replied: "If you let the time run over one day, the soldiers will be there to drive you on to the reservation, and all your cattle and horses outside of the reservation at that time will fall into the hands of the white men."

I knew I had never sold my country, and that I had no land in Lapwai; but I did not want bloodshed. I did not want my people killed. I did not want anybody killed. Some of my people had been murdered by white men, and the white murderers were never punished for it. I told General Howard about this, and again said I wanted no war. I wanted the people who lived upon the lands I was to occupy at Lapwai to have time to gather their harvest.

I said in my heart that, rather than have war, I would give up my country. I would give up my father's grave. I would give up everything rather than have the blood of white men upon the hands of my people.

General Howard refused to allow me more than thirty days to move my people and their stock. I am sure that he began to prepare for war at once.

When I returned to Wallowa I found my people very much excited upon discovering that the soldiers were already in the Wallowa Valley. We held a council, and decided to move immediately, to avoid bloodshed.

Too-hool-hool-suit, who felt outraged by his imprisonment, talked for war, and made many of my young men willing to fight rather than be driven like dogs from the land where they were born. He declared that blood alone would wipe out the disgrace General Howard had put upon him. It required a strong heart to stand up against such talk, but I urged my people to be quiet, and not to begin a war.

We gathered all the stock we could find, and made an attempt to move. We left many of our horses and cattle in Wallowa, and we lost several hundred in crossing the river. All of my people succeeded in getting across in safety. Many of the Nez Perces came together in Rocky Cañon to hold a grand council. I went with all my people. This council lasted ten days. There was a great deal of war-talk, and a great deal of excitement. There was one young brave present whose father had been killed by a white man five years before. This man's blood was bad against white men, and he left the council calling for revenge.

Again I counseled peace, and I thought the danger was past. We had not complied with General Howard's order because we could not, but we intended to do so as soon as possible. I was leaving the council to kill beef for my family, when news came that the young man whose father had been killed had gone out with several other hot-blooded young braves and killed four white men. He rode up to the council and shouted: "Why do you sit there like women? The war has begun already." I was deeply grieved. All the lodges were moved except my brother's and my own. I saw clearly that the war was upon us when I learned that my young men had been secretly buying ammunition. I heard then that Too-hool-hool-suit, who had been imprisoned by General Howard, had succeeded in organizing a war-party. I knew that their acts would involve all my people. I saw that the war could not then be prevented. The time had passed. I counseled peace from the beginning. I knew that we were too weak to fight the United States. We had many grievances, but I knew that war would bring more. We had good white friends, who advised us against taking the war-path. My friend and brother, Mr. Chapman, who had been with us since the surrender, told us just how the war would end. Mr. Chapman took sides against us, and helped General Howard. I do not blame him for doing so. He tried hard to prevent bloodshed. We hoped the white settlers would not join the soldiers. Before the war commenced we had discussed this matter all over, and many of my people were in favor of warning them that if they took no part against us they should not be molested in the event of war being begun by General Howard. This plan was voted down in the war-council.

There were bad men among my people who had quarreled with white men, and they talked of their wrongs until they roused all the bad hearts in the council. Still I could not believe that they would begin the war. I know that my young men did a great wrong, but I ask, Who was first to blame? They had been insulted a thousand times; their fathers and brothers had been killed; their mothers and wives had been disgraced; they had been driven to madness by whisky sold to them by white men; they had been told by General Howard that all their horses and cattle which they had been unable to drive out of Wallowa were to fall into the hands of white men; and, added to all this, they were homeless and desperate.

I would have given my own life if I could have undone the killing of white men by my people. I blame my young men and I blame the white men. I blame General Howard for not giving my people time to get their stock away from Wallowa. I do not acknowledge that he had the right to order me to leave Wallowa at any time. I deny that either my father or myself ever sold that land. It is still our land. It may never again be our home, but my father sleeps there, and I love it as I love my mother. I left there, hoping to avoid blood-shed.

If General Howard had given me plenty of time to gather up my stock, and treated Too-hool-hool-suit as a man should be treated, there *would have been no war.*

My friends among white men have blamed me for the war. I am not to blame. When my young men began the killing, my heart was hurt. Although I did not justify them, I remembered all the insults I had endured, and my blood was on fire. Still I would have taken my people to the buffalo country without fighting, if possible.

I could see no other way to avoid a war. We moved over to White Bird Creek, sixteen miles away, and there encamped, intending to collect our stock before leaving; but the soldiers attacked us, and the first battle was fought. We numbered in that battle sixty men, and the soldiers a hundred. The fight lasted but a few minutes, when the soldiers retreated before us for twelve miles. They lost thirty-three killed, and had seven wounded. When an Indian fights, he only shoots to kill; but soldiers shoot at random. None of the soldiers were scalped. We do not believe in scalping, nor in killing wounded men. Soldiers do not kill many Indians unless they are wounded and left upon the battle-field. They then kill Indians.

Seven days after the first battle, General Howard arrived in the Nez Perces country, bringing seven hundred more soldiers. It was now war in earnest. We crossed over Salmon River, hoping General Howard would follow. We were not disappointed. He did follow us, and we got back between him and his supplies, and cut him off for three days. He sent out two companies to open the way. We attacked them, killing one officer, two guides, and ten men.

We withdrew, hoping the soldiers would follow, but they had got enough fighting for that day. They intrenched themselves, and next day we attacked them again. The battle lasted all day, and was renewed next morning. We killed four and wounded seven or eight.

About this time General Howard found out that we were in his rear. Five days later he attacked us with three hundred and fifty soldiers and settlers. We had two hundred and fifty warriors. The fight lasted twenty-seven hours. We lost four killed and several wounded. General Howard's loss was twenty-nine men killed and sixty wounded.

The following day the soldiers charged upon us, and we retreated with our families and stock a few miles, leaving eighty lodges to fall into General Howard's hands.

Finding that we were outnumbered, we retreated to Bitterroot Valley. Here another body of soldiers came upon us and demanded our surrender. We re-fused. They said, "You cannot get by us." We answered, "We are going by you without fighting if you will let us, but we are going by you anyhow." We then made a treaty with these soldiers. We agreed not to molest anyone, and they agreed that we might pass through the Bitter Root country in peace. We bought provisions and traded stock with white men there.

We understood that there was to be no more war. We intended to go peace-ably to the buffalo country, and leave the question of returning to our country to be settled afterward.

With this understanding, we traveled on for four days, and, thinking that the trouble was all over, we stopped and prepared tent-poles to take with us. We started again, and at the end of two days we saw three white men passing our camp. Thinking that peace had been made, we did not molest them. We could have killed or taken them prisoners, but we did not suspect them of being spies, which they were.

That night the soldiers surrounded our camp. About daybreak one of my men went out to look after his horses. The soldiers saw him and shot him down like a coyote. I have since learned that these soldiers were not those we had left behind. They had come upon us from another direction. The new white war-chief's name was Gibbon. He charged upon us while some of my people were still asleep. We had a hard fight. Some of my men crept around and attacked the soldiers from the rear. In this battle we lost nearly all our lodges, but we finally drove General Gibbon back.

Finding that he was unable to capture us, he sent to his camp a few miles away for his big guns (cannons), but my men had captured them and all the ammunition. We damaged the big guns all we could, and carried away all the powder and lead. In the fight with General Gibbon we lost fifty women and children and thirty fighting men. We remained long enough to bury our dead. The Nez Perces never make war on women and children; we could have killed a great many women and children while the war lasted, but we would feel ashamed to do so cowardly an act.

We never scalp our enemies, but when General Howard came up and joined General Gibbon, their Indian scouts dug up our dead and scalped them. I have been told that General Howard did not order this great shame to be done.

We retreated as rapidly as we could toward the buffalo country. After six days General Howard came close to us, and we went out and attacked him, and captured nearly all his horses and mules (about two hundred and fifty head). We then marched on to the Yellowstone Basin.

On the way we captured one white man and two white women. We released them at the end of three days. They were treated kindly. The women were not insulted. Can the white soldiers tell me of one time when Indian women were taken prisoners, and held three days and then released without being insulted? Were the Nez Perces women who fell into the hands of General Howard's soldiers treated with as much respect? I deny that a Nez Perce was ever guilty of such a crime.

A few days later we captured two more white men. One of them stole a horse and escaped. We gave the other a poor horse and told him he was free.

Nine days' march brought us to the mouth of Clarke's Fork of the Yellowstone. We did not know what had become of General Howard, but we supposed that he had sent for more horses and mules. He did not come up, but another new war-chief (General Sturgis) attacked us. We held him in check while we moved all our women and children and stock out of danger, leaving a few men to cover our retreat.

Several days passed, and we heard nothing of General Howard, or Gibbon, or Sturgis. We had repulsed each in turn and began to feel secure, when another army, under General Miles, struck us. This was the fourth army, each of which outnumbered our fighting force, that we had encountered within sixty days.

We had no knowledge of General Miles's army until a short time before he made a charge upon us, cutting our camp in two, and capturing nearly all of our horses. About seventy men, myself among them, were cut off. My little daughter, twelve years of age, was with me. I gave her a rope, and told her to catch a horse and join the others who were cut off from the camp. I have not seen her since, but I have learned that she is alive and well.

I thought of my wife and children, who were now surrounded by soldiers, and I resolved to go to them or die. With a prayer in my mouth to the Great Spirit Chief who rules above, I dashed unarmed through the line of soldiers. It seemed to me that there were guns on every side, before and behind me. My clothes were cut to pieces and my horse was wounded, but I was not hurt. As I reached the door of my lodge, my wife handed me my rifle, saying: "Here's your gun. Fight!"

The soldiers kept up a continuous fire. Six of my men were killed in one spot near me. Ten or twelve soldiers charged into our camp and got possession of two lodges, killing three Nez Perces and losing three of their men, who fell inside our lines. I called my men to drive them back. We fought at close range, not more than twenty steps apart, and drove the soldiers back upon their main line, leaving their dead in our hands. We secured their arms and ammunition. We lost, the first day and night, eighteen men and three women. General Miles lost twenty-six killed and forty wounded. The following day General Miles sent a messenger into my camp under protection of a white flag. I sent my friend Yellow Bull to meet him.

Yellow Bull understood the messenger to say that General Miles wished me to consider the situation; that he did not want to kill my people unnecessarily. Yellow Bull understood this to be a demand for me to surrender and save blood. Upon reporting this message to me, Yellow Bull said he wondered whether General Miles was in earnest. I sent him back with my answer, that I had not made up my mind, but would think about it and send word soon. A little later he sent some Cheyenne scouts with another message. I went out to meet them. They said they believe General Miles was sincere and really wanted peace. I walked on to General Miles's tent. He met me and we shook hands. He said, "Come, let us sit down by the fire and talk this matter over." I remained with him all night; next morning Yellow Bull came over to see if I was alive, and why I did not return.

General Miles would not let me leave the tent to see my friend alone.

Yellow Bull said to me: "They have got you in their power, and I am afraid they will never let you go again. I have an officer in our camp, and I will hold him until they let you go free."

I said: "I do not know what they mean to do with me, but if they kill me you must not kill the officer. It will do no good to avenge my death by killing him."

Yellow Bull returned to my camp. I did not make any agreement that day with General Miles. The battle was renewed while I was with him. I was very anxious about my people. I knew that we were near Sitting Bull's camp in King George's land, and I thought maybe the Nez Perces who had escaped would return with assistance. No great damage was done to either party during the night.

On the following morning I returned to my camp by agreement, meeting the officer who had been held a prisoner in my camp at the flag of truce. My people were divided about surrendering. We could have escaped from Bear Paw Mountain if we had left our wounded, old women, and children behind. We were unwilling to do this. We had never heard of a wounded Indian recovering while in the hands of white men.

On the evening of the fourth day General Howard came in with a small escort, together with my friend Chapman. We could now talk understandingly. General Miles said to me in plain words: "If you will come out and give up your arms, I will spare your lives and send you to your reservation." I do not know what passed between General Miles and General Howard.

I could not bear to see my wounded men and women suffer any longer; we had lost enough already. General Miles had promised that we might return to our own country with what stock we had left. I thought we could start again. I believed General Miles, or *I never would have surrendered*. I have heard that he has been censured for making the promise to return us to Lapwai. He could not have made any other terms with me at that time. I would have held him in check until my friends came to my assistance, and then neither of the generals nor their soldiers would have ever left Bear Paw Mountain alive.

On the fifth day I went to General Miles and gave up my gun, and said, "From where the sun now stands I will fight no more." My people needed rest—we wanted peace.

Suggested Further Reading

Joseph, Chief. "An Indian's View of Indian Affairs," the *North American Review* 128 (1879): 421-433.

Josephy, Alvin M., Jr. *The Nez Perce Indians and the Opening of the Northwest*. New Haven: Yale University Press, 1965.

Wilfong, Cheryl. *Following the Nez Perce Trail: A Guide to the Nee-Me-Poo National Historic Trail with Eyewitness Accounts*. Corvallis, OR: Oregon State University Press, 1990.

C.E.S. Wood
1852-1944

Charles Erskine Scott Wood was one of Oregon's most complex and colorful figures. Born in Pennsylvania, Wood graduated from the United States Military Academy in 1874, served ten years in the Army, then settled in Portland as a lawyer. In 1918 he divorced his wife and moved to California with the poet Sara Bard Field. Wood's personality was bifurcated. While becoming wealthy from the practice of corporate law, he also defended advocates of birth control, feminism, anarchism, and syndicalism. Possessing versatile literary talents, as poet, journalist, and satirist, Wood concentrated on attacking injustice and hypocrisy. He also celebrated nature, as in his best poem, *The Poet in the Desert*. While aide to General O.O. Howard, Wood was present in the final days of the Nez Perce campaign and rendered into English Chief Joseph's eloquent words at the time of his surrender, which he published in an article: "Chief Joseph, the Nez Perce" (1894), from which the following excerpt is taken.

Chief Joseph, the Nez Perce

On September 12, General Howard sent word to General Miles that Joseph had foiled all attempts to stop him, and earnestly requested him to make every effort to intercept the Indians. This dispatch was received by General Miles September 17, and the next day he began the march which resulted in Joseph's capture. Joseph, who did not know of any other available troops in the field, and was watching only generals Howard and Sturgis, was encamped along Eagle Creek. The country around was all bare, rolling, grass prairie, at this time covered with a light fall of snow. The camp lay in the sheltering hollows—the lowest, and therefore for fighting purposes the worst situation. A blinding snow-storm shielded General Miles's approach on the morning of September 30, till he was almost upon them. Instantly, on discovering the advance, the Indians seized the crests of the knolls immediately surrounding their camp, and the cavalry charge was successfully repulsed. Every officer or non-commissioned officer who wore a badge of rank was killed or wounded, save one. Joseph and his elder daughter were on the other side of the creek, among the horse-herd, when the first charge was made. Calling to the girl to follow, he dashed across and joined his men, taking command; but his daughter and many others were cut off by the cavalry charge, which captured and drove off the herd. These people fled to the distant hills; some were murdered by the Sioux; some probably perished from the severe weather; but Joseph's daughter was restored to him some six months afterward. The troops held most of the higher crests commanding the camp. The Indians with wonderful labor and ingenuity literally honeycombed a portion of the site of their camp, and the other more advantageous transverse gulches, with subterranean dwelling-places, communicating galleries, etc. Their dead horses were utilized as fortifications and as food. Here they held their own, refusing all offers of surrender, and saying in effect: If you want us, come take us. Joseph visited General Miles under flag of truce, but at that time would not surrender. His people held Lieutenant Jerome as a hostage till Joseph was returned to them. Had he not lost the herd that moved his motley horde, it is more than probable that Joseph would have made another of his successful fights in retreat. On October 4 General Howard, with two aides, two friendly Nez Perces (both of whom had daughters in the hostile camp), and an interpreter, arrived in Miles's camp while the firing was still going on. The two old Nez Perces, "George" and "Captain John," rode into Joseph's camp next day. They told

him General Howard was there, with promises of good treatment; that his whole command was only two or three days behind him. With tears in their eyes they begged Joseph to surrender. Joseph asked if he would be allowed to return to Idaho. He was told that he would, unless higher authority ordered otherwise.

Then old "Captain John" brought this reply (and his lips quivered and his eyes filled with tears as he delivered the words of his chief):

"Tell General Howard I know his heart. What he told me before—I have it in my heart. I am tired of fighting. Our chiefs are killed. Looking-Glass is dead. *Too-hul-hul-suit* is dead. The old men are all dead. It is the young men, now, who say 'yes' or 'no' [that is, vote in council]. He who led on the young men [Joseph's brother, Ollicut] is dead. It is cold, and we have no blankets. The little children are freezing to death. My people—some of them—have run away to the hills, and have no blankets, no food. No one knows where they are— perhaps freezing to death. I want to have time to look for my children, and to see how many of them I can find; may be I shall find them among the dead. Hear me, my chiefs; my heart is sick and sad. From where the sun *now* stands, I will fight no more forever!"

It was nearly sunset when Joseph came to deliver himself up. He rode from his camp in the little hollow. His hands were clasped over the pommel of his saddle, and his rifle lay across his knees; his head was bowed down. Pressing around him walked five of his warriors; their faces were upturned and earnest as they murmured to him; but he looked neither to the right nor the left, yet seemed to listen intently. So the little group came slowly up the hill to where General Howard, with an aide-de-camp, and General Miles waited to receive the surrender. As he neared them, Joseph sat erect in the saddle, then grace-fully and with dignity he swung himself down from his horse, and with an impulsive gesture threw his arm to its full length, and offered his rifle to General Howard. The latter motioned him toward General Miles, who received the token of submission.

Those present shook hands with Joseph, whose worn and anxious face lighted with a sad smile as silently he took each offered hand. Then, turning away, he walked to the tent provided for him.

Suggested Further Reading

Bingham, Edwin R. *Charles Erskine Scott Wood*. Boise: Boise State University, 1990.
Wood, C.E.S. "Chief Joseph, the Nez Perce," *Century* (May 1894): 135-142.
———. *Heavenly Discourse*. New York: Vanguard, 1927.
———. *The Poet in the Desert*. Portland: F. W. Baltes, 1915. Reprint: New York: Vanguard, 1929.

Jeff Riddle
1863-1941

The Modoc War took place in northern California and southern Oregon in 1872-73. Clashes between white miners and the local Indians led to the Native Americans' being placed on the Klamath Reservation. When they defied their agent and left the reservation under their leader, Captain Jack, soldiers were ordered into the field against them. The small band of Indians, heavily outnumbered, held their ground for many months but were finally defeated. Jeff Riddle, a Modoc Indian, describes some of the incidents of the war from the vantage of his people. Riddle was a rancher in southern Oregon and wrote *The Indian History of the Modoc War. . .* (1914), from which this selection is taken.

The Indian History of the Modoc War

November 28th, 1872, the agent at Klamath agency sits in his office reading a telegram from the Secretary of War at Washington, D. C. The message read like this: "Major Jackson, Fort Klamath, Oregon: Go to Lost River and move Capt. Jack and band of Modoc Indians onto the Klamath Indian reservation, Oregon; peaceable if you can, but forcible if you must."

The soldiers rode right up to Capt. Jack's lodge and stopped. Then they advanced a few steps on foot and halted. By that time the braves were all around through the village. Major Jackson demanded Capt. Jack. Scar-Face Charley told the major he would go and get him. Jack appeared in a few minutes. A few of his men were with him. Every Indian had his gun with him. Jackson told Capt. Jack that the Great Father had sent him to go and get him, Jack and all his people and put them on the Klamath reservation. Jack replied, saying, "I will go; I will take all my people with me, but I do not place any confidence in anything you white people tell me. You see you came here to my camp when it is dark. You scare me and all my people when you do that. I won't run from you. Come up to me like men, when you want to see or talk with me." The major assured Jack he did not want any trouble. He says: "Jack, get all your men up here in front of my men." Jack called his men together. They did it, eyeing the soldiers closely. Some of the old men were saying, "Maybe this man wants to repeat what Ben Wright did to us Modocs years ago." When all the Modocs got in front of Jackson and his soldiers, Jackson says to Capt. Jack: "Now, Jack, lay down your gun here," pointing to a bunch of sage-brush. Jack hesitated. At last Jack says: "What for?" Jackson told him, "You are the chief. You lay your gun down, all your men does the same. You do that, we will not have any trouble." "Why do you want to disarm me and my men for? I never have fought white people yet, and I do not want to. Some of my old men are scared of what you ask me to do." Jackson said: "It is good, Jack, that you do not want to fight whites. If you believe what you say, Jack, and you will give up your gun, I won't let anyone hurt you." Jack looked at his own men and ordered them to lay down their guns. Every Indian stepped up smiling, and laid down his trusty muzzle-loading rifle. Scar-Face Charley laid his gun down on top of the pile of guns the Indians had stacked, but he kept his old revolver strapped on. Jackson ordered him to take his pistol off and hand it over. Scar-Face said: "You got my gun. This pistol all lite. Me no shoot him you." Jackson ordered his lieutenant, Boutelle, to disarm Scar-Face, where-upon Lieutenant Boutelle stepped forward and said: "Here, Injun, give that pistol here, d—m you, quick." Scar-Face Charley laughed and said: "Me no dog. Me man. Me no fraid you. You talk to me I just like dog. Me no dog. Talk me good. I listen you." Boutelle drew his revolver, saying, "You son — b—, I will show you now to talk back to me." Scar-Face said, "Me no dog. You no shoot me. Me keep pistol. You no get him, my pistol." Boutelle leveled his revolver at Scar-Face's breast. Scar-Face drew his pistol. At the same instant, both pistols made but one report. The Indian's bullet went through Boutelle's coat sleeve. Scar-Face jumped and got his gun. Every Indian then followed suit. The soldiers opened fire on the Indians.

Not more than thirty feet from them, the Indians piled on one another, trying to get their guns. After the Indians got their guns they gave battle. The soldiers retreated after a few minutes of firing, leaving one dead and seven severely wounded on the field. The Modocs lost one warrior killed and about half a dozen wounded. The Modoc warrior killed was known as Watchman; his Indian name was Wish-in-push.

When the Indians saw that their comrades on the south bank were into it, they jumped in their dugouts to go across and assist in the fight. When they were about in the middle of the river, the settlers on the north bank fired on them. George Faiuke fired the first shot, saying: "Up at them, boys!" The Indians returned the fire from their dugouts. They turned around and paddled back to the north side. By the time the Indians got on the bank the settlers were way back in the thick, tall sage-brush, shooting all the time with but little effect, only killing one old squaw on the north side, killed one little baby, shot out of its mother's arms while she was running to get in the thick tules. One man had his arm broken. His name was Duffey. On the white side three men were killed. On the south side one able-bodied warrior was killed; one girl about fifteen years old killed; two small children killed; one old woman, help-less, very old, burned up; Skukum Horse shot below the right nipple, making a bad wound.

After the Indians repulsed the soldiers, the women took to their dugouts, many going along the river through the tules, towards the lake on foot. Some of them hid right close to their camp so they could leave under cover of dark-ness the following night. The warriors got together, some on both sides of the river. The older men started right for the Lava Beds, and quite a few of the women and children in their dugouts or canoes. The Indians on the north bank of Lost River collected together and decided to kill the settlers. The settlers had all gone home. About ten o'clock a.m. Hooker Jim led the Indians on to the settlers' homes. By sundown Hooker Jim and his men had killed eighteen settlers, but they never touched a white woman or child. Bogus Charley told Mrs. Boddy that she need not be afraid of him. He said this just as Mrs. Boddy used to tell it. "Don't be afraid, Mrs. Boddy, we won't hurt you. We're not soldiers. We men never fight white women; never fight white girl or baby. Will kill you women's men, you bet. Soldier kill our women, gal, baby, too. We no do that. All I want is something to eat. You give, I go. Maybe I see white man; I like kill him. No like kill white woman." She said she gave him flour, sugar, and coffee. He thanked her and went on his mission of killing.

Kind reader, would these settlers have been killed if they had stayed at their homes as they were requested to do by the Indians? No, sir. The settlers would never have been bothered, not a bit more than their wives were. The Modocs never harmed one child or woman since Capt. Jack became a chief. Major Jackson's soldiers shot down women and children in Jack's village. Mind, kind reader, these men that shot the squaws and children were white men, government soldiers, supposed to be civilized. Jack, a born savage, would not allow his men to do such a coward's work, as he called it.

When the soldiers saw that the Indians had all left their village along in the afternoon, they went back to see after their dead. The soldier boys found a very old squaw. She was so old she could not walk, was blind, could not see. The soldiers took tule mats and heaped them up on the old squaw till they got a big pile heaped on her, say like a load of straw. One of the boys lit a match and set the pile of tule mats on fire that they had heaped on that poor old helpless blind squaw and burned her up alive. After the mats burned up, the body of the old squaw was laying there drawn up burned to a crisp. One of the officers saw her. He said: "Boys, kick some sand over that old thing. It looks too bad!" Mind you, gentle reader, this happened right under the eyes of the officers of this United States government that was in command that twenty-ninth day of November, 1872.

I can write many and many such doings on the white's side. It was not the Indians altogether that did the dark deeds that happened in the early days in the West. The people at large never got the Indian side of any of the Indian Wars with the white people of the United States, although some tribes did some awful bad deeds. On the other hand, the white people did the same. The Modoc Indians never killed white women or children after Capt. Jack became chief of the Modocs. Jack would never allow such doings.

Suggested Further Reading

Murray, Keith. *The Modocs and Their War*. Norman: University of Oklahoma Press, 1959.

Riddle, Jeff. *The Indian History of the Modoc War and the Causes that Led to It*. San Francisco: Marnell & Co., 1914.

James Stevens
1892-1972

H. L. Davis
1894-1960

The single essay that probably had the greatest influence on Pacific Northwest literature was *Status Rerum* (1927). Written by James Stevens and H.L. Davis, the privately published polemic shook Oregonians out of their literary complacency. A vitriolic attack upon the romanticism and commercialism of Pacific Northwestern authors and professors of creative writing, it infuriated its targets, but inspired younger authors to write more honestly about their region.

James Stevens was born in Iowa and moved with his family to Idaho. He left home at an early age and worked in lumber camps and mills in Oregon and Washington. Later he became a spokesman and office manager for the West Coast Lumberman's Association. His numerous writings included four books on Paul Bunyan that brought the mythical logger to national attention. Stevens also wrote short stories and novels about the lumber industry. For information about H.L. Davis, see the notes preceding "Oregon" on page 3.

Status Rerum:
A Manifesto, upon the Present Condition of Northwestern Literature: Containing Several Near-Libelous Utterances, upon Persons in the Public Eye

I

The present condition of literature in the Northwest has been mentioned apologetically too long. Something is wrong with Northwestern literature. It is time people were bestirring themselves to find out what it is.

Other sections of the United States can mention their literature, as a body, with respect. New England, the Middle West, New Mexico and the Southwest, California—each of these has produced a body of writing of which it can be proud. The Northwest—Oregon, Washington, Idaho, Montana—has produced a vast quantity of bilge, so vast, indeed, that the few books which are entitled to respect are totally lost in the general and seemingly interminable avalanche of tripe.

It is time people were seeking the cause of this. Is there something about the climate, or the soil, which inspires people to write tripe? Is there some occult influence, which catches them young, and shapes them to be instruments out of which tripe, and nothing but tripe, may issue?

Influence there certainly is, and shape them it certainly does. Every written work, however contemptible and however trivial it may be, is conceived and wrought to court the approbation of some tribunal. If the tribunal be contemptible, then equally contemptible will be the work which courts it.

And the tribunals are contemptible.

From Salem, Oregon, from the editorial offices of one Col. Hofer, issues, in a monthly periodical somewhat inexplicably called "The Lariat," an agglomeration of doggerel which comprises the most colossal imbecility, the most preposterous bathos, the most superb sublimity of metrical ineptitude, which the patience and perverted taste of man has ever availed to bring between the covers. And Col. Hofer encourages it. He battens upon it. Somewhere within the dark recesses of this creature's—we will not say soul, but nebulous sentience—is some monstrous chord which vibrates to these invertebrate twitterings.

In a healthy condition of society, this state of things would be merely funny. As things are, it is not funny. It is deeply tragic. Northwestern poetry, seeking, in the ingenuousness of its youth, some center about which to weave its fabric, has done no less than bind itself in thraldom to Col. Hofer and his astounding magazine, and the results are all too pathetically apparent. Read some of it!

Or contemplate the panorama of emotional indigestion, the incredible conglomeration of unleavened insipidity, spread before your eyes in the works of the Northwest Poetry Society; the begauded pastries of the Seattle "Muse and Mirror," which surfeit without satisfying. Regard the versicles emanating from the poetry classes of Prof. Glenn Hughes, of the University of Washington—a banquet of breath-tablets, persistently and impotently violet! Regard—but enough! "Palms," exotic *frijole* congealing among the firs of Aberdeen, you need not trouble to savor.

II

If this were all, it would be too much. Regrettably, we have still to contemplate a literary influence which has been, if possible, even more degrading. The Northwest has not escaped, any more than other sections of the United States, its share of "naturals," mental weaklings, numskulls, homosexuals, and other victims of mental and moral affliction. Unfortunately, our advanced civilization has neglected to provide an outlet for their feeble and bizarre energies. Yet, many of these unfortunate creatures are unfit even to teach school. What are they to do? In Chicago, the problem would be simple. There, such unfortunates can devote themselves to the services of some gang-leader, and gain a livelihood in the professions of bootlegging, blackmail and murder. In the South, they are privileged to lead active lives as members of the Ku Klux Klan, and appear prominently at nocturnal whipping-parties and Fundamentalist crusades. Such inoffensive and normal employments have, unfortunately, no place in our Northwestern civilization. What, then, are these unfortunates to do? Such puerile faculties as they may chance to possess demand some exercise. To deny it them would be inhumane.

The earliest white colonies of the Northwest, more merciful than we, found them normal employment. The lumber companies of that age availed themselves of the unfortunates of their time, for the purpose of filing upon timber lands, then in the possession of a too suspicious government. They were found useful instruments for murdering Chinese laundrymen and track laborers, thus establishing the supremacy of the Caucasian race. For hanging Basque and Mexican sheep-herders, and destroying sheep, by theft, poison, firearms, or dynamite, civilization has gained much from their exertions. We do not grudge them their meed of veneration.

But civilization, with impersonal cruelty, has used them and passed on. The agriculture commonwealth has given place to the industrial empire. What can we give our own numskulls, "naturals," homosexuals, and mentally afflicted to do? How can we even rid ourselves of the annoyance of their society? To our industrial leaders, the answer is simple. Put them where their imbecility will be congenially occupied. Obviously, they could not be trusted to manufacture rocking-chairs, to pile lumber, to operate donkey engines, or combined harvesters; to shear sheep or castrate calves; in the operation of woolen, paper and flour mills, their employment would be a continual jeopardy, not only to themselves, but to the lives of men valuable in the industry which they serve. Fortunately, no doubt, for Northwestern industry, but calamitously for the welfare of Northwestern literature, an employment has been developed which offers the advantages of congeniality and inoffensiveness, without entailing the least risk to the continued prosperity of our factories, so much desired by all. The employment is, briefly, short-story writing.

III

From this cause, from the humane sentiments which desire to find harmless employment for these poor creatures, has come that pullulating institution, the short-story writing class. Teachers were, of course, easily recruited. As chiropractors, prohibition agents, saxophone players, radio announcers, and movie organists, have been seduced from more strenuous walks of life, such as pants-pressing, curve greasing, track-walking, lumber-piling, tin-roofing, and cascara-bark-stripping, by the superior usufructs of a life of authority without backache, so, and from these or similar walks, have been recruited our teachers of short-story writing.

Nor have they succumbed to this seduction without honor. On the head and shoulders of the most eminent apostle of short-story writing, Dean M. Lyle Spencer, have descended, suffocatingly, the cap and gown of the Presidency of the University of Washington. Candor compels us to add, that President Spencer's rise to eminence was due no less to his leadership of the youthful unfortunates of the State of Washington through the occult mysteries of short-story writing, than to his faithfully sustained administration of the office of Vice-President of the Seattle Chamber of Commerce. President Spencer's career has been aptly expressed in the slogans of the institutions with which he is allied, as follows: "Get the Seattle Spirit;" "Advertise Education;" "Produce Pecuniary Prose."

The University of Oregon can boast of no short-story instructor of the eminent attainments of President M. Lyle Spencer. If Professor W.F. Thacher's record includes a term of service as Vice-President of any Chamber of Commerce, we possess no knowledge of the fact. Professor Thacher has, nevertheless, certain individual claims to fame. He has been awarded honorable mention in the list of winners in a Chicago tire naming contest, in which more than two and one-half million names were submitted. Professor Thacher has offered the fruits of his intellect in other national name and slogan contests, and has won distinction in practically all of them, for the winsomeness and *chic* of his titles. A movement is reported to be on foot among Professor Thacher's more devout disciples to present him with a gift of 250 engraved calling-cards, bearing his name with the legend, neatly engraved in elegant script, "You Can't Go Wrong with a Thacher Title."

But these are the admirals, so to speak, of the service. To continue the figure, the lower decks offer a spectacle which, in charity, we do not encourage the reader to contemplate. What shall be said of Mme. Mable Holmes Parsons, the illuminatrix of the short-story writing department of the University of Oregon Extension Division? Not for her the Vice-Presidency of the Seattle Chamber of Commerce; not for her parched lips the fragrant moisture of Honorable Mention in a Chicago tire-naming contest. For her, only the enfeebled sighs, the emasculate twitterings, of the vapid ladies, trousered and untrousered, the mental unfortunates who inhabit the unstoried corridors in which her dictum runs as law. Hers only to feed her soul, between intervals pathetically wide, upon the empty honor of the kiddie poem in the Sunday Supplement of the *Portland Journal*. Let us not touch her further. There is enough, ay, more than enough, to engage us elsewhere. Scientists inform us, nature is an excess. In the field of the short-story classes in the Northwest, surely she has outdone herself.

Shall we descend still further into the recesses? We shall encounter the vertiginous galley in which Prof. Borah, of the University of Washington, concocts his flashy and injurious messes, to dazzle the eyes and ossify the intestines of the hapless intellectual paralytics of his short-story classes. What lies further? The stokehold! Formless shapes there labor and conspire, yearning for greater power to lead victims into the path of error. There bend the leaders of the Y.M.C.A. short-story classes. There toil, in groaning discontent, the teacher of short-story writing in the high schools. What lies further? Shall we look further? Dare we look further? In common pity, no! There is a point at which curiosity ends, and perversion begins. We had almost crossed it. Let us turn our faces away.

IV

Until lately, it was difficult—it was impossible—to have formed the faintest conception of the abysmal degradation into which Northwestern letters had fallen. We had noticed that, when we announced ourselves a practitioners of literature, people regarded us suspiciously, and treated us with a wariness which impressed us as unnecessary. We could not imagine why. We had not seen the Parliament of Letters in Seattle. It included all the Writers' Clubs, all the Poetry Societies. Now, we have seen it. We have seen it all.

We have sat in the gallery of the Parliament of Letters in Seattle, and gazed with dreadful awe upon the tossing sea of puerile and monotonous imbecility raging beneath us. Sterile and barren wave after wave of frustrated insipidity swayed beneath the apostolic trident of their pitiable Neptune, the above-mentioned Col. E. Hofer. As the presiding deity, so were the votaries. What hope that a bright-hued phrase might leap glittering from that desert sea? What hope of any act of reverence for life, for character? What hope of any fruition, except that of selling a plot, conceived in avarice, written in slavish and feeble-witted devotion to the dictates of a porcine mind, squalidly inhabiting the skull of a professor of a short-story writing class? We faced the appalling truth. This, then, was the image upon which the public had formed its impression of Northwestern writers!

But worse than this had to be faced. How many times had some tired Eastern editor, chained to his desk by the necessity of earning his daily bread, cringed from the gruesome monument of driveling manuscript, overshadowing, like some monstrous fungus, the desk which, perhaps, has felt the glory of the writings of such men as Theodore Dreiser, Sinclair Lewis, James Branch Cabell, Robert Frost, Carl Sandburg—men of whom American literature may be proud? How could we, as Northwestern writers, ever again demand courtesy of these editors? How could we ever again dare to commit our manuscripts to this devastating flood of imbecility? In our innocence, we had done that which the imagination rebelled to contemplate.

V

Our first impulse was to vow abstention from a pursuit which linked us with such posers, parasites, and pismires. Horror at contemplating a spectacle so blasphemous, so mortifying, so licentious, so extravagantly obscene, drove our sense of loyalty, duty and self-sacrifice from our minds. Our own thoughts were washed away in the black flood, and we could only repeat, with the Elizabethan, Webster:

Thou has led me, like a heathen sacrifice,
With music and with fatal yokes of flowers,
To my eternal ruin.

But it need not be eternal. It lies with us, and with the young and yet unformed spirits, to cleanse the Augean stables which are poisoning the stream of Northwestern literature at the source. Our Hercules has not yet appeared, but hope is surely not lacking. We have had a vision and we have gained faith boldly to prophesy his coming. We can yet cry, even in this darkest and most hopeless hour, from the mountain tops a vision—

Yet, Freedom, yet thy banner, torn, but flying,
Streams like a thundercloud against the wind!

Suggested Further Reading

Stevens, James. *Big Jim Turner*. New York: Doubleday, 1948.

———. *Brawnyman*. New York: A.A. Knopf, 1926.

———. *Paul Bunyan*. New York: A.A. Knopf, 1948 (originally published 1925).

———. *Timber! The Way of Life in the Lumber Camps*. Evanston: Row Peterson & Co., 1942.

———, and H. L. Davis. *Status Rerum: A Manifesto, upon the Present Condition of Northwestern Literature: Containing Several Near-Libelous Utterances, upon Persons in the Public Eye*. The Dalles, Oregon: private printing, 1927.

For references to H.L. Davis, see Suggested Further Reading, page 18.

Beatrice M. Cannady
1890-1974

Beatrice M. Cannady dedicated her life to journalism and to civil rights. Born in Texas, she became assistant editor of Portland's second black-owned newspaper, the *Advocate*, in 1912, and Oregon's first African-American lawyer in 1922. Active in the National Association for the Advancement of Colored People, she founded chapters of the organization in both Oregon and Washington, testified on behalf of the first civil rights bill in Oregon, and worked to desegregate the public schools in Vernonia and Maxwell. Her *Advocate* editorials and news stories, such as the one below from the issue of 8 December 1928, frequently dealt with matters of racial equality and justice. In 1929 the Portland Council of Churches nominated her for the Harmon Award for outstanding contributions to race relations.

Some of the Joys of Being Colored in Portland
A Regular Occurrence

P*lace:* Portland, Oregon, "The land of the free and the home of the brave."
Time: 7:00 P.M. on Saturday evening in the year of our Lord and Savior Jesus Christ, 1928.
Scene: Lobby of the Oriental Theatre, Grand Ave. at Morrison St. (at entrance auditorium).
Cast: One usher and three guests. Usher of white race, guests of colored race; usher's profession, ushering; guests' professions, editor and lawyer.

Act I

Usher: "Best seats upstairs."
Guest: "Haven't you any seats downstairs?"
Usher: "Yes, but I'm sorry I can't seat your people downstairs."
Guest: "Just what do you mean by 'Your People'?"
Usher: Silence

Act II

Guest (peering inside): "I see there are plenty of seats downstairs, and as I'm not in the mood to climb stairs, as I am a law-abiding citizen, presentable and have paid admission for three people, myself and two sons, I prefer to sit downstairs and shall do so. If, however, you do not care to see me do it, just close your eyes and go to sleep."

Usher (seeing guests proceed to seats downstairs, rushes up): "I'll seat you over on the side aisle—but it's against the rules to seat you downstairs in the center aisles."

Guest (tired out, who went to the show for rest): "Seats, please, it doesn't matter a particle in what aisle they are for just as soon as seats are vacant on the center aisle, we'll take them anyway."

Act III

Three lovely seats are vacated on the center aisle. Guests move over and occupy them and nobody moves because of their presence. Guests see show but can't enjoy it because of the humiliation in obtaining seats.

Suggested Further Reading

McLagan, Elizabeth. *A Peculiar Paradise: A History of Blacks in Oregon, 1788-1940.* Portland: The Georgian Press, 1980.

Oregon Lung Association. *Notable Women in the History of Oregon.* Portland: n. p., 1982.

Kathryn Hall Bogle
1905-

In most respects, Portland, Oregon, was a racially segregated city in 1937. African Americans could not patronize restaurants and hotels. Movie theaters placed them in special sections. Insurance rates were prohibitive. Unions shut them out. There were no African-American teachers, salespeople, or bank tellers. For many white Portlanders of those days, knowledge of segregation first came from a compelling article written for the (Portland) *Sunday Oregonian* on 14 February 1937. Its author, Kathryn Hall Bogle, then a young mother, in time became one of the city's most respected citizens.

Kathryn Hall was born in 1905 in Oklahoma Territory. As her stepfather was a railroad man, she moved many times with her family, attending eighteen schools before graduating from Portland's Jefferson High School in 1925. After her marriage to Richard Bogle in 1927, she raised a family and became a vigorous participant in community affairs as a social worker, member of the National Association for the Advancement of Colored People, and parishioner of St. Philip's Episcopal Church. The article below was written at the *Oregonian*'s invitation after she had protested the lack of news about African Americans in that newspaper. It is reprinted here, with bracketed additions to the text representing information supplied by Kathryn Bogle or Rick Harmon, from the *Oregon Historical Quarterly* (1988).

An American Negro Speaks of Color

Recent discussion in the press of the difficulties, real or imagined, of Negroes while attending school prompted the *Oregonian* to ask me for my own reaction to this problem. Perhaps my own experiences, both in school and later, will give readers an insight into the conditions the Negro child faces, for it is when he starts to school that he gains an inkling of a situation destined to confront him all through life.

It is my belief that the high schools present more difficulties for the Negro student than the elementary grades, unless he is an athlete or particularly talented. In that case his pathway is smoothed to a great extent.

The casual speaker during assemblies is an unknown quantity and a hazard to a brown-skinned student, until the guest has told his warming-up jokes. If it is a "colored" story, the speaker often uses offensive terms, and the theme of the tale is usually a colored man's laziness or ignorance. (These stories cannot be compared to the tales told on other races, for in the main, their shrewdness and thrift are played up.)

During the telling of this sort of yarn the colored youngster sits stony-faced, his soul shrivels, as his young neighbors turn amused eyes on this the representative of such a race. Certainly whatever else follows cannot be enjoyed by the young Negro listener, and his smile is on only his *face* for the rest of that day.

Textbooks the students use are not designed to help the colored boy or girl regain any lost "face" after such an experience. About the only reference any of the regular textbooks make to the Negro is his enslavement and the granting of his freedom.

The pictures shown, if any, are always of bowing, scraping, cap-in-hand creatures who have been denied any opportunity whatsoever to better their underdog positions, and whose earthly deity is quoted as being "Massah!"

Hardly one white student in a thousand knows that the first man to give his life for the new country in the revolutionary war was a Negro—Crispus Attucks.

If there is any time a Negro high school student would like to skip class it is his history class during the study of the Reconstruction period following the Civil War. If the teacher happens to be a thoughtful one, no undue emphasis is laid upon the doings of this period.

Perhaps she points out that no people could have succeeded, given such power with no training for it. Perhaps she explains that any man who has been under bondage all his life may be boisterous on finding himself really free, and that the reaction is perfectly normal. She may tactfully draw as a parallel the actions of the students themselves as the bell rings releasing them at the close of a school day. She certainly does not minimize the work of rascally "carpet-baggers."

During this period perhaps no rocks are thrown by hand, but there are subtle omissions, exceptions, and other differences made that wound the spirit. No attempt is made to help him to real pride of his own race. Rather, outside of his home, he is bombarded by assaults and propaganda against his race.

When at length the Negro student receives his diploma the extra applause usually accorded a colored student at this time is to him at once a recognition of his having surmounted (we hope) inconveniences encountered because of his color and approval of his accomplishment, and an expression of a hope that he may continue onward and upward!

Yet the student knows that this expressed hope for his future advancement is but a delicate wisp of nothingness, for where, in that throng of hand-clapping enthusiasts, is there one businessman who will hire that graduate in his office, or anywhere in his business with a real chance to advance?

The man does not exist.

The Negro student knows that as he says good-bye to those friends he has made in high school, it is a real farewell, for, unless he plans to enter one of the colleges in his own state, he has lost all contact with the members of his graduation class. When they enter the workaday world in this land where men are born free and equal, the white student and the brown one become as separate and as distinct as the two poles.

There would be nothing to weep over if these distinctions and separations were merely those of social contacts, for the brown student's happiness does not depend on being included in the social activities of his white friends.

But the separation and distinction which are discrimination do not end there.

For Negro folk are denied their first desire—an equal chance to develop well-rounded lives and the equal chance to provide their children with the same sort of atmosphere any other American parents can choose and claim as a right that has been earned by sweat and blood.

On the other hand, anyone coming here from foreign shores can exercise all his rights as an American citizen as soon as he is naturalized.

Let two students who received their educations at the same local institution together seek employment. Let one be white, the other brown. Perhaps at first neither is successful, but at last they are fortunate in being present where an employer admits he needs two new employees.

The white girl steps forward, and, after answering routine questions satisfactorily, is hired. The brown girl steps forward, happy in her friend's good fortune.

She is stared at in open-mouthed astonishment. She is told quickly and firmly, "We have no place for you."

These words echoed and reechoed in my own ears when I looked for work [in Portland].

I started out buoyant and fresh with the dream of finding an employer without prejudice. I opened each new door with a hope that was loath to leave me. I visited large and small stores of all descriptions. I visited the telephone company; both light and power companies. I tried to become an elevator operator in an office building. I answered ads for inexperienced office help. In all these places where vacancies occurred I was told there was nothing about me in my disfavor—except the color of my skin.

Here is an odd thing to balance. Several of those denying me employment in town offered me employment in their homes. There my color is not a bar! My employer will not be criticized if I am employed in his home in contact with his nearest and dearest!

Were it not for this little quirk in a white man's discrimination against a brown skin, many thousands of Negroes could not earn the bare necessities for life.

With nothing to renew it, my hope began to fade, but still I would not admit defeat. Perhaps if I attended a first-class business school to become the very best stenographer or secretary they could turn out, success would be certain.

A trim little Negro girlfriend and I visited one of the two largest business schools in town [Behnke-Walker Business College]. We were stunned when we were told without delay that because of our race we could not register there! We went to their nearest competitor, only to meet with the same statement.

We anxiously consulted the telephone directory and visited each school listed. Many told us in lowered voices, "Of course I myself have no prejudice. It is my partner in business"—or perhaps the buck was passed to the students registered there. Evening found both of us soul weary.

Subsequent discoveries did not help us. We found that no Portland hospital will accept the application of a Negro girl for nurse training; there are no Negroes in the employ of the state of Oregon; Negroes have not one representative in the clerical departments of the city.

Finally to gain regular employment I put an ad in the *Oregonian*. I was offered a good many places to do "general housework," but declined them in favor of a place where I could be a helper. I stayed exactly three weeks, for I found that my day there began at 6:30 a.m. and ended when I dropped down on a hard, narrow day bed at 10: 30 at night. If this came of being a "helper," I decided to hire out to do general housework and be paid for it.

Before I had attempted another job of this sort, a friend gave my name to an official of a large concern [Meier & Frank Co.]. He was contemplating placing a girl in the dispensary of one of the departments [beauty shop] and thought I could fit in. The pay was good, and the work was a cut above what I had been doing; so I was glad to take it.

I stayed there several years and made a number of friends within the organization and among its customers.

Some other cities have dealt differently with their Negro populations. In Los Angeles one sees Negro policemen, Negro window decorators in white stores, many brown-skinned salespersons, and a goodly number of Negro nurses in the county hospital. In Seattle there are several Negroes working harmoniously in white establishments.

Here in Portland there is one Negro secretary [Norma N. Keene]. This young woman has been in the employ of the same busy man [Joe F. Keller, National Automobile Theft Bureau] for several years. She is a model secretary in her quiet, genteel, and highly efficient manner.

Here, also, one large store has departed from custom and has employed a young Negro in a position with some responsibility, albeit behind the scenes.

An official declared that the young man is "one of the best" and "does his work as well as anyone and better than most."

Those are isolated cases, but they do point the way. They have proved that Negro help is efficient and loyal and that harmony can exist among mixed employees.

Upon what does a color discrimination stand when a white girl returns from her vacation with her skin darker than some of my colored friends and makes a purchase in a downtown store from a blonde colored girl who is so fair no one in the store dreams that two little brown girls are her own daughters? The brown white girl goes unmolested, but if it were known that the white brown girl is brown she would lose her job. A little complex, isn't it?

My own voice does not betray my color to one who does not see my face. Letters I write to my friends and those I receive from them do not suffer for having been written by brown hands—they still convey thoughts from one soul to another. My personal belongings will not tell I am colored.

My own home only says the occupant is poor in the world's goods; it does not shout to anyone that I am dark while my neighbor is white. My dog will not tell you that he is dissatisfied with my color, for, real friend that he is, he sees only me. Our canary does not glance around at his audience to ascertain its color before he trills his song.

The flowers in my garden do not turn away their bright heads when I walk among them, nor do they withhold a single breath of their sweetness when I pluck them.

It is left for people to make a difference.

Now that I myself have a little son [Richard Bogle, Jr.], I am glad to know that he attends school [Hosford] where there is a just man as principal and a group of real teachers who have been fair to other Negro children before him. I shall see to it that he has as firm a foundation in pride of race as I can give him, so that when he meets with an occasional blow later on he can stand steady and strong and have only pity in his heart for those few who cannot see him because they see only his color.

Suggested Further Reading

Bogle, Kathryn Hall. "An American Negro Speaks of Color." (Portland) *Sunday Oregonian*, 14 February 1937, p. 16. Reprinted in *Oregon Historical Quarterly* 89 (Spring 1988): 70-73, 78-81.

Harmon, Rick. "Interview: Kathryn Hall Bogle on the Writing of 'An American Negro Speaks of Color.'" *Oregon Historical Quarterly* 89 (1988): 82-91.

Maves, Norm, Jr. "Kathryn Bogle." (Portland) *Oregonian*, 10 September 1989, Section 6, p. 1.

Minoru Yasui
1916-1986

Minoru Yasui, born in Hood River and a graduate of the University of Oregon Law School, was one of the victims of the greatest violation of civil liberties in American history since slavery. But he was more than just a victim; he struck back peaceably against injustice and hatred. Shortly after Japan's attack on Pearl Harbor, the military issued an order confining Japanese and Japanese Americans to their places of residence from 8 p.m. to 6 a.m. Convinced of the unconstitutionality of the order, Yasui intentionally violated it by walking the streets of Portland after the deadline. The following selection is Yasui's closing statement to Federal Judge James A. Fee on 18 November 1942, just before he was sentenced to nine months in solitary confinement in Multnomah County jail. The statement first appeared in the *Minidoka Irrigator* on 9 December 1942. After being released from solitary, Yasui was then placed in a detention camp for more than a year for violating a law making it a criminal offense knowingly to disobey a military order.

In 1990, Governor Neil Goldschmidt proclaimed March 28 of that year as Minoru Yasui Recognition Day, declaring him "one of our greatest Oregonians, one of our greatest Americans."

For a complete account of Yasui's experience, see *And Justice For All* in Suggested Further Reading, at the end of this selection.

Dearer Than Life Itself Is U.S. Citizenship

YOUR HONOR:

If the court pleases, I should like to say a few words. There is no intent to plead for leniency for myself or to request a mitigation of the punishment that is about to be inflicted upon me.

Despite the circumstances, I am compelled to pay tribute and give my unreserved respect to this honorable court for its clear-cut and courageous reaffirmation of the inviolability of the fundamental civil rights and liberties of an American citizen.

As an American citizen, it was for a clarification and the preservation of those rights that I undertook this case, confident that the American judiciary would zealously defend those rights, war or no war, in order to preserve the fundamental democratic doctrines of our nation and to perpetuate the eternal truths of America.

My confidence has been justified and I feel the greatest satisfaction and patriotic uplift in the decision of this honorable court, for it is full of significance for every American, be he humble or mighty.

I say that I am glad, regardless of the personal consequences to me, because I believe in the future and in the ultimate destiny of America. Ever since I was a child, I have been inculcated in the basic concepts and the traditions of those great patriots who founded our nation.

I have lived, believed, worked and aspired as an American. With due respect to this honorable court, in all good conscience, I can say that I have never, and will never, voluntarily relinquish my American citizenship.

The decision of this honorable court to the contrary notwithstanding, I am confident that I can establish in law and in fact that I am an American citizen, who is not only proud of that fact, but who is willing to defend that right.

When I attained majority, I swore allegiance to the United States of America, renouncing any and all other allegiances that I may have unknowingly owed. That solemn obligation to my native land has motivated me during the past 12 months upon three separate and distinct occasions to volunteer for active service in the United States army, wheresoever it may be fighting to preserve the American way of life.

For I would a thousand times prefer to die on a battle front as an American soldier in defense of freedom and democracy, for the principles which I believe, rather than to live in relative comfort as an interned alien Jap.

The treacherous attack on Pearl Harbor, the bombing of Manila, the aggressor policies of the war lords of Japan are just as reprehensible to me as to any American citizen.

If America were invaded today, I and 70,000 other loyal American citizens of Japanese ancestry would be willing, eager, to lay down our lives in the streets, down in the gutters, to defend our homes, our country, and our liberties!

Be that as it may; I reiterate, regardless of the personal consequences, even though it entail the sacrifice of my American citizenship which I regard as sacred and more dear than life itself, I pay homage and salute this honorable court and my country, the United States of America, for the gallant stand that has been taken for the preservation of the fundamental principles of democracy and freedom!

Suggested Further Reading

Buan, Carolyn M., editor. *The First Duty: A History of the U.S. District Court for Oregon*. Portland: U.S. District Court of Oregon Historical Society, 1993.

Commission on Wartime Relocation and Internment of Civilians. *Personal Justice Denied*. Washington, DC: U. S. Government Printing Office, 1982.

Daniels, Roger. *Concentration Camps USA: Japanese Americans and World War II*. Hinsdale, IL: Dryden Press, 1971.

Yasui, Minoru, in Tateishi, John, editor. *And Justice for All: An Oral History of the Japanese American Detention Camps*. New York: Random House, 1984.

Richard Neuberger
1912-1960

Richard Neuberger was born in Portland. In his first career as a journalist and popular writer, he produced hundreds of articles and several books on topics ranging from Nazi Germany, to the Lewis and Clark Expedition, to the Bonneville Dam. A liberal Democrat in politics, he was elected a member of the Oregon House of Representatives in 1940, and to the Oregon Senate in 1948 and 1952. In 1954 he was the first Democrat elected to the United States Senate from Oregon in over forty years. In the Senate he sponsored legislation on highway beautification, wilderness preservation, and historic preservation. The selection below is a slightly abridged version of "The Day We Passed the Oath Bill," an essay published in *Adventures in Politics: We Go to the Legislature* (1954) which deals with an aspect of the "red-baiting" McCarthyite era of American politics.

The Day We Passed the Oath Bill

T he day we passed the teacher's oath bill in the Oregon Senate was the most uncomfortable day I ever have spent during my service in minor political posts, which includes membership as an Oregon state representative before the war and now as a state senator.

It was unlike any other issue. An atmosphere of tension prevailed from the start. Ordinarily, the senators gossiped and bantered with each other before a day's session, trading opinions about the bills on the calendar for that particular date.

But on this day there was no swapping of early-morning views. A strange and ominous silence hung over most of us. A member of a veterans' organization to which I belong had come to my desk and said he hoped I would "vote for America." I told my veteran friend that according to the best of my poor lights I always voted for America. Aside from this, no one mentioned Senate Bill 323. Curiously, however, I did overhear some minor observations about trivial bills on the docket.

Several of my colleagues had tried hard to bottle up the bill in committee. They were opposed to a teacher's oath, felt it was bad legislation. Yet, now that the measure had been forced to the floor, I knew they intended to cast a *Yea* vote. They had brilliant careers ahead of them in the Republican party. They could not afford to have their patriotism and loyalty impugned.

The first speeches for the bill were reasonably calm and logical. Why should anyone hesitate to sign such an oath in a period of national crisis? But, then, the speeches began to take on fire and brimstone. Hearst editorials were quoted, and so were statements by U. S. Senator McCarthy. Some of the most zealous promoters of loyalty oaths for schoolteachers turned out to be senators who had sponsored bills calling for greater financial returns to the operators of pari-mutuel racetracks, to promoters of irrigation districts and to fly-by-night stock salesmen.

As I mused on the irony of this, a Republican senator strolled over and sat beside me at my walnut desk. "How are you going to vote?" he asked.

"I believe against the bill," I said somewhat tentatively.

"Then I will, too," he said and returned to his own chair.

This had never happened before. On many measures a senator often was willing to cast a solitary *Nay* vote. Indeed, it could be a sign of independence. But this was not the case on the oath bill. No one desired to be without partners on such an issue. In fact, the brief visit from my Republican colleague helped considerably to fortify my own attitude. Truth compels me to admit that I still am uncertain how I would have voted had I been completely alone in opposition to the bill. His visit bolstered my courage.

The speeches resumed and at last we voted. The bill passed 25 to 5.

II

The five who voted *Nay* were a diverse lot. Three were Democrats, two Republicans. One was a Union Pacific railroad brakeman, a Mormon, from the rugged Blue Mountains of Oregon. Another was the manager of radio station KAST. A third was a wealthy logging-equipment wholesaler who drove a big tan Cadillac and was lay head of the Presbyterian Church synod in the state. Another was a quiet, earthy farmer who was a bellwether of the most conservative wing of the G.O.P., although he told me after the vote that he was pleased to learn that Mr. Eisenhower opposed teacher oaths. And there was I, a journalist.

Lunch that day in the Senate lounge was a dismal occasion. One or two of the speakers for the oath bill ate their sandwiches with gusto and talked of the victory. But most of the senators munched and said little. As I looked around me in the lounge, I could see that the so-called normal measurements of liberalism and conservatism were no gauge in such a fight. The oath bill had been supported by men who regularly voiced the aphorisms of the New Deal, who always voted against the corporations and with the "common people." On the other hand, one of the adversaries of the oath bill was a Hoover Republican who made a fetish of governmental economy and who talked frequently for "the old-fashioned virtues."

Suddenly I realized that there was a whole lot to the old-fashioned virtues, after all—particularly when a citizen believed in them with sufficient faith to brave political perils in their defense. All at once, integrity seemed more important to me than ideology. As one of the youngest members of the Senate, I fear that this was a comparatively new set of values. In the past, zeal had dictated otherwise.

One of the conservatives said to me, "I am glad you and I voted together against the oath bill. It shows that freedom is more important than the budget." Perhaps he knew what I had been thinking, for his words paraphrased my thoughts.

It was not an historic or world-shaking episode and it occurred in a state with 1 per cent of the national population. Yet it told me many things. Liberalism may have more to do with the heart than with the stomach. And we do not tread the trail of Jefferson just because we may remark occasionally that Jefferson was a great man. Did not the President buried at Monticello tell us that "each generation must make its own fight for liberty"?

Looking back, I have decided that the day we passed Senate Bill 323 was one brief sortie in that fight. But there was no clear division as to sides, and this will make me more circumspect in my political judgments during the future.

Suggested Further Reading

Neuberger, Richard. *Adventures in Politics: We Go to the Legislature*. New York: Oxford University Press, 1954.

———. *Our Promised Land*. New York: Macmillan Co., 1938.

———. *They Never Go Back to Pocatello: The Selected Essays of Richard Neuberger*. Editor. Steve Neal. Portland: Oregon Historical Society, 1988.

Stephen Dow Beckham
1941-

The Rogue River people were a small group of Southwestern Oregon Indians whose life was largely destroyed by miners, beginning in the early 1850s. Later in that decade, the remainder of the tribe was placed on a reservation on the Oregon Coast. Stephen Dow Beckham chronicles their final journey in this section from his *Requiem for a People* (1971).

Beckham was born in Oregon and educated at the University of Oregon and the University of California, Los Angeles. He has written several books on Northwestern—and especially Indian—history and folklore, and is the editor of *Many Faces: An Anthology of Oregon Autobiography*, volume two in the *Oregon Literature Series*. He is currently a professor of history at Lewis and Clark College, Portland.

Requiem for a People

During the hot June days the blind, lame, sick, fearful people yet gathered. On the tenth the cavalcade of soldiers and prisoners set out for Port Orford. Ord was deeply stirred about forcing these people to leave on a long journey to an unknown land. "It almost makes me shed tears to listen to them wailing as they totter along," he wrote, as the final exodus began through the mountains.

While the people were on the trail, the volunteers from the Rogue Valley and the coast searched for refugees and fought skirmishes at Pistol River and the Chetco. They brought the Indians they captured to the garrison at Port Orford. On June 20 the steamer *Columbia* left the small harbor with 600 persons aboard. These Indians sailed up the coast to Astoria, up the Columbia River to Fort Vancouver, up the Willamette River to the Yamhill; then they boarded barges for a short passage toward the coast mountains. At the head of navigation they began a forced march through the hills to their new home on the Siletz Reservation.

"John," the last hostile leader in southern Oregon, surrendered near Port Orford at the end of June. The wily old man had kept together 35 men, 90 women, and 90 children of his band. Since the *Columbia* was taking a full load of 592 additional persons to the reservation, "John's" band was compelled to walk nearly 125 miles up the coast.

Although the Indians suffered on their long journey, either by land or by sea, they were fortunate compared to the stragglers left scattered through the hills of southern Oregon. During the summer and the following winter, the refugees were hunted down, murdered, and, occasionally, captured. The government hired William Tichenor to bring those survivors he could find to the new reservation. After eight months in the field, he had found 152 holdouts. The "fire-eaters" ambushed these half-naked, starving Indians when they were camped near the charred ruins of the cabin of John Geisel. When the captives marched on, they left the bodies of 19 of their kinsmen in the forest.

The rains came again to the Rogue country. The streams cleared as the miners rushed away for new diggings and pursued richer dreams of wealth. Along the mountain creeks the beaver gnawed the maple, the alder, and the dogwood. Sea otter yet swam and dived in the surf near the coast. In the summers the smelt returned to the coarse sand beaches, and in the fall the salmon surged up the streams, fought against the riffles and the rapids, and returned to their spawning grounds. Acorns formed, dried, and fell from the oaks. Camas lilies bloomed white and blue in the meadows—yet all was different in this land.

No longer did the buckskin-clad women, wearing their basket caps, wander through the fields with their digging sticks and collecting baskets. No longer did the stakes and poles of the weirs channel the salmon into netting ponds in the rivers. Sand and grass crept into the house pits amid the charred and rotting planks scattered along the river bars. Moss and lichens inched across the boulders to fill the rock mortars where for centuries the pestles had ground the acorns into flour for leaching. Occasionally the sun reflected from the iridescent fragments of shattered mussel and abalone shell, but never again would new layers of pearly refuse be tossed on the middens.

The opening of southwestern Oregon had begun slowly—ships of discovery sailing along the coast, a hearty band of fur trappers, a botanist seeking cones and twigs, the government exploring expeditions, and the surveying of the Southern Emigrant Route. Then the influx accelerated with the boom of gold rush and the scramble for donation land claims. The wealth of the Rogue country—furs, gold, rich lands, timber—was responsible for luring the white man.

The opening of this region was little different from the conquest of other frontiers in western America. The long-familiar elements of the frontier experience—the trapper, the trader, the cattle drover, the miner, and the settler—were all present. Nor was the resistance of the Indians unique; their desire to retain their homeland was only natural. Nevertheless, the forces of the newcomers, their diseases, vices, tools, and technology spelled change for the Rogues.

Change in the Rogue country was tragedy for her first people. The nearly ninety-five hundred Indians who had held this land when the white men first penetrated it became in increasing numbers victims of "civilization." The wars, the massacres, and the final struggles of 1855-56 forced the bands through the mountains in their exodus to the sea. Then over the Pacific, on the smoky, rumbling old steamer *Columbia,* the two thousand survivors journeyed north to the reservation, a land that had never held the bones of their ancestors or heard their chants, their shouts at the shinny game, or the singing of the shamans.

Near the spruce thickets north of the mouth of the Rogue River, near a clearing in the forest where once stood the cabin of a German settler and his family, near the weathering granite marker inscribed with the fate of those pioneers named Geisel, still lay the scattered and unburied bones of the last of the Rogues on their way from their homeland.

Suggested Further Reading

Beckham, Stephen Dow. *Hathaway Jones: Tales from Rogue River.* Bloomington: Indiana University Press, 1974. Reprinted by Oregon State University Press as *Tall Tales from Rogue River: The Yarns of Hathaway Jones,* 1991.

———. *The Indians of Western Oregon: This Land Was Theirs.* Coos Bay, OR: Arago Books, 1977.

———. *Requiem for a People: The Rogue Indians and the Frontiersmen.* Norman: University of Oklahoma Press, 1971.

Helen Murao
1926-

Helen Murao was born in Oregon. After her parents died, she was raised by Portland neighbors, a young Caucasian couple. In the following excerpt from her oral history, she describes her early life and her experiences in the wartime relocation camps, first published in *And Justice For All* (1984). The genesis of the camps was President Franklin D. Roosevelt's order of 19 February 1942 ordering the relocation of Japanese and Japanese Americans from their homes west of the Cascade Mountains. The order, justified as a military necessity to prevent sabotage and spying, sent Oregonians of Japanese ancestry to camps in Idaho, Wyoming, and California, although U.S. citizens from the nation's other enemies in the war, Germany and Italy, were not relocated.

After the war Murao worked in retail merchandising and interior design, and as a primary school teacher. Her undergraduate education was at the University of Wisconsin and her graduate degree is from Northeastern Illinois University. She now lives in retirement in San Jose, California.

Minidoka

I made my own decision. Nobody even approached me about it. I made my decision to go into camp with the two boys. At that point, as loving as my foster parents were, I did not think that they were good for me, and I think it's a good thing that I did not continue living with them. But I didn't know it at the time. They took me to the Portland Assembly Center and said good-bye to me. My foster mother had helped me pack, and we packed camp clothes, summer-camp clothes. You know how you pack shorts and tennis shoes and things like this. And I packed for maybe three weeks and thought this is only for a while, I'll be back. So I left school clothes, good clothes, cold-weather clothes and things like this, and books. I just took enough necessities for three weeks, thinking I surely would be back. She let me feel this way; she let me believe this way and let me prepare this way and took me to camp.

This was the first experience I'd ever had with living among Japanese people. Our home had been in the north part of Portland where we were the only Japanese family. So that, as children, we went to school as the only Japanese family in school, and our peer associations were not with Japanese people at all, so this was my first experience among Japanese people.

There was an overwhelming, confusing feeling, and it was just all negative—all bad feelings that I had. Not only the country having done this—causing us to have to be evacuated—but the Japanese people having done this to us. So I really was a very unhappy, bitter child, and I really entertained, at fleeting moments, some feelings that maybe I'd be better off if, you know, I tried to . . . I felt it might be a solution if I just did away with my brothers' and my own life. I thought that. I entertained that as a possibility, as a solution, and then abandoned it. But I thought this because it was so black for me at one point, you know. If your country is doing this to you, and if your people are doing this to you . . . I just couldn't see a way out of a big black hole. But I gave that idea up, obviously.

We spent the summer, through the end of August 1942, when we were evacuated into Idaho, in the Portland Assembly Center, which had been where they had stock shows. I remembered that from the time my parents took us to things like county fairs and stock shows. This was the county-fair grounds. All the places were very familiar to me as a child, and I recognized the place where we were assigned as the pavilion where they kept animals. They had these one by sixes or one by nines, however large those boards are, with big knotholes, just over the pens. It was a huge pavilion with twelve-foot-high plywood walls and with curtains as doors. Row after row after row of these. My two brothers and I were assigned to one of these. We had cots, and a curtain to cover the door, and our belongings. You've heard it all before. We ate in the community mess hall. We were given salt tablets because the weather was so hot.

I didn't know a soul. I knew a few kids, peers; but I didn't know them well, because I didn't live in the community. I was just beginning to feel like a teenager, and, you know, this is the time when peer relationships begin to be very important. Boy-girl relationships begin to be very important. It was a very brief period, but there was a nice feeling that I had when I first started to meet the kids. With them I was a social equal.

You probably have not experienced this yourself, but in the late thirties and forties in my neighborhood where I grew up with Caucasian kids, we were all just one big family. But as we approached our teen years, you know, sex started to become important, and boys and girls started to pair off. While I was just great as a neighbor and a friend, all of a sudden I wasn't right to be dated.

So, I had very strange feelings. I discovered that among the Japanese people I was really kind of an oddity, because I had lived among Caucasians, and I was a novelty. When the guys started really coming around, I was thinking, Boy, this is terrific. I was getting offers for dates and stuff like that, and I thought that this was just going to be great. It was this racial thing that I was just beginning to become aware of, and I was trying to sort that out in my mind. And I discovered that among the Nisei people I was an equal, that I could compete with the other girls for the boys' attention, and I could be very successful at it.

When I went into camp I was just overwhelmed with the numbers of Nisei boys and girls and everybody. But also I would remember taking walks with my sister's boyfriend and telling him how I felt about how angry I was at the Japanese people, at the world, people in general, the country in general, the war, the everything. And that I wanted to have nothing to do with the Japanese people. And he would say, yes, but so-and-so wants a date with you. And I'd say, that's terrific, but I don't want to have anything to do with him, not at all. And he would say, now you think about it. You may feel different, but you aren't different. You're one of us. Like it or not, you are here. You chose to come here. Face it and live with it.

That summer I had this sorting out and coming to terms with my own self and my own life. It was not an easy time. When my brothers and I got to the Portland Assembly Center there were no persons, no agency, no group there to counsel not only me but anybody. No social workers, no social-service agency of any kind. There was an infirmary for cuts and bruises, but nothing else. I

know, because I went seeking help one day when I can't tell you how low I felt. If a kid fifteen years old could even consider suicide, you know that she's got to be awfully unhappy. I went seeking some help and was directed by someone in charge to the infirmary. That's not what I needed.

There was nobody to give me any kind of emotional support of any sort—no Caucasians or Japanese personnel. I guess that this probably was the worst experience of my life, the hardest period of my life. I somehow got it all in my mind that it was the United States government, and it was this country, and it was the Japanese people—everybody was really out to do this to us. At that point, even if it hadn't been for the war, I might have felt this way. But I think that evacuation just heightened it all, because it was just heaping one indignity after another onto me. It was just almost more than I could handle, it really was.

By Labor Day 1942, when we were to be moved inland to Idaho, I guess I was beginning to feel that I had no choice. I had to quit being so angry and to quit being so hateful. I had a job to do with my brothers, and I ran them like a drill sergeant, and people who met me in those years smile and laugh and talk about it now; they say, "Helen ran those boys like she was a drill sergeant." I wouldn't let them be out after nine o'clock, I made them go to school, I made them study, I made them . . . you know. I had them help me scrub their clothes so that they would be clean. Then somewhere during that time I came to feel, well, we're going to show these people. We're going to show the world. They are not going to do this to me; nobody is going to make me feel this miserable. The United States government may have made me leave my home, but they're going to be sorry. You know what I mean; I came around to feeling that nobody's going to do this to me. *I'm going to prevail, my will is going to prevail, my own life will prevail.* I'm not going to kill myself, I'm going to prevail.

I made up my mind that my two brothers and I would show everybody. We were orphans, yes; we had come from an unhealthy family, a tubercular family, and we were like pariahs, but I made up my mind, and I told my brothers that we will excel, and we will be better than anybody so that they'll be sorry. Not that they would be proud of us, but they would be sorry, the whole world would be sorry that they did this to us. It was not a healthy attitude on my part.

At Idaho's Minidoka we were assigned our barracks. Well, the end rooms of the barracks were the small rooms, quite small, the smallest. We were given one of those. It was usually for two people, but since we were kids and we didn't take up so much space, three of us were put in one of those end barracks. But I do remember managing to get a bed by using feminine wiles because the guys in camp were teenagers, and they were running up and down the block saying, "There's one over there," and "There's a good one over here." They were pegging the families that were coming in that had—you know—good-looking girls. They came running up to me, ran in and looked, and they saw that it was me, that there were no parents around. They asked how many beds? The camp was giving out pillow ticking that you filled with straw, and cots. The old and the infirm got beds with mattresses, and the younger people got cots and pillow ticking. I managed to finagle a real bed with a real mattress from these guys. I thought that was pretty neat. That's all we had, that's absolutely all we had.

I had no skills, and I did not want to work as a waitress. So, I lied and said I could type, and I worked in a steno pool. Well, the fellow watched me and he knew damned well I couldn't type. I couldn't. But, again, I used whatever I could muster up and batted my eyelashes and said I would be a hard worker. He let me stay, but not because of any typing expertise, he just let me do that. So I had a job for which I was paid. A stenographic job was sixteen dollars a month, and I was part-time, so I got eight dollars a month.

I was still in high school, so I had to go to class. My two brothers had to go too, and I lied a lot because I didn't want to go. I would stay at home, because the hot water in the mess hall and in the laundry rooms was available in the morning. I would scrub my brothers' blue jeans and their clothes on a washboard and try to wring them out and also launder our sheets in the morning. Then I would write a note saying, "Please excuse Helen for being absent, she was busy." And then I'd sign it, and the teacher would accept it. I still managed to get good grades. But I never, never, was in class.

I insisted that my two brothers and I eat together in the mess hall as a family unit. I insisted that we have grace before meals. And I insisted that they be in our room at eight o'clock at night. Not because I wanted to see them but because I thought that's what we should do as a family unit—we should be together, spend our time together, and live as a family group—and I tried in all the really childish ways to maintain us that way. It's incredible, as I think about it now, how we did it; but we lived as a family unit. I don't know what gave me the strength to do it, but I can't help but feel that those early years with my parents must have given it to me. It must have been that, because that year and half from evacuation until the time when I left camp were terribly hard times. Not only for me emotionally, but just keeping body and soul together. And that whole time we had absolutely no money, absolutely no financial support. No emotional support either. No adult nurturing of any kind. The people were so wrapped up in their own misery in camp, in their own unhappiness, in their own problems, which is only to be expected, that nobody had anything to give to anybody else. It didn't occur to them that maybe we were needy in other ways.

We got out of camp because we had a sponsor. It was in August 1943. The same woman who helped me plan my sister's funeral worked for the Baptist Home Mission Society. I wrote to her, and I said it was imperative that I get out immediately. I said, "Will you find me a place?" And, again, there's something that's marvelous about being young and ignorant; you just ask and somehow things materialize. She had access to homes throughout the country willing to take students. She sent me a list of several, and one of them was a family, a Presbyterian minister and his family, in Madison, Wisconsin. They wanted an evacuee. I didn't stop to think whether that was going to be all right or not; it just meant getting out. So I went. They were a terrific family. When I came out of camp, they gave me the support that I really sorely needed, and they have been friends ever since.

I felt wonderful the day I left camp. We took a bus to the railroad siding and then stopped someplace to transfer, and I went in and bought a Coke, a nickel

Coke. It wasn't the Coke, but what it represented—that I was free to buy it, that feeling was so intense. You can get maudlin, sentimental about freedom; but if you've been deprived of it, it's very significant. When I ran in there as a teenager to buy that Coke, it was the freedom to buy it, the freedom to run out and do it.

Something my parents did for me provided the glue that held me together from age fifteen through seventeen. In my adult years the experience made me a very strong person, very strong. My two brothers—one is an M.D. and one is a Ph.D.—are very successful professionally. I have a master's degree. We all did this on our own. Nobody helped us.

Suggested Further Reading

Tateishi, John, editor. *And Justice for All: An Oral History of the Japanese American Detention Camps.* New York: Random House, 1984.

William Kittredge
1932-

The central encounter of the Native American people is with the natural environment that sustained their bodies, minds, and spirits. Nowhere in Oregon was nature more evident in the lives of the original inhabitants than in the semi-arid regions of its southeastern corner. William Kittredge here describes the intimate relationship of the Northern Paiute people and their land before the coming of the whites. Kittredge was born in Portland, and after graduation from Oregon State University he operated a cattle ranch in the Warner Valley of southeastern Oregon for ten years. He has edited and written many books and contributed stories and articles to more than forty magazines. He is currently professor of English at the University of Montana. This selection is from *Witness* (1989).

Ghosts

Not so long ago the scattering of native people in southeastern Oregon believed you could slip into caves under the rimrocks, and descend into an underworld in which there existed a heaven of creatures. Trout were thick in little streams, and would rise like ghosts to a grasshopper in the soft aftermath of an afternoon thunderstorm; the green moss would be soft and rich underfoot and the ripe berries would fall into your hands.

Mule deer would look back at you without apprehension, ears twitching at the little flies. This was where game animals lived before they emerged to share the world with us.

It is not altogether a fantasy; it is also a fairly precise description of the tiny fishing streams which collect in the isolated Great Basin ranges of desert mountains and work down to the swamplands where waterbirds congregate in flocks beyond numbering. Maybe those stories about an underworld populated by that richness of animals were not dreams at all. No one knows what those people thought, or what their dreams were like, but it's certain their descendants were neither unintelligent or unimaginative.

Maybe their stories were simply ways to celebrate what they loved about the world in its actualities; maybe the part about fantasies and dreams is my invention. I should be careful about projecting sadness from my disconnected times onto them.

The Northern Paiutes who lived in that country can be thought of as a deeply primitive people. They did not have much in the way of what anthropologists call "cultural items," which includes everything from spoons to ideas of magic. They lived sparse and traveled light. The country did not reward them for owning very much.

The clans who lived in Warner Valley were known as "The Groundhog Eaters," a name wonderful in its inelegance. But you have to wonder what it meant to them as they managed lives which likely did not seem either splendid or numbing or even simple.

Many of us like to imagine the people we understand as native as living in quietude with a world which is entirely holy. That is not altogether a sentimentalization; there are people who seem to regard existence as a series of communal ceremonies; many of them do in fact seem to think everything is alive and holy.

But what we know for sure is simpler, and brutal: such people are almost gone from the earth; in another generation their dreams will be extinct.

In the best book on the subject of pre-white narrative in eastern Oregon, *Coyote Was Going There; Indian Literature of the Oregon Country,* Jarold Ramsey writes:

> The white response, organized during the Civil War, was brutally simple: extermination. The unpublished "Field Journals" of Lt. William McKay (a medical doctor who was himself part Indian) make it vividly clear that Army detachments like McKay's, aided by Indian scouts from Warm Springs and elsewhere, went through the upper reaches of the Great Basin country hunting Paiutes and other Shoshoneans down like deer, killing for the sake of what in the Vietnam era became known as "body count."

As those people moved through the yearly cycle of their so-called hunting/gathering, their existences turned on few actual mileposts (birth, initiation, marriage, children, death), and the content of their days is hard for us to imagine with any accuracy (how would we know if it was accurate?). It is even more difficult for most of us to value.

They existed in an endless sway of time many of us find frightening; we like to think they lived in communality; we like to think they did not ever consider themselves alone, since the world around them was alive; we like to think they knew it was a useless idea to consider anyone exceptional since everything was part of every other thing. We like to think such things, but we don't know if we want such lives. We are still infected by our urge to go conquer time, to go out, and be individual.

In Warner Valley there is a long curl of high ground along the eastern side of Crump Lake (known locally as "The Bar"), where native people camped in waterbird season, spring and fall, over millennia. Up until the early 1930s The Bar was thick with wild roses and native berry brush. Then, in the devastating series of dry seasons which accompanied the economic ruination of the Great Depression, a lot of that tule-ground flood-plain country around Crump Lake got afire, and the thickets of dead chest-high brush burned away, leaving reefs of ashes across a litter of beautiful chipped obsidian artifacts which had been lost, accumulating over centuries.

Each fall at that latitude and elevation there are days when the sunlight lies like glory over the dying red-orange reeds of the tulebeds and the muddy soft water of the lake. Think of afternoons out on that bar amid the rosebushes, the waterbirds clattering as they come and go.

You could voyage into that country and try the art of sitting still in the silences alongside a seep spring deep in the hidden backlands. You could study the singular beauty at the heart of a desert flower while long-legged insects walk the surface tension of the water, and you could find your concern with the passage of time easing out of you, and you could be inclined to attempt the slow day-to-day dance of creatures, and imagine you have gone somewhat native. And probably you would be kind of right; the native people were much like us; we are the same species; it's just that some of our people killed them like animals, drove them away, gave them our diseases and taught them the arts of farming and rodeo; we live surrounded by ghosts. Some of us think we yearn to live like they do, but not enough, not yet.

Suggested Further Reading

William Kittredge. "Ghosts," *Witness* 3 (Winter 1989): 31-33.

——. *Hole in the Sky: A Memoir*. New York: Alfred A. Knopf, 1992.

——. *Owning It All*. St. Paul: Graywolf Press, 1987.

Ramsey, Jarold, compiler and editor. *Coyote Was Going There; Indian Literature of the Oregon Country*. Seattle and London: University of Washington Press, 1977.

Elizabeth Woody
1959-

Gloria Bird
1951-

In recent years there has been a burgeoning interest in the history and culture of the Native-American peoples. Both Native and non-Native scholars, artists, and writers have flourished in all regions of the United States. In the following selection, taken from *Dancing on the Rim of the World* (1990), Elizabeth Woody and Gloria Bird examine the state of Native American literature in the Pacific Northwest.

Elizabeth Woody was born in Arizona. She is a poet and writer whose works have appeared in many volumes. A member of the Confederated Tribes of Warm Springs, Oregon, Woody has won numerous awards, competitions, and fellowships. Gloria Bird, a member of the Spokane tribe, was born in Washington State. A poet and essayist whose work has appeared in several journals, she is currently teaching literature and creative writing at the Institute of American Indian Arts. In 1992 she received the Diane Decorah Memorial Award for Poetry for her collection *Full Moon on the Reservation*.

Dancing on the Rim of the World

The Northwest, "the rim of the world," like the rest of the "New World" of centuries ago, is a complex place of diverse, original peoples, ecosystems, and masterworks of art and language. As Northwest Native Americans, our perception of the boundaries of our region are quite different from the generally accepted ones that recognize arbitrary state lines; the reaches of our language groups suggest a greater territory, which, expressed in present political boundaries, includes southern Alaska, southwestern Canada, Montana, Washington, Oregon, Idaho, western Nevada, and northern California.

Our lives are exceptional from the new Americans in that we can claim a heritage that involves no fewer than forty thousand years with this continent. For example, a site called Celilo Falls (Wyam) was one of the longest continuously inhabited sites in the Northwest, lived in for well over twelve thousand years. Although it now lies inundated by the backwaters of the Dalles Dam (1956), its omniscience is evident in writing by Native Americans of this region. Earle Thompson writes, "One of my poems 'Dancer' has a particular line that lingers: 'Dancing on the rim of the world' from this vantage point we can see the sky so blue and the water and the shoreline; we can see Celilo Falls; the fishing platforms, and we survive in harmony with our inner and outer natures." Celilo Falls of Earle Thompson's poetry illustrates how Native individuals *define* themselves through relationships that include one's associations with family, household, or village. As writers, also, we know our strengths are our native languages, histories, and traditions that respect what is shared in common.

It needs to be stressed here that by our (Native American writers') active participation in contemporary literature, we should recognize the simultaneous existence of a living ancestral literature that shines through the eclipse of non-Native chronicles. In this light we can understand why the *voice* of the Northwest is a tribal one, rooted as it is in the oratorical visions of accessible past leaders such as Smohalla, Chief Joseph, Chief Leschi, and Chief Tommy Thompson, to name only a few. Like the Aborigines of Australia who sing dream songs that describe to the listener the geography of their origins, we, too, have a land-shape in our stories and songs. You can hear this in the observances of land cycles in our Indian communities as we give thanks for life. The Plateau tribes, which we are most familiar with, have first fruits and first salmon ceremonies to offer communal respect and rejoice in the return of our relatives to nourish us. This continued interdependence with land may well be the only principle that will save our planet.

Our literature has suffered and our history has been misrecorded in poor translations. It has been stereotyped as "shamanic," "mythic," or "primal," and overall thought to be naive by the general population. Before we can address the literary merit of our work as Native American writers, we must first deconstruct the myths about us. In many anthologies of Native American literature we see the perpetuation of the myth of the Vanishing American. It is repeated consistently in the overattention given to "surrender speeches," as if oratory exists as a part of our past.

We are confronted with the continuation of this aspect in some Native American literature courses, which sometimes serve as the only introduction students have to Indian people's existence, past or present. We no longer live with the assumption that the efforts of ethnologists and the literary milieu have the exclusive responsibility to preserve, and therefore the right to own, our work. At the same time, we recognize there has been much responsible scholarship on our people. We ourselves must often look to archives or works of non-Native scholars in our personal research to document and study the taproot of our conditions, but through literature we have the opportunity to express some important concepts, not exclusively Native American or Northwestern, but imparted to us from the environment.

On the other hand, there are specific instances of cultural appropriation that weaken that healthy exchange. Recently Skamania County Historical Society registered the symbol of the well-known petroglyph of the lower Columbia River, Tsagaglalal (She Who Watches), for their trademark. They have claimed *ownership* of an image without sensitivity to the Indian people who acknowledge her in their legends. The Yakima Nation has stepped forward to protect and preserve its traditional cultural and religious interests in the petroglyph's image and has challenged the notion that such a figure can become a clichéd commercial instrument. It is not enough simply to recognize oratorical traditions. What is needed is an understanding from our perspective of why it is so important for us to remember.

In the Northwest we have a number of native scholars and teachers actively writing and teaching from the background of their traditions. Especially notable are Vi Hilbert, author of *Haboo,* a collection of Skagit legends; Allen P. Slickpoo, Sr., author of *Nee-Me-Poom Tit Wah Tit* (Nez Perce Legends); as well as Gail Tremblay of Evergreen State College; Elizabeth Cook Lynn, editor of *Wicazo Sa Review* (Eastern Washington University, Cheney, Washington); and Roger Jack of Eastern Washington University. These are only a few of the many Native American scholars who teach in our Northwest system of higher education. What compels us to continue to write and teach in colleges and universities, to study linguistics or learn old languages, is that, for us, the *traditional* storytellers, elders, and orators, still exist. As we continue to "write the voice down," we are in a position to shape the emerging patterns.

Non-Indians may find themselves uncomfortable facing the cultural suppression, disease, political repression, and dispossession that we have endured and often write about. These disturbing issues are not a part of the silent past, but extend into modern society. During the 1980s, for example, we have lived with active neo-Nazi cults, eviction of Indian families from traditional livelihoods, and Indian grave-robbing—all of which confront Indian writers of the Northwest. Writers and artists have always been a threat to tender ideologies. We accept this challenge, as writers traditionally have, knowing that socially, we represent a microcosm of situations that plague everyone throughout the world. Somewhere, someone will assert that suppression is not a reality in contemporary America. Yet, remember that in 1988 Father Ernesto Cardinal was denied entrance to this country to tour and read his poetry. The irony is that while we create in a political hotbed, we *can* choose to let politics ride shotgun. It is different for each writer, but it is still part of our serious literature to play upon the incongruities of our lives.

The urge has been to *write down* the old stories before the old people have gone, or *write down* the language while there are elders who speak it. Humishuma (1888-1936), or Crystal Quintasket, an Okanagon woman, gathered stories in her time from the elders, and worked on a dictionary of the dialects of the Okanagon. She is known for *Cogowea, The Halfblood* (1927), one of the first published novels by a Native American. Her book illustrates the dilemma of being a half-blood: one was not accepted fully by either group. This theme has repeated itself both literally and in literature, although we have come a long way since Humishuma's time. By pulling away from a trusting status with the United States and its imposing definitions of blood quantum, we are all in a sense "half-bloods," a metaphor for walking in two worlds. In writing, we are taking back control of our tribes and our lives.

Even though American culture freely borrowed Native American democratic concepts from the Great Laws of Peace of the Iroquois Confederacy to create the Constitution of the United States, it has continually ignored the fact that there are people of the original spirit among us: entire tribes whose prerogatives are for a free society and a livable environment for the forthcoming Seventh Generation. From the Arctic Circle to the tip of South America we have indigenous people dedicated to this cause, making a statement—be it in literature, or voiced orally in a Sundance ceremonial, in Canada or Montana, in a sweatlodge with Buddhist monks during the Long Walk of 1978, or lobbying in Congress—to incite our generation to responsive self-government or land and wildlife preservation.

Already our central figures of legend, Coyote and Raven, are common cultural motifs in mainstream art. Archetypal, they still breathe through the facsimiles of the original trickster/changers, achieved in the pre-Euro-American traditions by the storyteller poet. Some of our applications, perhaps, are direct crossovers from this old medium, but each of us reflects deeply upon the complexity of our indigenous status in the context of our lives and our literary craft. We have a responsibility to the movement that began centuries ago. Our issues arise from that ancient body of thought and extend outward. There is a resurgence of participation in the Longhouses, Smokehouses, traditional dances, and the arts. The force of this movement also extends to contemporary theater, dance, and art, which deserve contemplation in their connection to our literature. This connection, however, cannot be covered in this specific essay, except to mention that many of the writers that we represent from the region are also visual artists, actors, scriptwriters, and filmmakers. As Ward Churchill, the Creek-Cherokee social historian, pointed out during a packed discussion in a Portland bookstore in 1988, "Indians are the barometers of the country." At best, we exemplify the great hope and ability of people to turn disaster around. Our contemporary progression in literature is analogous to human development in myth: of becoming complete, reawakened within the laws of the universal. The making of symbols and images is directly entwined with our Northwest homeland, family, ancestors, their graves, teachings, and specific sites that mark our tenure. Literature, funneled through these channels, surfaces alive and wonderful for all our children. To highlight this aspect of our primal and universal function is to insure the integrity of our literature.

The light at the rim spreads from collectives and combinations of talent, that specific "injin-uity," to enrich our communities. Aboriginal consortiums, such as the one surrounding Theytus Books, Ltd., whose most visible members include Viola Thomas and Janet Armstrong, work in association with En'Owkin Centre in British Columbia; The Institute of Alaska Native Arts in Fairbanks, Alaska; Press Gang Publishers, Vancouver, British Columbia (Chrystos's *Not Vanishing*); and the three-year-old Northwest Native American Writers Association of Portland, Oregon (NWNAW *Broadsides Collections*) exemplify Native American efforts to publish books that exist throughout the region.

The elders are sharing through people like Bruce Miller, Virginia Beavert, Allen P. Slickpoo, Sr., and P. Y. Minthorn—people who work silently, without acclaim, to collect stories and songs correctly. Virginia Beavert, as an example, compiled a text of legends and unselfishly gave the copyright to the Yakima Tribe.

We do not fail to recognize such efforts to inform one another. On the global level, Maori traditionalists visit Northwest Washington communities to build and race canoes in *Waterborne*, a native canoe project. Aboriginal radio broadcasters tour the Northwest to gather programs to air. This light is seen as part of a necessary shared spiritual culture that circles the globe, and sheds the "minority" veil in which history has draped us.

World interest in native culture is further illustrated in foreign language translations, groups of touring artistic emissaries, and medicine people crossing the oceans. Native American communities will prove an asset as our region moves to the forefront in a world economy that is now focused on the Pacific Rim. Major components of Northwest industries are inextricably tied to Indian lands. Many countries have interest in, and some sympathy for, Indian cultures by merit of our reputed ecological sense, and the "green trend" similarly embraces our aesthetics and philosophy. The overflow of this interest in our literature directs a growing awareness that could positively unite the dichotomous factions of Native and Non-native, right and left, East and West. We believe it will be through our images, again, that we will meet as equals. The challenge we face today is whether to maintain our literature as *Indian*, that is, as this ethnic fragment, or to reclaim the original place of honor as participants of a dynamic cultural force.

We look to the future in anticipation of more films by Sandra Osawa. *(In the Heart of Big Mountain* was included in the Annual Rainbow Film Festival in Portland, Oregon, 1988.) There will be more productions of award-winning plays such as those by William Yellow Robe, Jr. *(Independence of Eddy Rose).* The wealth of native playwrights of the Northwest includes Ed Edmo (*Through Coyote's Eyes)* and Monica Charles, whose plays originated at the Institute of American Indian Arts in Santa Fe and were performed across the country by the nationally recognized Native American Theatre Ensemble. Bruce Miller tells myths at the Haystack summer workshops on the Oregon coast, and is part of the Dreamkeepers film productions. Our writers are visible in events, such as Bumbershoot in Seattle, the Portland Poetry Festival, the Portland Arts and Lectures Series, the Fishtrap Gathering in the Wallowas, and the Oregon Institute for the Literary Arts fellowships and awards. The applause, anthologies of prose and poetry, novels, awards to plays, film, and video have been earned by our Native writers as contemporary artists, not as ethnic constituents enriching a popular culture.

In this light, contemporary Native American literature is a tribute to the keenness, tenacity, and intellect of our forebears. The many unheard voices, the invaluable record keepers of tribe and family, as well as the lesser known writers in this anthology deserve recognition as well. This is to cite the people who struggle alone to write what they have learned in their communities, but who may not consider themselves writers. They are possibly our most valuable asset, next to our children, in that they link our words from one generation to another.

We are greatly indebted to our "elders in the field," including James Welch, Mary TallMountain, Adrian C. Louis, Bill Oandasan, Nora Dauenhauer, Duane Niatum, Gladys Cardiff, Ed Edmo, Monica Charles, Liz Sohappy, Phil George, Ted Tomeo-Palmanteer, Janet Campbell Hale, Agnes Pratt, and R. A. Swanson, to name a few. They are the founders of a heritage of fine writing from the Northwest. From Humishuma's time to the present, we are now related through the strength of their voices "dancing on the rim of the world."

Suggested Further Reading

Bird, Gloria. *Full Moon on the Reservation.* New York: Greenfield Review Press Book, 1993.

Lerner, Andrea, editor. *Dancing on the Rim of the World: An Anthology of Contemporary Northwest Native American Writing.* Tucson: University of Arizona Press, 1990.

Woody, Elizabeth. *Hand into Stone.* New York: Contact II Publications, 1988.

Erasmo Gamboa
1941-

The Hispanic Oregonians are the largest minority population in the state today, but they are also a people well-rooted in its past. Over 450 years ago Spanish sailors first coasted Oregon, and Hispanics played important roles in the exploring, mining, and cattle industries of the eighteenth and nineteenth centuries.

Erasmo Gamboa, born in Texas, is associate professor of history and director of the Chicano Studies program at the University of Washington. He is the author of several scholarly historical articles and numerous essays on Hispanic history and culture. The following selection is a portion of his essay, entitled "Oregon's Hispanic Heritage," which first appeared in *Oregon Humanities* (1992). This selection surveys the Hispanic peoples of twentieth-century Oregon, their economic and cultural challenges, and their responses to them.

Oregon's Hispanic Heritage

The Early Twentieth Century

When Mexican *rurales* (soldiers) paraded through downtown Roseburg as part of Buffalo Bill's Wild West Show on August 7, 1902, they were harbingers of things to come. During the next four decades countless other Mexicans and Mexican Americans immigrated and migrated to Oregon. In doing so, they established the enclaves that developed into Oregon's present Hispanic communities.

In more ways than one, twentieth-century Hispanic migration to Oregon was keyed to events in Mexico and in other parts of the United States. In Mexico, two decades of civil war on the heels of an oppressive dictatorship prompted one in ten Mexicans to seek sanctuary in the United States between 1910 and the 1920s. Across the border in the United States, jobs were plentiful, as incredible economic development took place in the Southwest. Even as European and Asian immigration was restricted, land needed to be cleared, railroads constructed, irrigation projects developed, and farm production expanded. Much of this growth relied extensively on a cheap and plentiful supply of Mexican labor. In the urban areas of the Southwest, a similar demand for Mexican labor pulled many Mexican immigrants to industrial jobs in Los Angeles and El Paso.

Driven by events in their own country and invited to the United States by the promise of employment and an official open-border policy, families and sometimes nearly entire communities immigrated. Until 1927 the border separating the two nations did not present a problem—political, legal, physical, or otherwise—for Mexican emigrants. During World War I and until 1921, for example, the Secretary of Labor waived all immigration restrictions against Mexico in order to meet large-scale labor shortages.

In the Pacific Northwest region, a similar economic development took place. Railroads, irrigation projects, and agricultural expansion began to draw Mexican immigrants and Mexican-American migrants. By 1920, the outward ripples of Mexican immigration had extended into Oregon and farther north into Washington and into Idaho. No one knows, or will ever know, how many people came. Nonetheless, Mexican immigrant families were living in Nyssa and other places by the 1920s.

The Great Depression

The Great Depression and rising unemployment effectively ended Mexican immigration. Beginning in 1930 and lasting until World War II, employment opportunities evaporated and Mexican laborers were no longer welcomed in the U. S. In states like California nonlegal resident Mexicans, along with some United States citizens of Mexican descent, were forcefully repatriated back to Mexico to free up jobs for the unemployed.

Oregon's budding Hispanic communities were also halted. In many ways, Hispanics who had arrived during the 1920s were directly and indirectly encouraged to leave the state. And when Mexicans lost their jobs, they discovered that President Roosevelt's promise of government relief or employment was not always an option open to them as it was to many of Oregon's other residents. For the greater part of the Depression, penniless Mexican people found it difficult to reside permanently in Oregon.

On the other hand, even as unemployment soared, the hard "stoop" agricultural jobs went begging for workers. Therefore, in the midst of a depression and record unemployment, Oregon farmers began to recruit substantial numbers of Mexican-American migratory laborers from the Southwest—enough that Congress singled out the state as one of the principal users of interstate Mexican migratory labor.

Although farmers required migratory help, as soon as the work season ended these same workers were expected to leave the state so that they would not become public charges.

The Bracero Program

The turning point in the establishment of permanent Hispanic communities came with World War II. More than any other period, World War II pulled Mexican Hispanics in unprecedented numbers to Oregon and the rest of the Pacific Northwest. They came for one reason—to fill the critical labor shortages that threatened agricultural production. In Oregon, labor was desperately needed everywhere, but the most serious want developed on Oregon's farms. The reasons were simple. The war exerted pressure on farms to produce unprecedented amounts for national consumption and for distribution abroad, yet among non-Hispanics, farm jobs went begging because they paid poorly and work conditions remained poor. Under such circumstances, these men and women sought industrial employment or men were drafted for military service.

To avoid losing the crops, employers and state officials tapped all potential sources of labor, including school children, housewives, business employees, and state prisoners. Even so, labor shortages continued to threaten Oregon's farm production. One year into the war, Oregon farmers turned to Mexico for help.

In August 1942, Mexico and the United States signed a binational wartime labor agreement. Under this pact, the federal government began to contract with Mexican men (*braceros*) for temporary employment in the United States.

The agreement guaranteed, among other things, that the men would be paid a minimum wage; receive health care, adequate housing, and board; and not be subject to social discrimination.

In Oregon the Emergency Farm Labor Supply, or "Bracero" Program, as it was popularly called, was administered by the State College at Corvallis and by federal labor officials. In the next five years approximately 15,136 braceros contracted for farm employment in Oregon. The number alone was impressive; but more important was its labor potential. Once in the state, the men were organized into a highly regimented and effective labor force. They were housed together, sometimes in mobile tent camps that dotted the farming areas from Ontario to Salem and from Hood River to Medford. The men were on call on a daily basis, including Sundays, and could be transferred at a moment's notice to meet labor shortages elsewhere.

In Oregon and throughout the Pacific Northwest, the bracero labor force was a decisive factor in the state's ability to sustain critical agricultural production. In this regard, the Mexican men played a significant role in winning the war. Governor Earl Snell recognized their contribution in a letter to the Mexican Government, in which he expressed the sincere appreciation of all Oregonians for the men's work.

Governor Snell was not alone in expressing his gratitude. Farmers, more than anybody else, understood that Mexican labor was essential to Oregon farms. One farmer from Columbia County summarized it best. These "Mexican boys," he stated, were "God-sent."

Although the braceros were praised for their labor, the war contract farm labor program was not without problems. Oregon employers soon tired of having workers complain about poor wages, harsh living conditions, hard work, and racial discrimination. They tired of braceros refusing to work or walking away from the labor camps and their employers in protest.

Post-War Years

When the war ended, the Bracero Program was gradually phased out and migratory Mexican-American workers began to replace those who had earlier been imported. Now, Mexican-American laborers were recruited from Colorado and Wyoming, Texas and California, through an elaborate federal and state farm labor program. And, although the war was over, the new workers were just as necessary as the wartime braceros had been, for there was no letup in farm production. Moreover, many of the non-Hispanic men and women who had left farm employment during the war never returned. Instead, they remained in the more rewarding industrial sector in cities like Portland, Salem, and Seattle.

During the post-war years, Mexican Americans who migrated to Oregon gradually became permanent residents. As their numbers increased, they began to change the cultural and racial landscape of Oregon's smaller rural communities like Independence, Woodburn, Nyssa, and Ontario.

Throughout the state, the pattern of settlement was similar. Initially, one family or person came to work in Oregon; the next year, others from the immediate or extended family followed. In the process, the traditions of the Mexican-American family played a crucial role in helping the newcomers adjust to life in Oregon.

In the Northwest, Mexican Americans found themselves separated from the cultural ambiance of their former hometowns. To a large degree, they also felt alienated from the social, political, and economic institutions of Oregon's established communities. Through the family, baptismal and marriage celebrations, food preparation, folk healing, dances, fiestas, and other traditional cultural practices became the pillars of transplanted post-war Mexican-American life.

By the mid 1950s and early 1960s, the seeds sown by the first post-war generation began to bear fruit. Spanish language movies began to appear in theaters. In some dioceses, parishes scheduled Sunday mass in Spanish, especially during the summer months. During the state centennial celebration in 1959, Mexican-American floats appeared in parades in eastern Oregon communities. In Woodburn the Mexican-American community and the Club Latino Americano recognized the importance of celebrating a sense of self-worth and pride by organizing a Mexican Fiesta in 1966. (Over two decades later this particular event has become an annual cultural affair that draws thousands of persons.)

These and similar activities formed the early social matrix of Hispanics in Oregon. Since then, Hispanic immigrants from other parts of Latin America, Central America, and the Caribbean, and migrants from elsewhere in the United States, have added their own cultural values and traditions. This has resulted in a Hispanic community that is a rich and complex mosaic of many cultures.

Hispanic Life in Oregon Today

Oregon has changed in a dramatic fashion from the days of the early Hispanic pioneers. In place of discrimination, Hispanics are beginning to find broad avenues of equality. In employment, equity has begun to replace the norm of dead-end agricultural jobs. Greater opportunity for Hispanics is the result of a more accepting and tolerant society, but it is also the outcome of repeated demands by the increasing voice of Hispanics for full citizenship in the state.

Today, the Hispanic population in Oregon is growing at a remarkable rate, nearly doubling every ten years since the 1970 census. Since World War II, the Hispanic population has increased dramatically, numbering 112,707 in 1990. Yet the speed with which many of Oregon's rural communities have changed is even more remarkable.

In some locales in the Willamette Valley, Central Oregon, and the Ontario-Nyssa area, true Mexican-American zones have emerged. There, much exists to feed the cultural souls of Hispanics—Mexican restaurants, *panaderías* (bakeries) and *tortillerías;* dances, *conjuntos,* and *mariachis;* Spanish radio and television programming; and stores that sell everything from *nogales* (cactus) and *chorizo* (sausage) to Spanish-language videos. Traditional celebrations such as *Cinco de Mayo, Posadas,* and *quinceañeras* are commonplace. Hispanics have their own newspapers. Each year the number of Hispanic students grows, their culture reflected in classrooms and school activities. Cultural centers, health clinics, and other community organizations with bilingual staffs exist.

Over the years, Hispanics have given much to Oregon. Through effective utilization of resources within themselves and through the good will of many other Oregonians, they have been able to make gains and now occupy new ground. Nevertheless, Hispanics in Oregon still face scorn, ridicule, and discrimination. External groups are trying to force Hispanics and others back in time through the use of racist literature distributed in public areas in communities like Woodburn.

These manifestations of prejudice occur because people do not know or have forgotten that Hispanics have been a part of Oregon history from its beginning. Still today the significance of Hispanic contributions to Oregon history go unappreciated in the written accounts.

When history is presented as an inclusive portrait of all the peoples who have played a hand in Oregon, the value of our state's history will be more substantial. Hispanics can learn to appreciate and take pride in knowing that their ancestors helped to settle Oregon and have worked persistently ever since to improve it. Non-Hispanics can understand that Oregon does not belong to one people, it is the collective result of many peoples.

Suggested Further Reading

Gamboa, Erasmo. "Braceros in the Pacific Northwest: Laborers on the Domestic Front, 1942-1947," *Pacific Historical Review* 56 (August 1987): 378-398.

————. *Mexican Labor and World War II: Braceros in the Pacific Northwest.* Austin: University of Texas Press, 1990.

————. "Mexican Mule Packers and Oregon's Second Regiment Mounted Volunteers, 1855-1856," *Oregon Historical Quarterly* 92 (Spring 1991): 41-59.

————. "Oregon's Hispanic Heritage," *Oregon Humanities* (Summer 1992): 3-7.

SECTION III
Responding to Nature

Thomas Condon
1822-1907

Thomas Condon, born in Ireland, came to the United States in 1833, and to Oregon in 1852. The next year he was ordained as a Congregational minister. Condon later became interested in geology, and was a professor of geology at the University of Oregon from 1876 to 1907. His book, *The Two Islands* (1902), was the first comprehensive work on Oregon geology and one of the earliest examples of scientific writing about Oregon.

While living at The Dalles as a minister in 1862, Condon discovered fossil remains in the John Day River Valley. This discovery, which became nationally famous, was used by supporters of the new belief in Darwinian evolution in controversies with religious traditionalists who retained their belief in special creation. Condon traces the geological and paleontological history of the John Day region, and relates it to the debate over evolution, in the following article, which first appeared in the *Overland Monthly* (1871).

The Rocks of the John Day Valley

In the controversies of the day on the Origin of Species, any record of the past as authoritative as that of a good geological field, covering an extensive range, and filled with minute details of events, can hardly fail to be instructive. The basin of the Columbia River with its tributaries offers such a history to the world, at once continuous and authoritative, reaching, in its field of operations, from the Rocky Mountains to the Pacific Ocean; and, in the time it covers, from the Cretaceous period to the Recent. It covers even the laying of the foundations of the country, and defines the narrow strips of land that first emerged from the ocean to become the framework of the great mountain-chains. As the elevation and extent of the land increased, the ocean water that first occupied the depressions between was displaced, and fresh water took its place, brought there by the now greatly increased flow from the land. Henceforth history written by the ocean ceased; history written by lakes and rivers commenced, in the storing away of specimens of tree, and beast, and bird, and their effectual preservation as material facts in an unerring record. The sea, thus excluded, never returned to the region east of the Cascade Mountains. A vast lake-system took its place, and began at once to make, as well as to write, its own history.

There are many residents of the Pacific Slope who will remember having journeyed from The Dalles, on the Columbia River, to Canyon City, among the Blue Mountains. For sixty miles or more the road passes over volcanic materials, which have drifted there from the Cascade Range. Twenty miles farther, and this outflow thins out into a mere capping of basalt on the hill-tops. The hills themselves, and the foundations on which they stand, are here found to be sedimentary rock, wonderfully filled with the abundant records of former animal and vegetable life. Oldest of all in sight is the old ocean-bed of the Cretaceous period, with its teeming thousands of marine shells, as perfect to-day in their rocky bed as those of our recent sea-shores; their cavities often filled with calcareous spar or chalcedony, as if to compensate for the loss of their own proper marine hues. Next in ascending order come the fresh-water deposits of the earlier Tertiaries, so full of the leaf-prints of the grand old forests that, during that age of semi-tropical climate, covered those lake-shores. The marine rocks form the outer rim, or shoreline, of what was in those early times a lake, of irregular outline, extending from Kern Creek Hill on the west to Canyon City on the east and from the hills north of the John Day River to the Crooked River Valley on the south. Within this lake-depression, whose former muddy sediment is now elevated into chalky hills, so despised for their alkaline waters and unproductive soils, the geologist feels at home. How strangely out of place a score of palm-trees, a hundred yew-trees, or even a bank of ferns, would seem here now! And yet here these once lived, and died, and were buried; and beautiful beyond description are their fossil remains even now, as they are unburied.

Seen from the summit of Kern Creek Hill—its western border—this vast amphitheatre of lesser hills presents a wild, wonderful grouping of varied out-lines and colors. A spur of the Blue Mountains—its nearest point, forty miles away—covered with a dense forest, forms the dark background of the view. The varying shades of brown that characterize the older marine rocks rise in vast border masses, almost treeless and shrubless, in an inner, irregular circle, while the lighter shades that fill the deeper depressions of the central portion mark the later sedimentary deposits; and then, like vast ink-blots on a painting, one sees, here and there, a protruding mass of dark-colored trap. Through the heart of this wild region winds the John Day River, running westward until it passes the middle ground of the picture, and then turning northward to join the Columbia.

This stream, so insignificant in appearance, has done wonderful work among these hills. The river itself was, in the olden time, merely a series of connecting-links between a chain of lakes that extended from the Blue Mountains to the Cascades of the Columbia. It has for unnumbered ages gone on excavating vast gorges and *cañons,* as all other streams in central Oregon have done, till lake after lake was drained off, and their beds laid dry, stripped of enduring moisture, and slowly changed to a treeless desert. The deep excavations that resulted could hardly fail to lay bare important records of the past, cutting as they do through the whole extent of the Tertiary periods. In a deep *cañon,* through which runs a branch of Kern Creek, may be found the remains of the fan-palm, with abundant remains of a beautiful fern—gems of their kind—which no thoughtful mind can see without wonder and admiration. In another ravine are seen in great numbers the remains of a yew, or yew-like tree that sheds annually, not its leaflets, but its branchlets; for in this form they are found imbedded in the rocks, of almost uniform length and structure. This tree was evidently abundant upon those ancient shores, for it can be found at almost every spot where a little stream washed its miniature delta into the lake. Oaks, too, and occasionally a fine impression of an acorn, or acorn-cup, are found at intervals from this place to the Blue Mountains.

But the great geological importance of that old lake-depression does not arise from the fossil remains of its forests—beautiful, varied, and abundant as these are—but from its finely preserved fossil bones. Two species of rhinoceros lived their quiet, indolent lives among the reeds that lined that old lake-shore. A little beyond the southern spur of that distant mountain there evidently emptied a stream of some size, for its delta is strewn with fragments of silicified bones. Among these the bones of the rhinoceros are frequent; but the remains of an extinct animal, allied in some things to the camel, in others to the tapir family, are most abundant. Paleontologists have designated the *genus* by the name of *Oreodon*. The remains of three or four species of this animal are found in central Oregon. One of these, new to science, was discovered thirty miles from here, and was named by Doctor Leidy *Oreodon Superbus,* from its superior size. The shaly rocks in which these remains are found are very brittle; and the inclosed fossils partake of that brittleness to such an extent, that, if not handled with the utmost care, they crumble into small fragments. Two nearly entire heads were discovered, last spring, in a ravine that opens into Bridge Creek Valley. They had been exposed all winter to rain and frost, and were very brittle—almost ready to drop to pieces. They were passed by until the following day, when a careful treatment to several coats of good flour-paste was rendered the more efficient by additional pasting on of common paper. This was kept on for awhile, when it was carefully washed off, and a more permanent preparation applied. These specimens now make a very passable appearance. Mute historians are they of the far-distant past, uniting with hundreds of others to tell strange stories of the wonderful wealth of forest, field, and lake-shore of that period. A tapir-like animal, to which the name of *Lophiodon* has been given, lived here, too. His remains indicate an animal of the size of the living tapir. Not far from these last were found some bones of a fossil peccary, of large size. Another of the denizens of these ancient lake-shores bore some resemblance to the horse. The remains of this animal, the *Anchitherium,* were first discovered in the Tertiary rocks of France, a few years ago; more recently, they were found in the "Bad Lands" of Nebraska, and within the past year, here, in the John Day Valley. But the richest chapters in the history of the Horse, in Oregon, are not from these rocks of the lower valley; for another, and a later, record in the upper part of the valley contains these.

Doubtless both portions of the valley were once continuous and formed one lake, but a stream of lava from the Blue Mountains seems to have run into it near the present site of Camp Watson, dividing it into an upper and a lower lake. The lower one seems to have drained off first, the upper one remaining a lake into the late Tertiary period, and receiving into its archives the remains of the animal types of a later age. The river was apparently turned northward by that outpouring of volcanic materials; and cutting for itself a new channel in

the deep *cañon*, thirty miles or more away, formed a great bend, and excavated an immense basin, in these nearer and lighter-colored Tertiary rocks. Above that bend, that *cañon*, and that volcanic outflow, the valley opens again; and there, extending from Cottonwood Creek to Canyon City, are the remains of the upper lake-depression of the John Day Valley. This later lake-depression received into its sediment a larger amount of volcanic ashes and cinders than the lower one did. Several of its strata are pure volcanic ashes, rough to the touch as ground pumice-stone, which must have fallen in vast quantities. The purest was evidently that which had fallen directly into the lake; the less pure that which, first falling on surrounding hills, had subsequently drifted from them by the action of the winds and waters, and become part of the lake-sediment.

Upon the hills that overlooked these lake-shores, there lived three or four different species of the horse family. Their remains are easily distinguished; for the teeth are well preserved, and the teeth of the horse are well marked. Almost as well marked as these equine remains, were some teeth that apparently represented a member of the camel family—found there, too, in a fine specimen of a lower jaw, silicified completely, and in solid rock. Fossil remains of other species, too, giving a wide range of life-record, were found, all of which are now in competent hands, for determination and description.

But the most remarkable thing about this upper lake record is that which reveals the way in which its history of this period was brought to a close. The last rock of the series fills the place of a cover to the volume. Never was cover better defined, nor more distinctly separated from the well-written and well-illustrated pages it serves to protect. The cover itself, too, has a history worth reading. It extends for miles, varying but slightly in thickness, which amounts to twenty or twenty-five feet, and is throughout so entirely volcanic as to leave no room for mistake. Its materials are volcanic ashes and cinders; the cinders ranging from an inch across downward to the minuteness of the ashes. One can hardly look at a piece of this rock without recalling the younger Pliny's vivid description of that shower of cinders from Mount Vesuvius, from which he saw people escaping, with pillows tied on their heads, for protection. Such showers fell here, certainly, over hundreds of square miles, and in such vast bulk, that, pressed by the hydraulic force of later masses above it into a solid plate of rock, it now in this form measures from twenty to twenty-five feet through. No wonder it closed one of the finest life-records of that remote period, and with the record that volume—becoming at once the proximate cause of the change, and the upper cover of the volume it closed.

But this violent destruction of the life of the period did not destroy that lake-depression: it only partially filled its shallower portions, and added thirty feet or more of sediment to the rest. The lake remained, and still continued to receive, into its archives of hidden sediment, tokens of the forces at work among the hills around it. One remarkable change marked that transition: the laboratories of the hills seem thereafter to have lost the power to send forth from their secret recesses heated vapors laden with mineral materials, as they had done, capable of changing every thing they touched to stone. The old sediments of that lake, if originally clay, are found changed to argillaceous rock; if sand, changed to sandstone; if washed gravel, they are found cemented into conglomerate. The new sediments, if clay, remained clay; if sand, remained sand; if gravel remained so, unaltered even now.

Long after that heaviest deluge of ashes had settled down into permanent rock, a new chapter was opened in the life-record of these lake-shores. The stratified materials that received these later records were washed from either shore into remarkably uniform slopes toward the middle line of the lake-depression. These slopes were evidently once continuous along both sides of the valley; but since the lake was drained off by the deeper wearing of its outlet, every little stream from the surrounding hills has cut its own ravine through these stratified sands, gravels, and clays, until what was once continuous, is now cut up into a remarkably uniform series of ridges, whose summit outlines stand in fine perspective, as far as the eye can reach. In the ravines that separate these ridges, the gold of this region is found; and in the diggings that result, the bones, teeth, and tusks of the elephant are often uncovered—a few of which have been preserved. In the loose materials that form these ridges, the closing annals of that remarkable lake-period of central Oregon may be read as in a book. The last facts noted there are the records of the mammoth, horse, the ox, and their contemporaries.

We have thus attempted to give four or five glimpses into the grand old panoramic life-record of the past in central Oregon—successive day-and-night glimpses of the past, along the shores of a series of lakes that once occupied the valley, now depressed, through which meanders the John Day River.

The first one of these views is characteristic of the old marine life of the original sea-bed. It is made up of a number of patches of sea-beach, strewn with shells; a tooth or two, of some extinct reptile; a vertebra of another—and the marine record closes. The shoals on which these marine remains lived became elevated into the frame-work of the future Oregon; while in the depressions between them, her earliest historic records at once began. Oregon's Eocene, Oregon's dawn! strange, beautiful coincidence of fact with system!

The next glimpse we get is of the Middle Tertiary period. It is distinct enough to enable us to recognize upon those lake-shores the rhinoceros, the oreodon, the tapir; and then closes abruptly, to give place to a record of fire and of violence—the fire of the volcano, and the violence of the earthquake—bringing upon the life of the period a blotted, illegible night-record in its history.

But another dawn came then; and we see among the forms that move along those shores, the familiar ones of the horse and the camel. Again the legible record closes, and thirty feet or more of ashes and volcanic cinders cover the land, and choke and poison the waters.

A long, dark, nearly illegible part of the record follows, during which no life-history was written; but during which the old throes of violence seem to have passed away, and the laboratories of the earth seem to have lost the power of forcing heated vapors to the surface, capable of changing all to stone that they touched.

The mammoth, the horse, and the ox appear in the light of the dawn that follows this long geological night; and not fire, as before, but frost, seems to have closed the record marked by their fossil remains.

This alternating of light of life, and darkness of death, as read in the rocks of that region, leaves us long periods of its chronology unwritten save by fire and flood. What are these blanks in that life-record? Have the materials upon which they were originally written been partially or wholly destroyed, or washed away? No; for, in a neighboring mountain, 1,500 feet in vertical section still remain, protected by a heavy capping of basalt. The pages are there, but they are defaced by fire and ashes. But were there not, or at least might there not have been, vast periods during which no record was made?

This supposition, too, is inadmissible. A lake existed here through the whole Tertiary period; and a continued lake-depression, surrounded by elevated ridges of hills, rising in many places into mountain magnitude, implies the deposit of continued sediment, and this necessarily becomes the page upon which the history of the life along its shores is written. The winds would always blow into the waters of the lake their burden of leaves, and the floods of winter wash there some fragments of the bones of the animals that characterized the period. It must have happened, then, that at the close of each great period, as indicated here, the animal life of these ancient lake-shores was entirely destroyed, by fire, flood, and the poisonous vapors that tainted earth, air, and waters, or else those to whom migration was possible, escaped to some other region. The supposition of their entire destruction encounters this difficulty: the destruction of the entire fauna of Oregon, and even of the whole western slope of the continent, would not have secured the results observed, unless we suppose a like destruction extending to the Atlantic coast; for the same animals lived there, when they lived here. Their remains are found, even to identity of species, from Nebraska to New Mexico. It is difficult to assign their destruction there, to the same causes that destroyed them here; or to any cause operating at once, over a whole continent, while the climate remained unchanged, and food continued abundant. On the other hand, the supposition of the escape of a portion from these destroying agencies meets, among others, this difficulty: when here, in this John Day Valley, quiet had been again restored, the hills had been again clothed in verdure, and the waters had precipitated not only, but covered out of sight, their vast strata of volcanic ashes, then animal life returned too, but not the same that had previously existed. The whole fauna was changed; and even where the same type was restored, as in the case of the horse, it is in some new species: the old has passed away, and forever.

If any one supposes that all the difficulties that beset these lines of inquiry and research rest only in the path of the theologian who claims a separate creation for each great type of animal life, he greatly misapprehends the present state of these investigations. But it was no part of the plan of this article to advocate any existing theory, or to start a new one, in this difficult field of inquiry, so full today of conflicting views; but rather, to call attention to the importance of the Columbia basin as a field filled, to an extraordinary degree, with the very facts needed to throw light on the question of the Origin of Species.

Three great ranges of mountains, and several minor ones, were elevated across its watershed, making so many immense dams, holding back the waters in extensive lake-depressions, among which the river itself was, for ages, but a series of connecting-links. It is now almost certain that these vast lake-depressions continued, from their first formation, to be such, until the bones of the modern horse, ox, and elephant were received into their sedimentary deposits; thus including records covering nearly the whole period of ancient mammalian life upon the earth. Add to these facts that all the rocks through which the streams of this region, during this long geological period, have been wearing their way, were those of the later and softer materials, and therefore the more rapidly worn down, not only in the *cañons* of the larger streams, but the ravines of the smaller ones, and upon every hillside, and we have a combination of favoring conditions, such as must make its geology accessible, very full, and important.

Indeed, one can hardly look over its historic archives of the Tertiary period, without a conviction that this Columbia basin is destined yet to be the great battle-ground of conflicting theories, upon the question of the Origin of Species.

Suggested Further Reading

Clark, Robert D. *The Odyssey of Thomas Condon: Irish Immigrant; Frontier Missionary; Oregon Geologist.* Portland: Oregon Historical Society Press, 1989.
Condon, Thomas. *The Two Islands and What Came of Them.* Portland: The J.K. Gill Co., 1902.

Anne Shannon Monroe
1873-1942

Anne Shannon Monroe was identified with the West
through her lineage, her residence, and her writings.
Born in Minnesota, the descendant of a member of the
Lewis and Clark Expedition, she attended the
University of Washington, and spent much of her life in
Oregon. Monroe was an accomplished speaker as well as
writer, and campaigned for Woodrow Wilson and
Franklin Roosevelt, lectured on western literature, and
spoke in behalf of the sale of war bonds in World War I.
The author of a dozen books and a regular contributor
to national magazines, she wrote often on Oregon
themes. The selection below, a chapter from her last
work, *Sparks from Home Fires* (1940), which she
described as an "all-Oregon book," illustrates her
romantic approach to nature.

A Porch by a Lake

"To live here alone! Isolate yourself in this way! Why, it's unthinkable! If you felt you must have a home of your own in the country—though I don't see why, what with taxes and everything—why couldn't you have found one convenient to clubs and libraries and things where you'd at least be in touch with world movements and people you know?"

My friend, who had driven the dozen miles out from town to look me up, drove off thoroughly exasperated with me, and I sank down on the day bed on my wonderful new view porch—I almost said "perch"—to repent. For that day I had moved in, bag and baggage, at the far end of a little woodsy lake— the sparsely settled end—where I didn't know a soul. And I had bought, so it was irrevocable.

I had been away from America for some time . . . away across the ocean looking on the heaped-up agony of the old world; on oppression and want and hideous living; on gently nurtured people huddled together in sordid little rooms, working desperately at any and everything they could find to do to earn the privilege merely of staying alive. I had felt their terrible loneliness in a strange land—the torture in brains, the ache in hearts, the fear in nerves, the waste in fine abilities adrift. People lost in chaos, darkness closing in, madness . . . suicide. Tired old world . . . weary old world. Why live? Why go on?

I had run away from it all.

Standing on the deck of the ship bringing me home, I had breathed a prayer of thanksgiving: "Thank you, ancestors, thank you, *thank you* for coming to America." Fresh new buoyancy had swelled within me. "Thank you, ancestors, thank you!"

And so I had come home, and I had rushed across the continent, getting away from things. By chance I had stumbled onto this lovely region of scattered farms and acre-tract homes along a lake and a river, and all impulsively I had made an acre of it my own. A little piece of American earth—how good and safe and sound it seemed! And mine, not for toiling and wresting, not for fighting and taking, but for a price in honestly earned coin. It seemed marvelous that someone had power to sell me a piece of America! Could anyone sell me also a piece of the sun and the moon? But someone had, for I had them in the full swing of their arc . . . and nothing could take them away from me ever.

And so I had moved in, into a little old farmhouse set high on the side of a ridge that broke sharply down to the lake's edge. From my wide eastern porch I looked across masses of hillside treetops—maples and alders and dogwoods. On this early autumn day they made great splashings of color that laughed and brushed together in one vast Turner painting. And all this gorgeous color picture was repeated in the lake below which in turn laughed and sparkled in its own happy radiance, its surface undisturbed save by a pair of majestic white swans moving smoothly across it.

But the lake wasn't merely a placid body of water doing a grand job of reflecting. Midway from its other more orderly and thickly settled end, it made a sharp turn and came running on, vagrantly, as if to say: "I've behaved myself thus far . . . now I guess I can do as I please!" It darted up numerous bayous in little runaway venturings of its own. And besides the bayous—to add to its delightful irregularity—there rippled into it a charming little river up which you could paddle for miles on end, completely closed in by the richest verdure in all the world! Maidenhair and sword ferns and vine maples and sweet brier roses; dogwood trees and hazels and willows! Such greenness! Such mossiness! And such ripply, lively water and still dark pools! You could drop a line most anywhere, if you wished, and catch fish!

But on beyond the lake—on its other shore directly opposite my view porch— there were somber hills heavy with forests of fir. The wooded hills gave stability to the little runaway lake. Like some severe matron they held it on a leash. However friskily it might dart here and there up its winding bayous, the solid old hills permitted it to go just so far and no farther. And away up on the very tiptop of the highest hill of all there was a clearing where some pioneer— probably back in those years when pioneers sturdily followed any wilderness dream that beckoned—had dug out for himself a farm and planted it to grain. Now, in the season of its ripening, it lay—a patch of gold against the blue sky—lifted as on a high altar to the god of abundance.

But through all this hypnotic beauty—which when first seen had so completely captured my imagination that I had bought without rhyme or reason—my friend's words pricked disturbingly. Perhaps she was right. I came back to it. An isolated life—no, that wasn't the American ideal. We mixed in things over here, did something about things, acted, took steps. All Europe calling. All America calling. Was this a time to hide away? No. By all the rules my friend was terribly right.

Depressed, I went to bed early, curled up in the day bed on the porch. I lay there, filled with a terrible awareness of the troubles out in the world of cities and towns and peoples, trying desperately to think things through, to arrive at what was right, what was wrong, what was wise, what was foolish. Gradually the blue of the early night sky settled down over the lake world—a blue shot through somehow with star dust. A crescent moon lifted above the dark neighboring hills. Presently there were two moons, one down in the water. Stars looked on, near and twinkling . . . a cricket chirped . . . a tree toad began to croak . . . a red-winged blackbird called once to his mate—then all was quiet. Earth's fragrances ascended around me like incense of divine origin. . . .

Gently the silent night took hold . . . doubts and questionings lifted. Weighing and measuring, deciding and redeciding vanished like a miasma under a warming sun. . . . I swung off into another world, a world where there was forgetting of troublous man-made conditions, a world of fresh realizing of the eternal harmonies. . . .

With a new song in my heart I swept off into God's perfect rest—dreamless slumber.

Suggested Further Reading

Monroe, Anne Shannon. *Feeling' Fine! Bill Hanley's Book*. Garden City, NY: Doubleday, Doran & Co., 1930.
———. *Happy Valley: A Story of Oregon*. Chicago: A. C. McClurg & Co., 1916. Reprinted by Oregon State University Press, with an introduction by Karen Blair, 1991.
———. *Sparks from Home Fires*. New York: Doubleday, Doran & Co., 1940.

William O. Douglas
1898-1980

William O. Douglas served on the United States Supreme Court for thirty-six years, longer than any other justice. Known on the court for his vigorous defense of individual liberties guaranteed by the First Amendment, Douglas was also an author of over twenty books, a world traveler, and a conservationist.

Douglas was born in Maine, but grew up in Yakima, Washington. Overcoming an attack of poliomyelitis as well as family poverty, he graduated from Whitman College and Columbia University Law School. President Franklin D. Roosevelt appointed him to the Securities and Exchange Commission in 1936 and to the Supreme Court in 1939. Douglas traveled all over the world: to the Himalayas, Malaysia, Russia, China, and the Middle East, and he wrote books expressing his awe and wonder about nature, and his desire to help conserve it. He also spent many of his vacations in the Wallowa Mountains of Oregon, where he owned a cabin for many years. One of his favorite places was the Hart Mountain Antelope Refuge in Oregon, which he describes below in a chapter from *My Wilderness* (1960).

Hart Mountain

Hart Mountain—thirty miles long—rises like a gargantuan loaf from the dry prairies of southeastern Oregon. Its main ridges are over 7,000 feet high; Warner Peak, its southernmost point, reaches nearly 8,100 feet. This is a mountain of lava rock whose cliffs show streaks of yellow and red. The west and the north sides are almost sheer walls that drop precipitously 3,000 feet to Warner Valley that is as smooth as a table top. The valley is dotted with marshy lakes, which trappers of the Hudson's Bay Company called *lacs des plants.* They are, indeed, rich in tules, sedges, and pond weeds. The rugged northern wall has been fenced off as a vast pasture for bighorn sheep, which once occupied this range and recently have been reintroduced. The east and south sides have easier slopes. The east slope rises gently; the south is broken by moderately level benches. The whole of Hart Mountain and much of the valley land to the south and east make up the Hart Mountain Antelope Refuge, established in 1936.

The pronghorned antelope is truly American in ancestry, having lived here for some millions of years. It is small, as horned ruminants go, the does averaging a little over 90 pounds and the bucks 114 pounds. The antelope is faster than any of its other relatives. I once clocked a Hart Mountain antelope at 60 miles an hour. This American antelope—cinnamon-brown and white—is different from other horned ruminants in other respects also. It is the only one that has hollow horns; and it sheds the outer shell once a year. Its hair, which is hollow, is so controlled by muscles that it can be made to lie flat or to stand up. This gives the animal the power to retain warmth in the Winter or to arrange its pelage in a cooling pattern for the hot days of Summer. Thus it can remain comfortable whether the temperature is 20°F. below zero or 120°F. above. Moreover, the eyes of the antelope have an extraordinarily wide angle of vision, being able to see behind them as well as in front and to catch the slightest movement on a distant horizon. Its saucy white rump flashing over the prairie is probably as distinctively American as anything our wilderness offers.

Hart Mountain, with pronghorned antelopes at its base, is, therefore, a choice sanctuary.

My first climb of Hart Mountain is in memory like a haunting melody. This is an exotic ridge, different from any I have known. Guano Plateau stretches to the south and east as far as the eye can see. The rainfall is not more than ten inches annually. Here is a vast expanse of dry, windblown land that to the untrained eye paints a picture of desolation. One can look to the horizon and see no tree except an occasional western juniper. Far to the southeast Steens Mountain lies against the skyline—a great hulk of land with a bluish tinge. On the plateau there are light green spots that from a distance look like pastures. They are called lakes—Spanish Lake, Desert Lake, Flook Lake—because water gathers there in the Spring. But by June they are dry, and the antelope feed there during the summer months. A type of salt grass, known as alkali sacaton, grows in these lake beds. The antelope eat some of it. But when they forgather at these lakes they usually come to eat the plants and blossoms of the yellow flowered primrose and other wild flowers that flourish there.

The Idaho fescue grows on these plains. There is also the Sandberg (or little) bluegrass and the famous bluebunch wheatgrass for which the dry slopes of the Pacific Northwest are famous. These are excellent forage for the antelope. There is also the cheat grass that invades the ranges of the West on the heels of overgrazing. The antelope eat it when it starts up in the Fall after the rains.

The antelope consume the flowers and leaves of the lupine and desert clovers, and even the blossoms of the death camass. And for winter forage they rely mainly on rabbit brush, bitter brush, and sagebrush. These latter are, indeed, an important item in the antelope's diet the year around. Studies by Olaus J. Murie show that sagebrush and other browse plants arc vital to the pronghorned antelope as well as to the sage grouse. So it is alarming to those who want these species perpetuated to hear of proposals for the removal of sagebrush from Hart Mountain.

A large shoulder of the mountain, thick with sagebrush, recently caught fire by accident, and hundreds of acres were burned. Bunch grass took over on the heels of the fire, and this shoulder now boasts a thick stand of it. Some want to burn or spray other sagebrush areas to bring on richer stands of grass. This is good news to cattlemen, who enjoy grazing rights in this refuge. The political pressures are toward improving the ranges of Hart Mountain for cattle grazing as, under federal law, Lake County, where the refuge is located, gets 25 per cent of all grazing fees earned by the refuge; and that amount goes into the local school and road fund. Though it amounts to only a few thousand dollars a year, the allies against sagebrush are powerful. This promises no good for either the antelope or the sage grouse. For as grass invades, the margin of subsistence for wildlife dependent on sagebrush narrows. If we are to give antelope the preference they deserve, sagebrush and the other browse on which they are dependent must be allowed to flourish.

The plains at the base of Hart Mountain are in the Upper Sonoran life zone. Here will be found, along with the sage grouse, hawks, horned owls, ash-throated flycatchers, gray flycatchers, bushtits, and Oregon lark sparrows. And among the mammals there are, in addition to the pronghorned antelopes, rabbits, chipmunks, ground squirrels, mice, coyotes, and skunks.

As one climbs Hart Mountain he enters three other life zones. The Transition zone is characterized by the ponderosa pine. It harbors a great variety of birds—Oregon poorwill, nighthawks, flickers, woodpeckers, western wood pewee, warblers, robins, western chipping sparrow, Warner Mountain fox sparrow, and valley quail.

The Canadian zone starts around 6,500 feet, and during the wet seasons carries snow well into the Summer. This is the home of the cony, Arizona weasel, golden-mantled ground squirrel, and western white-tailed jack rabbit. Here are forests of quaking aspen and thickets of willow, mountain mahogany, mountain alder, and wild gooseberries. The western goshawk, red-naped sapsucker, mountain bluebird, Oregon white-crowned sparrows, and meadowlarks make this their habitat.

At about 7,500 feet the Hudsonian zone commences. There the aspen and mountain mahogany have thinned out, leaving most of the top open and exposed. Some of the mammals of the Canadian zone are found here and many of the birds, particularly the sparrows and bluebirds.

It was mid-July when I first climbed Hart Mountain. Most of the bloom had left the plateau. Only yellow desert snowballs and wild onions were flowering there. Higher up I came across some startling wild-flower effects. In open places on the lower shoulder of the mountain I found fields of the delicate rose-colored Clarkia, the flower that Lewis and Clark first discovered on the Clearwater in Idaho and which bears the name of Captain William Clark. David Douglas rediscovered this Clarkia on the Columbia and sent it to England.

I had not gone far before I came across a hillside of the greenbanded mariposa lily—with three lavender and lilac petals whose yellow base is dotted with dark purple and violet spots. Scattered lavishly among these lilies were the waxen blooms of the delicate bitterroot. The soft, bright colors of the flowers and their delicacy were in vivid contrast to the heavy dullness and coarseness of the sage.

At about 6,500 feet I found hundreds of acres of lupine in bloom—mostly blue but some white and some mixed. It stood at times almost knee-high, dominating the bunch grass with which it grew. As I climbed higher I came across patches of soft pink alpine phlox, clinging tenaciously to sandy outcroppings as if it had pledged its life to prevent even the coarse topsoil from blowing away.

This had been a late summer, and the grasses—fescue, squirreltail, and native bunch—were thick and lush. Near the top I sat down among them. There was lupine at my feet, and at my back was a small stand of mountain mahogany. The mahogany, which stood about eight feet high, had a bushlike appearance, and its top had been browsed upon so much by deer and antelope that it looked as if it had been carefully clipped with shears by some meticulous gardener.

Below me lay the Guano Plateau, stretching almost a hundred miles to the Steens Mountain on the far horizon. The dry lakes of the plateau gave a light greenish touch to the somber gray and dust of the sage. Long fingers of grease-wood were thrust out into the sage, marking the places where the soil is alkaline. Darker green dots were scattered in a patternless scheme across the plateau. These marked the western juniper, the tree that is good for fuel and fence posts in this vast and empty domain.

The view from the top of Hart Mountain creates a feeling of greater depth and expanse than even the Great Plains. Valleys are as flat as a table top for seventy-five miles. The land is bleak and gray. Yet a shimmer of blue against the skyline says that there is water to be had. A streak of green along a distant hillside tells of springs and creeks. Patches of light green across the plateaus show where the rich native hay grows. And one has only to watch the plateau through glasses or walk through its sagebrush to learn that it virtually teems with life. This is land to possess and embrace. It is land to command as far as the eye can see. Here is the ultimate for the possessive instinct.

Across a ravine a buck antelope was standing in the open, alternately burying his nose in sagebrush and scanning the slopes for signs of danger. A mule deer crossed the field below me and then, sensing danger, ran for a cover of mahogany.

The late Stanley Jewett counted 120 species of birds on Hart Mountain, and the list is not yet complete. Not far below the point where I was resting, I had seen a black-chinned humming-bird feeding its young in a nest on the side of an aspen. Now a turkey buzzard was circling below me, looking for carrion. Farther down, a grebe was flying east to some nesting grounds. A few ducks streaked by as if they were frantically trying to find their flock before day's end. I looked up, and there in the sky—perhaps a mile above me—were white objects flying in wide circles. These were white pelicans that nest in the Malheur National Wildlife Refuge some miles to the east. Now they were wheeling in great circles ten thousand feet or more above Guano Plateau. They were promenading in the sky like a fleet of bombers on display.

I also climbed Hart Mountain in the dry cycle when Guano Plateau was parched and even the grass on the slopes was suffering. I camped under ponderosa pine by clear and cold Guano Creek where the Order of the Antelope has its annual outing. This group, formed to honor and perpetuate the refuge, had forgathered; and Samuel M. Smith, business executive from California who also loves Hart Mountain, and I sat in the shade listening to officials of the refuge give an accounting of this dry cycle. The dry season had not noticeably affected the deer population. They have, indeed, become so abundant that the refuge is open to hunters. Hunting deer by bow and arrow is permitted; and the archers have a success ratio of less than eight per cent. The drought, however, had a very serious effect on the pronghorns. The antelope herd had been down to 100 before the refuge was established in 1936. When I first visited the area, the herd had increased to 2,000. The dry cycle of the late fifties had reduced them to 700. The dry cycle was proving that Hart Mountain as a refuge was necessary if antelope were to survive.

This time I climbed the mountain via Stockade Creek, one of the few streams that run off these ridges. At the point where Stockade Creek pours onto the plateau the antelope were gathering for food and water. When feed and water are plentiful they tend to scatter. Now they were bunching in herds of 100 and more—one evidence of the dry cycle. This creek, which rises at about 7,000 feet from a spring in the mountain's side, has clear, cold water. Aspen line its banks nearly to the source. I was serenaded most of the way by meadowlarks. I found the dainty water spring beauty in wet spots along the creek bed. Large monkey flowers nodded in the light, hot breeze that touched the ravine. The royal blue penstemon flourished here. The tiny, petty cinquefoil bowed graciously.

The blue American speedwell, so petite as to seem unreal, grew here. Along with it was the tansyleaf evening primrose—a bright yellow flower almost concealed by its tall serrated leaves. By its side was the gay spike checkermallow with an inflorescence of purple flowers.

As I left the creek bed and climbed the gentle slopes to Warner Peak, I found new glories of this mountain. First was the Wyoming paintbrush, flower of the State of Wyoming—orange-red against the dull sage. Yellow eriogonum were splashed lavishly across the mountain. Even though this was a drought year, the lovely mariposa lily—lavender with purple dots on its sepals—was flourishing in the shade of the sage. Another delicate creation was the longstalk starwort, whose single tiny white flower seemed almost out of keeping with the harshness of the sage. Perhaps loveliest of all were the scatterings of the western blue flax, whose bright blue flowers get protection from the shade of the sage. This is the flower that served the Indians well by providing them with cordage. It bears the name of Lewis of the Lewis and Clark Expedition.

Farther up Stockade Creek I found other evidences of the dry cycle. The golden-mantled ground squirrel was beginning to hibernate, though July was not ended. And the sage grouse had moved far up the mountain. As I worked my way along the ravine they went out from under my feet in large numbers. One covey of forty-two broke the stillness of the mountain with the roar of a bomber plane. Young hens weighing a couple of pounds escaped gracefully. Old toms weighing over five pounds worked hard to get elevation.

There were antelope fawn in the aspen groves, born in June. When the rabbits and rodents are in low supply, the predators turn to these fawn. The coyote and the golden eagle are the chief enemies. They actually follow an antelope doe until she discloses where the fawn is located or until the fawn makes a false move. But predator control is necessary only two years out of ten. Most of the time, nature supplies the necessary balance. Wildlife will continue to have its periods of decline and its periods of prosperity. As yet we do not know all the factors that play a role in these cycles. Food, of course, is important. And if we have sense enough to heed Dr. Murie's warning and leave the sagebrush unmolested, we will have done much to insure against the decline and extinction of the antelope.

I was thinking of these things as I last stood on the top of Hart Mountain, watching the lengthening shadows streak across the plateau far below me. It struck me that man sometimes seems to try to crowd everything but himself out of the universe. Yet he cannot live a full life from the products of his own creation. He needs a measure of the wilderness, so that he may relax in the environment that God made for him. He needs life around him in order to experience the true measure of living. Then only can he get a sense of the full glory of the universe. There is a place in man's life for the antelope, just as there is for the whir of sage grouse and the song of the thrush. There would be a great emptiness in the land if there were no pelicans wheeling in great circles over Hart Mountain, no antelope fawn in its aspen groves, no red-shafted flickers in its willow. I say the same for the coyote and golden eagle. We often downgrade them as predators. Yet they, too, play an important role in the cosmic scheme.

I always feel sad leaving Hart Mountain. Yet after I travel a few hours and turn to see its great bulk against a southern sky, my heart rejoices. This refuge will leave our grandsons and granddaughters an inheritance of the wilderness that no dollars could recreate. Here they will find life teeming throughout all the life zones that lead from the desert to alpine meadows.

Those who visit Hart Mountain next century will know that we were faithful life tenants, that we did not entirely despoil the earth which we left them. We will make the tradition of conservation as much a part of their inheritance as the land itself.

Suggested Further Reading

Douglas, William O. *The Court Years: The Autobiography of William O. Douglas.* New York: Random House, 1980.

———. *Go East, Young Man: The Early Years. The Autobiography of William O. Douglas.* New York: Random House, 1974.

———. *My Wilderness: The Pacific West.* Garden City, NY: Doubleday & Co., 1960. Reprinted by Comstock Editions, Sausalito, 1989.

Simon, James F. *Independent Journey: The Life of William O. Douglas.* New York: Harper & Row, 1980.

Ursula K. Le Guin
1929-

Nature reminded Pacific Northwesterners of its enormous destructive power in the eruption of Mount St. Helens on 18 May 1980, an event that sent volcanic ash around the world. Ursula K. Le Guin furnishes a description of this cataclysm in the following essay published in *Parabola* (1980).

Le Guin is an internationally acclaimed author and lecturer who has published over thirty books for adults and several books for young people. In addition to essays on many subjects, she has also written plays, novels, short stories, and poetry. Her writings have won all of the major honors for authors of science fantasy, and numerous other awards, including the 1992 Oregon Institute for Literary Arts best fiction award. Le Guin has been a visiting lecturer and writer-in-residence at universities in Australia, Great Britain, and the United States.

A Very Warm Mountain

An enormous region extending from north-central Washington to north-eastern California and including most of Oregon east of the Cascades is covered by basalt lava flows. . . . The unending cliffs of basalt along the Columbia River . . . 74 volcanoes in the Portland area . . . A blanket of pumice that averages about 50 feet thick . . .

Roadside Geology of Oregon
Alt and Hyndman, 1978

Everybody takes it personally. Some get mad. Damn stupid mountain went and dumped all that dirty gritty glassy gray ash that lies like flour and lies like cement all over their roofs, roads, and rhododendrons. Now they have to clean it up. And the scientists are a real big help: all they'll say is we don't know, we can't tell, she might dump another load of ash on you just when you've got it all cleaned up. It's an outrage.

Some take it ethically. She lay and watched her forests being cut and her elk being hunted and her lakes being fished and fouled and her ecology being tampered with and the smoky, snarling suburbs creeping closer to her skirts, until she saw it was time to teach the White Man's Children a lesson. And she did. In the process of the lesson, she blew her forests to matchsticks, fried her elk, boiled her fish, wrecked her ecosystem, and did very little damage to the cities; so that the lesson taught to the White Man's Children would seem, at best, equivocal.

But everybody takes it personally. We try to reduce it to human scale. To make a molehill out of the mountain.

Some got very anxious, especially during the dreary white weather that hung round the area after May 18 (the first great eruption, when she blew 1300 feet of her summit all over Washington, Idaho, and points east) and May 25 (the first considerable ashfall in the thickly populated Portland area west of the mountain). Farmers in Washington State who had the real fallout, six inches of ash smothering their crops, answered the reporters' questions with polite stoicism; but in town a lot of people were cross and dull and jumpy. Some erratic behavior, some really weird driving. "Everybody on my bus coming to work these days talks to everybody else; they never used to." "Everybody on my bus coming to work sits there like a stone instead of talking to each other like they used to." Some welcomed the mild sense of urgency and emergency as bringing people together in mutual support. Some—the old, the ill—were terrified beyond reassurance. Psychologists reported that psychotics had promptly incorporated the volcano into their private systems; some thought they were controlling her, and some thought she was controlling them. Businessmen, whom we know from the Dow Jones Reports to be an almost ethereally timid and emotional breed, read the scare stories in Eastern newspapers and cancelled all their conventions here; Portland hotels are having a long cool summer. A Chinese Cultural Attaché, evidently preferring earthquakes, wouldn't come farther north than San Francisco. But many natives were irrationally exhilarated, secretly, heartlessly welcoming every steam-blast and earth-tremor: Go it, mountain!

Everybody read in the newspapers everywhere that the May 18 eruption was "five hundred times greater than the bomb dropped on Hiroshima." Some reflected that we have bombs much more than five hundred times more powerful than the 1945 bombs. But these are never mentioned in the comparisons. Perhaps it would upset people in Moscow, Idaho, or Missoula, Montana, who got a lot of volcanic ash dumped on them, and don't want to have to think: what if that stuff had been radioactive? It really isn't nice to talk about, is it. I mean, what if something went off in New Jersey, say, and *was* radioactive—Oh, stop it. That volcano's way out west there somewhere anyhow.

Everybody takes it personally.

I had to go into hospital for some surgery in April, while the mountain was in her early phase—she jumped and rumbled, like the Uncles in *A Child's Christmas in Wales,* but she hadn't done anything spectacular. I was hoping she wouldn't perform while I couldn't watch. She obliged and held off for a month. On May 18 I was home, lying around with the cats, with a ringside view: bedroom and study look straight north about forty-five miles to the mountain.

I kept the radio tuned to a good country western station and listened to the reports as they came in, and wrote down some of the things they said. For the first couple of hours there was a lot of confusion and contradiction, but no panic, then or later. Late in the morning a man who had been about twenty miles from the blast described it: "Pumice-balls and mud-balls began falling for about a quarter of an hour, then the stuff got smaller, and by nine it was completely and totally black dark. You couldn't see ten foot in front of you!" He spoke with energy and admiration. Falling mud-balls, what next? The main West Coast artery, I-5, was soon closed because of the mud and wreckage rushing down the Toutle River towards the highway bridges. Walla Walla, 260 miles east, reported in to say their street lights had come on automatically

at about ten in the morning. The Spokane-Seattle highway, far to the north, was closed, said an official expressionless voice, "on acount of darkness."

At one-thirty that afternoon, I wrote:

It has been warm with a white high haze all morning, since six A.M.., when I saw the top of the mountain floating dark against yellow-rose sunrise sky above the haze.

That was, of course, the last time I saw or will ever see that peak.

Now we can see the mountain from the base to near the summit. The mountain itself is whitish in the haze. All morning there has been this long cobalt-bluish drift to the east from where the summit would be. And about ten o'clock there began to be visible clots, like cottage cheese curds, above the summit. Now the eruption cloud is visible from the summit of the mountain till obscured by a cloud layer at about twice the height of the mountain, i.e., 25-30,000 feet. The eruption cloud is very solid-looking, like sculptured marble, a beautiful blue in the deep relief of baroque curls, sworls, curled-cloud-shapes—darkening towards the top—a wonderful color. One is aware of motion, but (being shaky and looking through shaky binoculars) I don't actually see the cavern-blue-sworl-shapes move. Like the shadow on a sundial. It is enormous. *Forty-five miles away. It is so much bigger than the mountain itself. It is silent, from this distance. Enormous, silent. It looks not like anything earthy, from the earth, but it does not look like anything atmospheric, a natural cloud, either. The blue of it is stormcloud blue but the shapes are far more delicate, complex, and immense than stormcloud shapes, and it has this solid look; a weightiness, like the capital of some unimaginable column—which in a way indeed it is, the pillar of fire being underground.*

At four in the afternoon a reporter said cautiously, "Earthquakes are being felt in the metropolitan area," to which I added, with feeling, "I'll say they are!" I had decided not to panic unless the cats did. Animals are supposed to know about earthquakes, aren't they? I don't know what our cats know; they lay asleep in various restful and decorative poses on the swaying floor and the jiggling bed, and paid no attention to anything except dinner time. I was not allowed to panic.

At four-thirty a meteorologist, explaining the height of that massive, storm-blue pillar of cloud, said charmingly, "You must understand that the mountain is very warm. Warm enough to lift the air over it to 75,000 feet."

And a reporter: "Heavy mud flow on Shoestring Glacier, with continuous lightning." I tried to imagine that scene. I went to the television, and there it was. The radio and television coverage, right through, was splendid. One forgets the joyful courage of reporters and cameramen when there is something worth reporting, a real Watergate, a real volcano.

On the 19th, I wrote down from the radio, "A helicopter picked the logger up while he was sitting on a log surrounded by a mud flow." This rescue was filmed and shown on television: the tiny figure crouching hopeless in the huge abomination of ash and mud. I don't know if this man was one of the loggers who later died in the Emanuel Hospital burn center, or if he survived. They were already beginning to talk about the "killer eruption," as if the mountain had murdered with intent. Taking it personally . . . . Of course she killed. Or did they kill themselves? Old Harry who wouldn't leave his lodge and his whiskey and his eighteen cats at Spirit Lake, and quite right too, at eighty-three; and the young cameraman and the young geologist, both up there on the north side on the job of their lives; and the loggers who went back to work because logging was their living; and the tourists who thought a volcano is like Channel Six, if you don't like the show you turn it off, and took their RVs and their kids up past the roadblocks and the reasonable warnings and the weary county sheriffs sick of arguing: they were all there to keep the appointment. Who made the appointment?

A firefighter pilot that day said to the radio interviewer, "We do what the mountain says. It's not ready for us to go in."

On the 21st I wrote:

Last night a long, strange, glowing twilight; but no ash has yet fallen west of the mountain. Today, fine, gray, mild, dense Oregon rain. Yesterday afternoon we could see her vaguely through the glasses. Looking appallingly lessened—short, flat—That is painful. She was so beautiful. She hurled her beauty in dust clear to the Atlantic shore, she made sunsets and sunrises of it, she gave it to the western wind. I hope she erupts magma and begins to build herself again. But I guess she is still unbuilding. The Pres. of the U. S. came today to see her. I wonder if he thinks he is on her level. Of course he could destroy much more than she has destroyed if he took a mind to.

On June 4 I wrote:

Could see her through the glasses for the first time in two weeks or so. It's been dreary white weather with a couple of hours sun in the afternoons. Not the new summit, yet; that's always in the roil of cloud/plume. But both her long lovely flanks. A good deal of new snow has fallen on her (while we had rain), and her SW face is white, black, and gray, much seamed, in unfamiliar patterns.
"As changeless as the hills—"
Part of the glory of it is being included in an event on the geologic scale.

Being enlarged. "I shall lift up mine eyes unto the hills," yes: "whence cometh my help."

In all the Indian legends dug out by newspaper writers for the occasion, the mountain is female. Told in the Dick-and-Jane style considered appropriate for popular reportage of Indian myth, with all the syllables hyphenated, the stories seem even more naive and trivial than myths out of context generally do. But the theme of the mountain as woman—first ugly, then beautiful, but always a woman—is consistent. The mapmaking whites of course named the peak after a man, an Englishman who took his title, Baron St. Helens, from a town in the North Country: but the name is obstinately feminine. The Baron is forgotten, Helen remains. The whites who lived on and near the mountain called it The Lady. Called her The Lady. It seems impossible not to take her personally. In twenty years of living through a window from her I guess I have never really thought of her as "it."

She made weather, like all single peaks. She put on hats of cloud, and took them off again, and tried a different shape, and sent them all skimming off across the sky. She wore veils around the neck, across the breast: white, silver, silver-gray, gray-blue. Her taste was impeccable. She knew the weathers that became her, and how to wear the snow.

Dr. William Hamilton of Portland State University wrote a lovely piece for the college paper about "volcano anxiety," suggesting that the silver cone of St. Helens had been in human eyes a breast, and saying:

St. Helens' real damage to us is not . . . that we have witnessed a denial of the trustworthiness of God (such denials are our familiar friends). It is the perfection of the mother that has been spoiled, for part of her breast has been removed. Our metaphor has had a mastectomy.

At some deep level, the eruption of Mt. St. Helens has become a new metaphor for the very opposite of stability—for that greatest of twentieth-century fears—cancer. Our uneasiness may well rest on more elusive levels than dirty windshields.

This comes far closer to home than anything else I've read about the "meaning" of the eruption, and yet for me it doesn't work. Maybe it would work better for men. The trouble is, I never saw St. Helens as a breast. Some mountains, yes: Twin Peaks in San Francisco, of course, and other round, sweet California hills—breasts, bellies, eggs, anything maternal, bounteous, yielding. But St. Helens in my eyes was never part of a woman; she is a woman. And not a mother but a sister.

These emotional perceptions and responses sound quite foolish when written out in rational prose, but the fact is that, to me, the eruption was all mixed up with the women's movement. It may be silly but there it is; along the same lines, do you know any woman who wasn't rooting for Genuine Risk to take the Triple Crown? Part of my satisfaction and exultation at each eruption was unmistakably feminist solidarity. You men think you're the only ones can make a really nasty mess? You think you got all the firepower, and God's on your side? You think you run things? Watch this, gents. Watch the Lady act like a woman.

For that's what she did. The well-behaved, quiet, pretty, serene, domestic creature peaceably yielding herself to the uses of man all of a sudden said NO. And she spat dirt and smoke and steam. She blackened half her face, in those first March days, like an angry brat. She fouled herself like a mad old harridan. She swore and belched and farted, threatened and shook and swelled, and then she spoke. They heard her voice two hundred miles away. Here I go, she said. I'm doing my thing now. Old Nobodaddy you better JUMP!

Her thing turns out to be more like childbirth than anything else, to my way of thinking. But not on our scale, not in our terms. Why should she speak in our terms or stoop to our scale? Why should she bear any birth that we can recognize? To us it is cataclysm and destruction and deformity. To her—well, for the language for it one must go to the scientists or to the poets. To the geologists, St. Helens is doing exactly what she "ought" to do—playing her part in the great pattern of events perceived by that noble discipline. Geology provides the only time-scale large enough to include the behavior of a volcano without deforming it. Geology, or poetry, which can see a mountain and a cloud as, after all, very similar phenomena. Shelley's cloud can speak for St. Helens:

I silently laugh
At my own cenotaph. . .
And arise, and unbuild it again.

So many mornings waking I have seen her from the window before any other thing: dark against red daybreak, silvery in summer light, faint above river-valley fog. So many times I have watched her at evening, the faintest outline in mist, immense, remote, serene: the center, the central stone. A self across the air, a sister self, a stone. "The stone is at the center," I wrote in a poem about her years ago. But the poem is impertinent. All I can say is impertinent.

When I was writing the first draft of this essay in California, on July 23, she erupted again, sending her plume to 60,000 feet. Yesterday, August 7, as I was typing the words "the meaning of the eruption," I checked out the study window and there it was, the towering blue cloud against the quiet northern sky—the fifth major eruption. How long may her labor be? A year, ten years, ten thousand? We cannot predict what she may or might or will do, now, or next, or for the rest of our lives, or ever. A threat: a terror: a fulfillment. This is what serenity is built on. This unmakes the metaphors. This is beyond us, and we must take it personally. This is the ground we walk on.

Suggested Further Reading

Le Guin, Ursula. *Dancing at the Edge of the World: Thoughts on Words, Women, Places.* New York: Grove Press, 1989.

———. *The Lathe of Heaven.* New York: Avon, 1973.

———. *Searoad: Chronicles of Klatsand.* New York: HarperCollins, 1991.

———. "A Very Warm Mountain," *Parabola* 5, 1980: 46-51.

Barry Lopez
1945-

Barry Lopez is one of America's most illustrious nature writers. Born in New York State, and currently a resident on the McKenzie River in Oregon, Lopez has written fictional narratives, fiction, essays, and articles. His first major work, *Of Wolves and Men*, appeared in 1978 to widespread critical acclaim. *Arctic Dreams* (1986) is a work of even greater renown. Lopez regards the natural environment from the perspectives of science, lore, and personal encounter, and throughout examines the moral issues that underlie these perspectives. His numerous honors include a National Book Award; an Award in Literature from the American Academy and Institute of Arts and Letters; and a Guggenheim fellowship. The following essay first appeared in *Pacific Northwest* (1982).

Children in the Woods

When I was a child growing up in the San Fernando Valley in California, a trip into Los Angeles was special. The sensation of movement from a rural area into an urban one was sharp. On one of these charged occasions, walking down a sidewalk with my mother, I stopped suddenly, caught by a pattern of sunlight trapped in a spiraling imperfection in a windowpane. A stranger, an elderly woman in a cloth coat and a dark hat, spoke out spontaneously, saying how remarkable it is that children notice these things.

I have never forgotten the texture of this incident. Whenever I recall it I am moved not so much by any sense of my young self but by a sense of responsibility toward children, knowing how acutely I was affected in that moment by that woman's words. The effect, for all I know, has lasted a lifetime.

Now, years later, I live in the rain forest in western Oregon, on the banks of a mountain river in relatively undisturbed country, surrounded by 200-foot-tall Douglas firs, delicate deer-head orchids, and clearings where wild berries grow. White-footed mice and mule deer, mink and coyote move through here. My wife and I do not have children, but children we know, or children whose parents we are close to, are often here. They always want to go into the woods. And I wonder what to tell them.

In the beginning, years ago, I think I said too much. I spoke with an encyclopedic knowledge of the names of plants or the names of birds passing through in season. Gradually I came to say less. After a while the only words I spoke, beyond answering a question or calling attention quickly to the slight difference between a sprig of red cedar and a sprig of incense cedar, were to elucidate single objects.

I remember once finding a fragment of a raccoon's jaw in an alder thicket. I sat down alongside the two children with me and encouraged them to find out who this was—with only the three teeth intact in a piece of the animal's maxilla to guide them. The teeth told by their shape and placement what this animal ate. By a kind of visual extrapolation its size became clear. There were other clues, immediately present, which told, with what I could add of climate and terrain, how this animal lived, how its broken jaw came to be lying here. Raccoon, they surmised. And tiny tooth marks along the bone's broken edge told of a mouse's hunger for calcium.

We set the jaw back and went on.

If I had known more about raccoons, finer points of osteology, we might have guessed more: say, whether it was male or female. But what we deduced was all we needed. Hours later, the maxilla, lost behind us in the detritus of the forest floor, continued to effervesce. It was tied faintly to all else we spoke of that afternoon.

In speaking with children who might one day take a permanent interest in natural history—as writers, as scientists, as filmmakers, as anthropologists—I have sensed that an extrapolation from a single fragment of the whole is the most invigorating experience I can share with them. I think children know that nearly anyone can learn the names of things: the impression made on them at this level is fleeting. What takes a lifetime to learn, they comprehend, is the existence and substance of myriad relationships; it is these relationships, not the things themselves, that ultimately hold the human imagination.

The brightest children, it has often struck me, are fascinated by metaphor—with what is shown in the set of relationships bearing on the raccoon, for instance, to lie quite beyond the raccoon. In the end, you are trying to make clear to them that everything found at the edge of one's senses—the high note of the winter wren, the thick perfume of propolis that drifts downwind from spring willows, the brightness of wood chips scattered by beaver—that all this fits together. The indestructibility of these associations conveys a sense of permanence that nurtures the heart, that cripples one of the most insidious of human anxieties, the one that says, you do not belong here, you are unnecessary.

Whenever I walk with a child, I think how much I have seen disappear in my own life. What will there be for this person when he is my age? If he senses something ineffable in the landscape, will I know enough to encourage it?—to somehow show him that, yes, when people talk about violent death, spiritual exhilaration, compassion, futility, final causes, they are drawing on 40,000 years of human meditations on *this*—as we embrace Douglas firs, stand at a river across whose undulating back we skip stones, and dig out a camas bulb, biting down into a taste so much wilder than last night's potatoes.

The most moving look I ever saw from a child in the woods was on a mud bar by the footprints of a heron. We were on our knees, making handprints beside the footprints. You could feel the creek vibrating in the soil. The sun beat down hot on our hair. Our shoes were soaking wet. The look said: I did not know until now that I needed someone much older to confirm the feeling of life here. I can now grow older and know it need never be lost.

The quickest door to open in the woods for a child is the one that leads to the smallest room, by knowing the name each thing is called. The door that leads to the cathedral is marked by a hesitancy to speak at all, rather to encourage by example a sharpness of the senses. If one speaks it should only be to say, as well as one can, how wonderfully all this fits together, to indicate what a long, fierce peace can derive from this knowledge.

Suggested Further Reading

Lopez, Barry. *Arctic Dreams: Imagination and Desire in a Northern Landscape.* New York: Scribner, 1986.

———. "Children in the Woods," *Pacific Northwest*, April 1982: 8.

———. *Desert Notes: Reflections in the Eye of a Raven*. Kansas City, Kansas: Sheed, Andrews & McMeel, 1976.

———. *Of Wolves and Men*. New York: Scribner, 1978.

SECTION IV
All Creatures Great and Small

Joaquin Miller
1837-1913

Joaquin Miller, talented, versatile, flamboyant, was Oregon's first internationally famous writer. Born in Indiana as Cincinnatus Hiner Miller, he came with his family across the trail to Oregon in 1852. As a young man he lived with the Indians in northern California, was arrested for horse stealing, and edited a pro-Confederate newspaper in Eugene. He became a lawyer in 1863 and was elected judge of Grant County, Oregon, in 1866.

Miller's first book of poetry was published in Portland in 1868. Beginning in 1871 his poetry, his frontier costume, and his accounts of his adventures in California and Oregon made him a literary lion in Great Britain and Europe, and helped create a romantic myth of the American West abroad. Although his reputation was never as large in the United States as overseas, Miller, who spent his last twenty-six years on a fantastic estate in Oakland, California, remained a well-known literary figure until his death. Besides his poetry, his many works included novels, articles, his fictionalized autobiography, *Life Amongst the Modocs*, and a book for children, *True Bear Stories* (1900), from which this selection is drawn.

Music-loving Bears

No, don't despise the bear, either in his life or his death. He is a kingly fellow, every inch a king; a curious, monkish, music-loving, roving Robin Hood of his somber woods—a silent monk, who knows a great deal more than he tells. And please don't go to look at him and sit in judgment on him behind the bars. Put yourself in his place and see how much of manhood or kinghood would be left in you with a muzzle on your mouth, and only enough liberty left to push your nose between two rusty bars and catch the peanut which the little boy has found to be a bad one and so generously tosses it to the bear.

Of course, the little boy, remembering the experience of about forty other little boys in connection with the late baldheaded Elijah, has a prejudice against the bear family, but why the full-grown man should so continually persist in caging this shaggy-coated, dignified, kingly and ancient brother of his, I cannot see, unless it is that he knows almost nothing at all of his better nature, his shy, innocent love of a joke, his partiality for music and his imperial disdain of death. And so, with a desire that man may know a little more about this storied and classic creature which, with noiseless and stately tread, has come down to us out of the past, and is as quietly passing away from the face of the earth, these fragmentary facts are set down. But first as to his love of music. A bear loves music better than he loves honey, and that is saying that he loves music better than he loves his life.

We were going to mill, father and I, and Lyte Howard, in Oregon, about forty years ago, with ox-teams, a dozen or two bags of wheat, threshed with a flail and winnowed with a wagon cover, and were camped for the night by the Calipoola River; for it took two days to reach the mill. Lyte got out his fiddle, keeping his gun, of course, close at hand. Pretty soon the oxen came down, came very close, so close that they almost put their cold, moist noses against the backs of our necks as we sat there on the ox-yokes or reclined in our blankets, around the crackling pine-log fire and listened to the wild, sweet strains that swept up and down and up till the very tree tops seemed to dance and quiver with delight.

Then suddenly father seemed to feel the presence of something or somebody strange, and I felt it, too. But the fiddler felt, heard, saw nothing but the divine, wild melody that made the very pine trees dance and quiver to their tips. Oh, for the pure, wild, sweet, plaintive music once more! the music of

"Money Musk," "Zip Coon," "Ol' Dan Tucker" and all the other dear old airs that once made a thousand happy feet keep time on the puncheon floors from Hudson's bank to the Oregon. But they are no more, now. They have passed away forever with the Indian, the pioneer, and the music-loving bear. It is strange how a man—I mean the natural man—will feel a presence long before he hears it or sees it. You can always feel the approach of a—but I forget. You are of another generation, a generation that only reads, takes thought at second hand only, if at all, and you would not understand; so let us get forward and not waste time in explaining the unexplainable to you.

Father got up, turned about, put me behind him, as an animal will its young, and peered back and down through the dense tangle of the deep river bank between two of the huge oxen which had crossed the plains with us; then he reached around and drew me to him with his left hand, pointing between the oxen sharp down the bank with his right forefinger.

A bear! two bears! and another coming; one already more than half way across on the great, mossy log that lay above the deep, sweeping waters of the Calipoola; and Lyte kept on, and the wild, sweet music leaped up and swept through the delighted and dancing boughs above. Then father reached back to the fire and thrust a long, burning bough deeper into the dying embers and the glittering sparks leaped and laughed and danced, and swept out and up and up as if to companion with the stars. Then Lyte knew. He did not hear, he did not see, he only felt; but the fiddle forsook his fingers and his chin in a second, and his gun was to his face with the muzzle thrust down between the oxen. And then my father's gentle hand reached out, lay on that long, black,

Kentucky rifle barrel, and it dropped down, slept once more at the fiddler's side, and again the melodies; and the very stars came down, believe me, to listen, for they never seemed so big and so close by before. The bears sat down on their haunches at last, and one of them kept opening his mouth and putting out his red tongue, as if he really wanted to taste the music. Every now and then one of them would lift up a paw and gently tap the ground, as if to keep time with the music. And both my papa and Lyte said next day that those bears really wanted to dance.

And that is all there is to say about that, except that my father was the gentlest gentleman I ever knew and his influence must have been boundless; for who ever before heard of any hunter laying down his rifle with a family of fat black bears holding the little snow-white cross on their breasts almost within reach of its muzzle?

The moon came up by and by, and the chin of the weary fiddler sank lower and lower, till all was still. The oxen lay down and ruminated, with their noses nearly against us. Then the coal-black bears melted away before the milk-white moon, and we slept there, with the sweet breath of the cattle, like incense, upon us.

Suggested Further Reading

Frost, O. W. *Joaquin Miller*. New York: Twayne Publishers, 1967.

Miller, Joaquin. *Life Amongst the Modocs: Unwritten History*. London: Richard Bentley & Sons, 1873.

———. *Songs of the Sierras*. London: Longman, Green, Reader, and Dyer, 1871.

———. *True Bear Stories*. Chicago and New York: Rand, McNally & Co., 1900.

Peterson, Martin S. *Joaquin Miller, Literary Frontiersman*. Palo Alto: Stanford University Press, 1937.

Ben Hur Lampman
1886-1954

For over forty years, Ben Hur Lampman edified and entertained Oregonians. His articles, books, editorials, essays, poems, and short stories demonstrated a rare versatility of genres, and the contents of his numerous works ranged from world affairs to the best place to bury a dog ("in the heart of his master").

Lampman was born in Wisconsin and moved with his family to North Dakota when he was four years old. He founded a newspaper in North Dakota and managed one in Gold Hill, Oregon, until he joined the (Portland) *Oregonian* in 1916, where he remained for thirty-five years, rising from police reporter to associate editor of the newspaper. The state legislature named him Poet Laureate of Oregon in 1951. The essay from which the excerpt below has been taken first appeared in *Nature Magazine* (1925).

The Fish Called Eulachon

The town of Troutdale stretches along the Sandy and climbs a hill to pause halfway, setting an outpost of roses. In mid-March the tourists have not come. There is little to do save to tallk of the last catch of salmon trout, the steelhead hooked and played below the wagon bridge, and the nearness of the eulachon run. Ought to be here most any time now. Never miss it more than a few days. In the main river long ago. Why, as a matter of fact. . . .

The gulls are yonder, screaming, dipping, whirling. And a breathless boy racing up from the stream. He has seen them, the advance guard. He is shouting the news, and within an hour the word has raced from village to city and across a county and is spreading far and wide through western Oregon. Even now men are wading into the stream, flourishing dip-nets, peering to mark the eulachon.

"Smelt are in the Sandy!"

The Sandy is a comely stream, either in the mountains of its birth, where it threads the canyon with hurrying silver, or where it flows in contemplative emerald to its union with the Columbia. Lewis and Clark gave it the name it bears, for the great burden of sand it carries down to its mouth and there arranges in a multiplicity of bars that never quite suit its fancy but must be shifted anew each season. The Sandy is a whimsical mother saying to her fishes that return from ocean—"I am here or perhaps there; seek for me, children!" But an Oregon river for all that, loved of salmon and trout and fishermen — and most of all by the eulachon.

A trifling fish, the eulachon, individually considered, scarce longer than the span of your hand, slit and rounded, and witless, as well, and of a dull leaden color untouched by any shimmering scales. But in the aggregate this least of anadromous fishes, commonly and wrongly called a smelt, to which it is but cousin, is almost an awesome evidence of the fecundity of river and sea. To deal with its numbers in mathematical calculation, where but a minor portion of the main run turns into the Sandy, is to clutch at the fringes of infinitude. For the current itself is clouded with them, the gravel of the river bed is obscured as by darkness, and that which the eye perceives from a given station is true of the river for a matter of miles—and this ceaseless advance of the eulachon to the spawning beds must continue not for days, but often for weeks.

One realizes the futility of estimate, when the pressure of the living tide thrusts from the water, to the sand at his feet, a luckless score of that myriad company. They yield to death most tamely, almost without struggle, as though dimly aware of their inconsequence. A gull slopes heavily over, curves, retraces his course, and mutely bids you begone.

In a single day 50,000 people have visited the river, along a frontage of two miles. They have made an outing of it, a festival—they are eager as gulls and thrice as clamorous. Hopeful novices from other parts bring trout rods and tackle and are laughed to scorn, since no lure diverts the eulachon from its propagative purpose. And some have nets rudely fashioned of wire mesh, and always there is an enthusiast who has lashed the family bird cage to a pole—but the regulation dip net is of linen mesh, its hoop two feet across, its bottom tapering to a point. Mounted on a ten-foot pole, the dip-net of an expert literally scoops the eulachon from the river in such quantity that the burden is lifted only with difficulty. You thrust the net upstream, downward to the required depth, and bring it forward at a rate to exceed the green current. Tick. Tick-tick. Tick. Tick-tick-tick. The captives signal their capture by those faint impacts. One draws the pole sharply backward, that the net may cross the hoop and seal itself—backward and upward, sagging with trophies.

Launch and raft are heaped as with silver ore. Men and women, burdened with dripping sacks, struggle and pant up the steep trail to the highway. A sprinkle of rain patters on rock and river. They laugh like children to feel it. What is rain to them? They are thigh-deep in the cold water, they are balanced on perilous ledges, they are teetering cheerfully on wet gray rock. They are sharing the bounty of the sea. A splash. A welter of foam and flailing arms, and up from the river rises one who leaned too far. No matter. He has regained the driftwood, dripping but undismayed, to resume his fishing. From the willows below the bridge a wisp of smoke rises into the moist March morning. Beside the fire sundry masterless men, strollers, vagrants, wandering workers are frying eulachon on a battered tin. In many a camp they will tell the tale of the river that ran black with fish.

Suggested Further Reading

Lampman, Ben Hur. *At the End of the Car Line*. Portland: Binfords & Mort, 1942.
———. *The Coming of the Pond Fishes*. Portland: Binfords & Mort, 1946.
———. "The Fish Called Eulachon," *Nature Magazine* (October 1925):204-207.
———. *How Could I Be Forgetting?* Portland: W. W. R. May, 1926.
———. *Where Would You Go?: Exploring the Seasons with Ben Hur Lampman*. Boise: R. O. Beatty & Associates, 1975.

Roderick Haig-Brown
1908-1976

No other creature is as intimately identified with the Pacific Northwest as the Pacific salmon, and no one has written of the salmon more gracefully or more scientifically than Roderick Haig-Brown. Haig-Brown was born in Lancing, Sussex, England. He came to Washington State in 1926, worked in British Columbia in 1927, and returned to England. He came back to British Columbia to stay in 1931. After working as a logger, fisherman, and trapper, he became a full-time writer, a judge, and an army officer in World War II. His novels and works of nonfiction dealt with salmon, history, lumbering, and conservation, and two of them, *A River Never Sleeps* and *Return to the River* (1941, from which the following selection is taken), are original and beautiful works of natural history, the latter set in the Columbia and Willamette river watersheds in Oregon.

Spring the Salmon Reaches the Ocean

In the night they reached the Columbia, Spring and her school traveled some three or four miles down the river before daylight turned them to rest and feed in the shelter of a sandbar. They were still sluggish and almost feeble, but they had worked over from the left bank towards the center of the river and were in good water, recovering rapidly. Spring searched the gray water about her and found chironomids rising through it occasionally. Behind a barely submerged hump in the sandbar which sheltered the school there was a rippled line of rejoining currents, and along this surface insects collected; the little fish rose to them quietly, touching the surface with tiny dimples that were almost instantly lost. But there was no real plenty of food even yet and the school slipped out and found the current again well before dusk.

In the big river they traveled a little faster than they had before, quite often in daylight, because they were safer in its great breadth and depth and because the silt-bearing water hid them from too strong a light and the searching eyes of their enemies. But enemies passed over them from time to time—eagles and ospreys, cormorants and, more and more frequently, the ravenous, searching herring gulls—forcing them to turn quickly down to deeper water. In the depths there were bullheads, many times larger than those in the Canyon Pool, wide-jawed and hungry. They passed among these dangers without the protection of fear, because fear would have delayed their journey, halted their feeding, broken the necessary order of their lives. But they were helped and driven by quick fear and quick reaction as soon as any danger became immediate.

They passed under Longview Bridge in the night, tasting pollution again below it. It was noon, two days later, somewhere off the mouth of Abernathy Creek, that they came in the path of the *Pacific Shipper*. The *Shipper* was bound upstream, to take on apples at Portland for the British Isles. Spring was aware of her as a great looming shadow in the midst of a thunderous vibration that had passed without harming her many times before. The shadow was new and terrifying and she sought to go down, away from it. The hissing bow wave caught her with the rest of the school and tossed her out in a tumble of foam. She struggled, found her balance and drove herself down through the water. She saw the squawfish clearly, open-mouthed and very close, swung from it and went up again; behind her it turned down, the struggles of a slower member of the school satisfyingly in its gullet.

A raven swept on slow black wings across the river, two or three feet above the surface. The shadow of his passing met Spring as she came up from the squawfish. She turned from it less wildly; the raven dipped, hovered, went on. A pale wide-winged shadow drew swiftly to his movement, drove a curved yellow beak below the surface. A moment later the gull was riding smoothly in the still disturbed wake of the *Shipper*, a second fish from the school gleaming silver in his beak. He threw his head back and swallowed. Spring and the rest of the school were already many yards downstream, deep under the surface, beyond sight, beyond fear. They continued downstream, heading into the current, until an eddy behind a small island drew them to feed.

Danger did not often crowd them so closely. Many gulls saw the school as it was passing over deep water, hesitated briefly on braking wings, then passed on. As the shadow crossed them the little fish sank a few feet deeper, slowly and deliberately, without changing the speed of their journey, then rose again as slowly. When a big fish drove at them from below they darted up, scattered and panicky, jumping clear of the water, turning and twisting, sending the encouraging flashes through the water behind them; usually it was the end of the migration for one or more of the school. But the school was not constant. Other schools joined it, traveled with it briefly or for long stretches, broke away, leaving room for yet others to join. At all times there were a hundred or more migrants in the water about Spring, traveling at the same pace, turning as she turned, resting as she rested, belonging with her. Sometimes there were as many as a thousand. The toll taken by the predators, birds and fish, was steady and large; but it left no mark upon the survivors.

Two or three days after the upstream passing of the *Pacific Shipper* the school came suddenly upon the gleaming, twisting bodies of half a dozen great chinooks. The bodies were invisibly restrained and suspended, but a line of dark floating blobs at the surface dipped and sent out ripples as they struggled. Two fish grew still and hung with spread gill-plates as Spring passed under them; she felt the touch of the net's twine along her side and swam quickly up from it, frightened. The current took her down again and she passed easily through the mesh, whose width was nearly twice her length. Above her the cork-line moved and the shining bodies of the chinooks moved with it. Later the school passed through other nets which held struggling fish; the flashes of the great bodies held no warning for Spring and she had felt terror only at the chance touch of the twine of that first net.

As they worked down the river, past the low-lying islands with their small farms and splendid cottonwood trees, past the orange-buff gashes that stood out against the dark green timber wherever the road cut through a point, past the sandbars and past the drift-lined beaches, the influence of the tide began to make itself felt. Off Cathalamet, where Puget Island broadly splits the river and the mountains mount steeply from the south shore, the tide mark shows clearly, several feet of dark silt-gray dampness on the piles at low water. There was still no faintest trace of salt in the water, but from this point on the migration of the school became less constant. A chart of its course would have seemed confused and almost purposeless, marked by delays in slack water or turned back upon itself by contrary currents; but the sum total was always downstream, towards the plenty of the ocean, until they came to Desdemona Sands and turned among the piles under the canneries of Astoria.

Here they found food in plenty, suddenly and easily. The fish-packing boats were still bringing in late-fall chinooks and dog salmon, from gill-netters and drag seiners, from traps and trollers; the machinery roared in the canneries, the gang knives clanked and rattled, cutting the fish for the cans. The offal poured down into the water around the piles, hearts and livers that were called waste and the great swollen ovaries with their thousands upon thousands of smooth, shining, orange-scarlet eggs. The migrant schools turned in from every direction towards the feast and hung on the downstream side of each cannery until the water was black with them. For nearly a month Spring held there and fed in the midst of a threshing, driving, competitive multitude of migrants. Above them the gulls screamed and struggled, breaking up the larger pieces of offal. Below them Dolly Vardens, squawfish and bullheads grew too fat and too lazy to prey on bright living things that could move away.

Spring grew fast. On her scales the concentric rings began to widen and record this intermediate growth, more rapid than that she had made in her own river or during her migration but still much slower than that she would make in the sea. Her whole body was now overlaid with silver, veiling parr-marks and spots until they were invisible except from certain angles and in certain lights. Like all animals whose safety or food depends in any degree upon concealment, she was dark on the back and lighter below; her back was a strong steel blue with fresh black spots in it; her sides were silver gray shading to pure silver and then to clear white on her belly. Her tail was spotted and forked and the fineness of the wrist above it was emphasized by the increasing bulk of her body.

By the end of November she was more than six inches long; a full inch of her growth had been made during the month she had spent under the cannery and, though there were individuals among the migrants still larger, she was at least half an inch above the average size of those collected under the cannery. Throughout the whole busy, active month her belly had been full, yet she had never lacked the drive and strength to compete vigorously for food whenever it appeared; had the supply of offal continued, her migration might have been delayed through many months, but early in December the cannery closed and the flow of easy forage was over. Spring hung hopefully nearby for two or three days, picking up such trifles as the current brought to her. But her belly was no longer full and there was a new restlessness among the young fish about her. Schools broke away from the main body and disappeared. There was constant stirring and circling and searching through the water among the piles. Then Spring found herself in the middle of a school of about two hundred fish, working away, out and down river; the piles became dim shadows standing faintly in the gray water; very soon they faded into the wall of grayness that edged the circle of Spring's vision.

Astoria is a little more than half way down the wide estuary of the Columbia. More than twenty miles long, nearly ten miles wide from Grays Bay to the Oregon shore, the estuary would be a great gulf opening upon the Pacific Ocean were it not for the weight of fresh water pressing through it and forcing the ocean to keep its place and halt its salt tides to the west of the line between Astoria and Point Ellice. In a man's ordinary conception a river can have but a little part in filling and sweeping such a place; the winds fleet across it and drive spume from the wave tops; from the Oregon side the sawmills and the canneries of Washington are slim plumes of white smoke against the heavy green mountainsides; from the Washington side Astoria is flattened into a dwarf and hazy city; Astoria itself looks down river upon an infinity of water that is still for a long time the Columbia before it becomes the Pacific Ocean.

In all the scope of the last ten miles of this great estuary Spring found yet more delay in her journey. With the school that had left the cannery she crossed the strong deep flow of the ship channel between Astoria and Desdemona Sands. The tide was ebbing and for the first time there was a taste of salt in the water which made her feel buoyant and strong; she swam with quickly moving tail and body, heading up into the current but drifting down with it as she had all through the long migration. Angling easily across, feeding upon what was swept down to it, the school was carried seawards by the current for nearly a mile before it reached the slacker water along the sands.

Here Spring fed easily, ranging over the shoals in the eddies of the returning tide. She found reddish copepods, queer-shaped, small, swimming with active strokes of feathered oarlike arms, and took them eagerly; occasionally a chironomid or some other winged insect was carried down on the water and crossed her sight; more rarely still she flashed in quick pursuit of Asellus the sow-bug, so like a wood-louse that one might easily have supposed he had slipped into the water from some floating chunk of rotten wood, or the jerkily swimming sand-hoppers whose sideways-flattened bodies drew across her vision in always curving passage.

The school fed out the flood tide on the sands, ranging, driving and pursuing for the first time as they would through their whole saltwater life. But there was still a restlessness in them and on the start of the ebb they swung out once more into the current of the ship channel. A strong wind from the Washington side raised short broken waves and piled the flow in towards the deep bay below Astoria. The young fish were carried gradually across in the drift and, as the flood tide started to make, they found themselves within the eddy of the bay. There was food there and they fed, working gradually deeper and deeper into the sheltered water, away from the flow that would have carried them on out to sea.

Suggested Further Reading

Haig-Brown, Roderick. *Return to the River: The Story of the Chinook Run*. New York: Morrow, 1941.

———. *A River Never Sleeps*. New York: Morrow, 1946.

———. *The Western Angler: An Account of Pacific Salmon and Western Trout*. 2 vols. New York: Derrydale Press, 1939.

Barbara Garson
1941-

Fishing and preserving fish have been important industries from the beginning of Oregon history. Barbara Garson here recounts life in the Astoria canneries in an excerpt from a chapter titled "Tuna Fish" published in *All the Livelong Day* (1975).

Garson was born in Brooklyn and has written books, plays, and articles in numerous periodicals such as the *New York Times, Harper's, Liberation*, and *Ramparts*. A social and political activist, she has worked against the United States' presence in El Salvador, the manufacture and deployment of atomic weapons, and Soviet Russian oppression of Poland. Her play *Macbird!*, a satire on the Lyndon Johnson years, has had more than three hundred productions and has sold over 500,000 copies.

Tuna Fish

Astoria, Oregon, is a town of ten thousand that sits on stone steps above the Columbia, just where it rolls into the Pacific. The town was first settled by one of Jacob Astor's fur-trading parties. Later it was settled by Scandinavian immigrants, many of them Finns, who came to fish. To this day most everyone in Astoria still does a little fishing, or puts their time in at one of the fish canneries.

Though it's August, the height of the salmon season, the big canneries have been letting out early. No one knows exactly what time they'll be let off. The time cards the women wear on their backs at Bumble Bee may be punched at 1:42 or 1:48 or 1:54. (Everything goes in tenths of the hour.) Whatever time it is, it will be too early for those who make their whole living at the cannery, though the youngsters who work for the summer may welcome the early release.

In every tavern in town there's the usual speculations: "It's just a bad season"; "It's the mercury they found near the docks"; "By God, we finally fished out the whole Columbia." These may be the long-range reasons for a declining catch, but the women in the canneries, those who face facts, know that the short-range reason for the short hours this summer is the contract they signed two years ago, a contract that was supposed to benefit the full-time workers at the expense of the seasonal help.

"It's the 'casual workers' clause," a few women will say, as adamantly as others avoid the issue. "And the strike didn't settle a thing."

But the casual workers (now called probationary workers) clause is a complicated story which I only came to understand slowly. So perhaps I'd better let it unravel for the reader as it did for me.

Since nobody knows exactly what time the skinners and the cleaners will run out of fish, I waited at Bumble Bee's main plant starting at 1 p.m. I sat on a curb in the smelly yard next to a whiney-eyed man of thirty-two. He told me that he had been a photographer for *Life* magazine, that he knew Lawrence Ferlinghetti, and that he was waiting for his girl friend Starlein, who was a tuna cleaner.

The names of cannery workers in this story have been changed. However, I have tried to produce reasonable facsimiles by using Pacific Northwest Finnish names. If by chance the names I chose resemble the names of people in Astoria, I apologize. And I repeat that real names are never used.

Starlein was one of the first cleaners out, after the skinners. She still had her white smock on, just like all the other women. But she came out undoing her white head scarf. She was already shaking her brown wavy hair free by the time she got to us. Most of the other women drove or walked home through town in their uniforms, with the white head scarves, knotted squarely in the front, covering every bit of hair.

Starlein's boyfriend hung on her from behind with his head dangling over her shoulder as he introduced us. I think it may have embarrassed or annoyed her. But I'm not sure, and no one else seemed to care.

Starlein was eighteen and pretty. She had a dreamy look when she talked or listened. She said she would be perfectly happy to tell me about her job.

"What do you do in the cannery?" I asked.

"I clean tuna," she said. "The loins come past me on a belt. [Loins are the skinned, headless, tailless, halved or quartered pieces of fish.] I bone the loin and take out the dark meat—the cat food. I put the clean loins on the second belt, the cat food on the third belt and I save my bones. You're not allowed to dump any garbage till the line lady okays it. Because that's how they check your work. They count your bones and see if they're clean."

"Do you talk a lot to the other women?" I asked.

"Not really," she answered.

"What do you do all day?"

"I daydream."

"What do you daydream about?"

"About sex."

"I guess that's my fault," her boyfriend apologized proudly.

"No, it's not you," she said. "It's the tuna fish." I asked quite curiously what she meant.

"Well first it's the smell. You've got that certain smell in your nose all day. It's not like the smell out here. Your own fish next to you is sweet. And then there's the men touching you when they punch the tags on your back and maybe the other women on the line. But it's mostly handling the loins. Not the touch itself, because we wear gloves. But the soft colors. The reds and the whites and the purples. The most exciting thing is the dark meat. It comes in streaks. It's red-brown. And you have to pull it out with your knife. You pile it next to your loin and it's crumbly and dark red and moist like earth.

"You're supposed to put the cat food on the belt as you finish each loin. But I hold it out to make as big a pile of dark meat as I can."

"Well," I said, "aside from liking the dark meat, what do you think of your work?"

"I don't think about it," she said. "When I get there I put on the apron—we each have a plastic apron with our name in felt pen—and go to the line and wait for the buzzer. The first fish comes along and I pull it off the belt. [She made a heavy movement to show me.] And I just do it.

"I try not to look at the clock so the time will pass more quickly. When I do sometimes I'm surprised at how it went but more often I look and it's not even two minutes later. But there's not that much to complain about. When you're really into it you don't notice it. And then it feels so good when you pull a loin with a big dark vein of cat food.

"I knew it would be dull and boring when I came here. But I had no idea of the sensuous things I would feel just from cleaning fish. I came just to make some money fast."

"How much do you make?" I asked.

"I get something like $2.70 an hour, I think. They don't tell you exactly and I never asked. Mine is lower now because I'm on probation."

"Oh," I asked, "what did you do?"

"Oh no. It's just a thing. When you first come you don't get your real salary."

"How long does it last?" I asked.

"I don't know. But I don't think I'll stay that long."

"How do you get along with the older women?"

"The other women they're very nice. They show you how to tie up the scarves and how to get a good knife. And the line ladies don't bother you much either. At first they're on your back, always counting your bones or checking your cat-food pile. But when they see you're a good worker they don't bother you."

"Are you a good worker?" I asked.

"Sure, what else is there to do. Besides, I like to see how much cat food I can pile up."

I liked Starlein very much. But I decided I ought to find some more normal cannery workers to talk to.

Suggested Further Reading

Garson, Barbara. *All the Livelong Day: The Meaning and Demeaning of Routine Work*. Garden City, NY: Doubleday & Co., 1975.

———. *The Dinosaur Door;* first produced off-Broadway at the Theatre for the New City, June 1976.

———. *MacBird!* Berkeley and New York: Grassy Knoll Press, 1966.

Irving, Washington. *Astoria*. . . . Norman: University of Oklahoma Press, 1964. (First published in 1836.)

Barbara Drake
1939-

Barbara Drake lives on a small farm near Yamhill, Oregon, where she raises sheep and maintains a vineyard. Born in Kansas, Drake is an accomplished writer in many genres. She is the author of several books of poetry, and a college textbook on writing poetry. Her poetry, fiction, and nonfiction have appeared in various magazines. She is now a member of the English Department and Director of Creative Writing at Linfield College. Her essay that follows first appeared in the (Portland) *Sunday Oregonian* (1990).

Birth of a Lamb

We'd gotten the sheep the year before, from an ad that read: "spinner's flock reduction." One of the ewe lambs, Amity, was undersized and none too vigorous, a cull in spite of her fine, dense wool. She was slow to mature, and when the other two ewes lambed at the end of winter, thereby "proving" (as they say in the livestock ads, like yeast that will rise) the virility of our young ram, Amity showed no sign of maternity. If our ram Ajax, a fine black Romney, had managed to breed the other two ewes but not Amity, perhaps our runty ewe was not going to produce. Production, sheep people kept telling us, was everything.

By June, when the new lambs were already outsizing their mothers, Amity showed signs she was going to lamb. Overnight, her udder was as long as her legs and she walked with a dwarfish sway that was as brave as it was awkward. With an out-of-season lamb it's hard to tell when to expect it. But one afternoon Amity took off for the barn early; we kept an eye on her.

I've never raised sheep before. Whenever I get a chance, I ask a sheep person for details. I have a copy of Paula Simmons' *Raising Sheep the Modern Way*. I've read it forward and backward as needed, studied relevant parts from parasites to subcutaneous injections, from breed types to tips on shearing. The day Amity went to the barn early I reviewed the section on lambing. With the other sheep, nothing out of the ordinary had happened during lambing except that one night at the end of winter I dreamed about sheep lambing. As if still in a dream, I went out to the barn in red rubber boots and nightgown and looked into the sheep pen. An older ewe, Why, was cleaning off a wet black lamb while the other sheep looked on.

Aurora, the yearling, did more groaning and pacing but she, too, delivered without assistance. Now I kept an eye on Amity, put her in a pen apart from the others, and hoped she would deliver well.

About 9 p.m. I went out to check Amity and found the lamb's nose protruding, but no front feet in sight. I went back to the house, where the light was better, and studied the drawings of "abnormal positions in lambing." A lamb is supposed to slide out with its head and front feet pointing downward. According to Paula Simmons, head first feet back is abnormal and requires assistance. Later I checked for signs of hooves tucked under the lamb's head that was now dangling under the ewe's tail like some strangely mounted trophy. No feet.

210

For people raised on farms and around animals, such sights may be commonplace. But I am a writer and a college teacher. At age 50, I am trying to learn how to raise sheep, and it's all new to me. *Raising Sheep the Modern Way* describes various obstetrical maneuvers for rearranging the lamb that goes off course in the birth process, most of which involve looping a cord around whatever part of the lamb that manages to present itself so as not to lose that part, and then gently pushing and turning and reaching in to straighten bent knees, and so on. Various cautions and commentaries warn about not pinching the umbilical cord, which supplies the lamb with oxygen until it's in a position to breathe on its own, and the occasional necessity for delivering a dead lamb, as well as cautions about sanitation and infection. Horrible possibilities presented themselves to my imagination.

I went back to the barn, hoping that Amity would have managed things on her own by then. Perhaps such a short-legged ewe was giving birth to an even shorter-legged lamb, and I was not able to see the feet because they were too short to have appeared yet, but such a possibility did not seem likely. I scanned Paula Simmons' index but there was no entry for "short sheep."

The dangling face of the unborn lamb looked both comical and touching. Baby lambs look as if they are smiling, and this head continued to smile with its eyes shut in the sleep of the unborn and its face waxy and wet and unreal, turned downward, absolutely still as if lifeless—and with no feet in sight.

To make things worse, Amity seemed to be giving up. She stood up and moved restessly, bumping the lamb's head against the wall of the barn. She turned dangerously, groaned and lay down. After a while she seemed to quit laboring. I bent to look again at the little animal face, unsure in my inexperience, if the lamb was in fact, alive. It was not breathing, but that would be normal if it was still getting oxygen through its umbilical attachment. I put the flashlight near the lamb's face, and its closed eyes twitched in reflex. It was alive. The lamb's ears were wetly crumpled to its head and as I reached out and barely touched one it unfolded like a paper flower in water. Amity lay back, her dreamy eyes resigned.

I went to the house for one last look at *Raising Sheep the Modern Way*. I tied three loops of cord as Paula Simmons described. I checked my fingernails for snags and rough spots, and scrubbed my hands and arms with iodine wash, trying self-consciously not to imitate a soap-opera surgeon on camera. Looking for a lubricant, as described, I found nothing that fit the definition of "antiseptic." So I took a bottle of aloe and vitamin E lotion, bought at a fashionable natural cosmetics store in Northwest Portland, and went to the barn.

Considerably more time had passed than the hour and a half advised by Paula Simmons. Still, the birth seemed at an impasse. My husband, Bill, who is steadier than I in giving animals shots and shearing sheep, decided his hands were too large to try what we were going to do. I slipped the loop around the back of the lamb's neck and through its mouth, as recommended (so as not to choke the lamb). Then I slathered my hands with aloe Vitamin E skin lotion and slid my right hand along the lamb's back, into the birth canal. The ewe groaned, as well she might, but she was still as my husband held her head and the flashlight.

I moved my hand as gently as possible along the lamb's body until I felt its shoulder. At one point I thought I felt the umbilical cord looped over the lamb's shoulder and I shrank from entangling it. My hand moved over the lamb's shoulder and down, but at first I could not get a sense of its leg. Then I felt the joint of its knee and slid my pointer finger into the bend, pulling the foot foward from where it was turned, slipping it back down the birth canal where it straightened along the lamb's neck and came out.

"The book says it can be delivered with just one leg out," my husband reminded me. I slipped a loop over the protruding foot and gently tugged this cord and the one that passed across the lamb's neck and through its mouth. The lamb slid out easily now, a limp, small, slippery thing, almost fishlike, but loose like a soapy washrag. I could not tell if it was alive. I eased it to the hay-covered floor of the stall and wiped its nose, then it gurgled and gasped, shuddered and began to breathe.

The ewe looked surprised; then she began to lick the lamb as it came alive in the straw. The night was warm—it was June after all, so we weren't too worried about cold. The lamb was bony and light, as lambs are, though it would fill out considerably in the next 24 hours, but it appeared to be a good-sized lamb. Soon it stumbled to its feet and, swaying amazingly on its tiny hooves, began to look for the ewe's nipple, which I had "stripped," or pulled in a milking motion, to clear it of wax. With what looked to me like an agonizing amount of fumbling, ewe and lamb finally got together, and she continued to lick it and sniff its rear end (the way ewes identify their own lambs) while it nursed in an awkward off-and-on way.

A newborn lamb makes a tiny baa, at first reminiscent of the waa cry of a human baby. The ewe answers with a soft nicker unlike any of the other voicings sheep make, a sound that attracts, comforts and quiets the newborn. My husband gave Amity a shot of penicillin to prevent infection. Then we left her with her lamb, a ewe lamb, as soon as she proved she was doing everything right, and went in to bed.

Around 3 a.m., and still awake, Bill and I went out to the barn to take another look. The lamb was dry now, and turned its head to the beam of the flashlight. The ewe nickered and moved defensively to place herself between us and the lamb. My role as obstetrical savior was not about to be appreciated by a sheep. Who ever knows how anything will turn out? But for that moment, it was all right. We went back to the house and slept.

Suggested Further Reading

Drake, Barbara. *Bees in Wet Weather.* Traverse City, MI: Canoe Press, 1992.
———. "Birth of a Lamb," (Portland) *Sunday Oregonian, Northwest Magazine,* 6 May 1990.
———. *Love at the Egyptian Theatre.* East Lansing, MI: Red Cedar Press, 1978.
———. *What We Say to Strangers.* Portland: Breitenbush Publications, 1986.
Simmons, Paula. *Raising Sheep the Modern Way.* Charlotte, VT: Garden Way Publishing, 1979.

SECTION V
Opportunities in a New Land

Jesse Applegate
1811-1888

Jesse Applegate, born in Kentucky, came over the trail to Oregon in 1843. He became a farmer in the new land, but also entered public life as a surveyor and road builder. Among his many projects were the original survey of Oregon City and the laying out of the Applegate Trail from Fort Hall in Idaho through northern Nevada and California to the Willamette Valley. Applegate helped reorganize Oregon's first government (the Provisional Government), served one term in its legislature, and was a member of the convention that drew up Oregon's constitution in 1857. Originally a Whig, he joined the new Republican Party and helped influence Oregonians to vote for Abraham Lincoln in 1860.

 A sensitive, literate, and prolific writer about politics, Applegate is best known for his inspired capture of one day's life on the Oregon Trail. The "cow column"that he describes comprised the overlanders who were accompanied by their cattle. Since the animals stirred up dust, and moved so slowly, they and their owners were forced to follow behind the first column of migrants who were traveling without stock. This famous essay, an excerpt of which follows, first appeared in the *Overland Monthly* in 1868 and is available in several reprint editions.

A Day with the Cow Column

F rom six to seven o'clock is a busy time; breakfast is to be eaten, the tents struck, the wagons loaded, and the teams yoked and brought up in readiness to be attached to their respective wagons. All know when, at seven o'clock, the signal to march sounds, that those not ready to take their proper places in the line of march must fall into the dusty rear for the day.

There are sixty wagons. They have been divided into fifteen divisions or platoons of four wagons each, and each platoon is entitled to lead in its turn. The leading platoon of today will be the rear one of tomorrow, and will bring up the rear unless some teamster, through indolence or negligence, has lost his place in the line, and is condemned to that uncomfortable post. It is within ten minutes of seven; the corral but now a strong barricade is everywhere broken, the teams being attached to the wagons. The women and children have taken their places in them. The pilot (a borderer who has passed his life on the verge of civilization, and has been chosen to the post of leader from his knowledge of the savages and his experience in travel through roadless wastes) stands ready in the midst of his pioneers, and aids to mount and lead the way. Ten or fifteen young men, not today on duty, form another cluster. They are ready to start on a buffalo hunt, are well mounted and well armed as they need be, for the unfriendly Sioux have driven the buffalo out of the Platte, and the hunters must ride fifteen or twenty miles to reach them. The cow-drivers are hastening, as they get ready, to the rear of their charge, to collect and prepare them for the day's march.

It is on the stroke of seven; the rushing to and fro, the cracking of whips, the loud command to oxen, and what seemed to be the inextricable confusion of the last ten minutes has ceased. Fortunately everyone has been found and every teamster is at his post. The clear notes of a trumpet sound in the front; the pilot and his guards mount their horses; the leading division of wagons move out of the encampment, and take up the line of march; the rest fall into their places with the precision of clockwork, until the spot so lately full of life sinks back into that solitude that seems to reign over the broad plain and rushing river as the caravan draws its lazy length towards the distant El Dorado. It is with hunters we will briskly canter towards the bold but smooth and grassy bluffs that bound the broad valley, for we are not yet in sight of the grander but less beautiful scenery (of the Chimney Rock, Courthouse, and other bluffs, so nearly resembling giant castles and palaces) made by the passage of the

Platte through the Highlands near Laramie. We have been traveling briskly for more than an hour. We have reached the top of the bluff, and now have turned to view the wonderful panorama spread before us. To those who have not been on the Platte my powers of description are wholly inadequate to convey an idea of the vast extent and grandeur of the picture, and the rare beauty and distinctness of its detail. No haze or fog obscures objects in the pure and transparent atmosphere of this lofty region. To those accustomed only to the murky air of the seaboard, no correct judgment of distance can be formed by sight, and objects which they think they can reach in a two hours' walk may be a day's travel away; and though the evening air is a better conductor of sound, on the high plain during the day the report of the loudest rifle sounds little louder than the bursting of a cap; and while the report can be heard but a few hundred yards, the smoke of the discharge may be seen for miles. So extended is the view from the bluff on which the hunters stand, that the broad river glowing under the morning sun like a sheet of silver, and the broader emerald valley that borders it, stretch away in the distance until they narrow at almost two points on the horizon, and when first seen, the vast pile of the Wind River Mountain, though hundreds of miles away, looks clear and distinct as a white cottage on the plain.

We are full six miles away from the line of march; though everything is dwarfed by distance, it is seen distinctly. The caravan has been about two hours in motion and is now extended as widely as a prudent regard for safety will permit. First, near the bank of the shining river, is a company of horsemen; they seem to have found an obstruction, for the main body has halted while three or four ride rapidly along the bank of a creek or slough. They are hunting a favorable crossing for the wagons; while we look they have succeeded; it has apparently required no work to make it passable, for all but one of the party have passed on, and he has raised a flag, no doubt a signal to the wagons to steer their course to where he stands. The leading teamster sees him, though he is yet two miles off, and steers his course directly towards him, all the wagons following in his track. They (the wagons) form a line three-quarters of a mile in length; some of the teamsters ride upon the front of their wagons, some march beside their teams; scattered along the line companies of women and children are taking exercise on foot; they gather bouquets of rare and beautiful flowers that line the way; near them stalks a stately greyhound or an Irish wolf dog, apparently proud of keeping watch and ward over his master's wife and children. Next comes a band of horses; two or three men or boys follow them, the docile and sagacious animals scarce needing their attention, for they have learned to follow in the rear of the wagons, and know that at noon they will be allowed to graze and rest. Their knowledge of time seems as accurate as of the place they are to occupy in the line, and even a full-blown thistle will scarce tempt them to straggle or halt until the dinner hour has arrived. Not so with the large herd of horned beasts that bring up the rear; lazy, selfish and unsocial, it has been a task to get them in motion, the strong always ready to domineer over the weak, halt in the front and forbid the weaker to pass them. They seem to move only in fear of the driver's whip; though in the morning full to repletion, they have not been driven an hour, before their hunger and thirst seem to indicate a fast of days' duration. Through all the long day their greed is never sated nor their thirst quenched, nor is there a moment of relaxation of the tedious and vexatious labors of their drivers, although to all others the march furnishes some season of relaxation or enjoyment. For the cow-drivers there is none.

But from the stand-point of the hunters the vexations are not apparent; the crack of whips and loud objurgations are lost in the distance. Nothing of the moving panorama, smooth and orderly as it appears, has more attractions for the eye than that vast square column in which all colors are mingled, moving here slowly and there briskly, as impelled by horsemen riding furiously in front and rear.

But the picture, in its grandeur, its wonderful mingling of colors and distinctness of detail, is forgotten in contemplation of the singular people who give it life and animation. No other race of men with the means at their command would undertake so great a journey; none save these could successfully perform it, with no previous preparation, relying only on the fertility of their invention to devise the means to overcome each danger and difficulty as it arose. They have undertaken to perform, with slow-moving oxen, a journey of two thousand miles. The way lies over trackless wastes, wide and deep rivers, rugged and lofty mountains, and is beset with hostile savages. Yet, whether it were a deep river with no tree upon its banks, a rugged defile where even a loose horse could not pass, a hill too steep for him to climb, or a threatened attack of an enemy, they are always found ready and equal to the occasion, and always conquerors. May we not call them men of destiny? They are people changed in no essential particulars from their ancestors, who have followed closely on the footsteps of the receding savage, from the Atlantic sea-board to the great valley of the Mississippi.

Suggested Further Reading

Applegate, Jesse. "A Day with the Cow Column," *Oregon Historical Quarterly* 1 (1900): 371-383.

Applegate, Shannon. *Skookum: An Oregon Pioneer Family's History and Lore*. New York: William Morrow, 1988.

Schafer, Joseph. "Jesse Applegate: Pioneer, Statesman, and Philosopher," *Washington Historical Quarterly* 7 (1907): 217-233.

Shannon Applegate
1944-

Shannon Applegate, great-grand niece of Jesse Applegate, here treats the saga of the Oregon Trail from a somewhat different perspective than does "A Day with the Cow Column." Born in Maryland, Applegate has been the director of a historical museum and editor of a historical society press, and has served on the publications and editorial advisory boards of the Oregon Council for the Humanities. She is co-editor of the *Letters and Diaries* volume of the *Oregon Literature Series.* This selection is excerpted from the Portraits section of *Skookum* (1988), which was an Oregon Institute of Literary Arts Book Award finalist in 1989.

The Marrow

Melinda Miller Applegate
Pioneer Wife and Mother
Born Clay County, Tennessee
Growing to Womanhood in Missouri
Came to the Oregon Territory
Wife of Charles Applegate

1879

It was the day of leaving; of their slow departure by wagon from the Missouri countryside she loved so well. The day she saw her father for the last time. He had ridden his powerful gray horse alongside the party as far as the river. It was comforting to see the old man on the horse beside them. He didn't say much. It was his way.

She had been feeling queer and half lightheaded and wondering whether or not to tell Charles she was expecting another child. There were already eight little ones to contend with.

But Charles was busy with his two brothers and some of the other emigrant men, organizing the wagons and stock. She felt the distance between herself and her husband. She felt cut off from her duties, her children, her will. How cumbersome would be this expedition of men, women, and children, and animals. Their wagons and herds streamed into the rendezvous place from all directions. She heard the nearly deafening accumulation of their sounds. Then, she remembered, she felt nothing except the certainty that she would soon vomit. She loosened her neckerchief, already dreading the pitch and jerk of the journey before her without yet having climbed atop the wagon.

Young Billy Doak was to be their teamster. Charles had been somewhere nearer to the front, meeting with some other men. At length he had made his way back to her, pausing briefly, brusquely relaying the plans of the day. Upon seeing him, the children had begun wailing, "Pappa, why cain't we take Ellis? Uncle Lindsay is taking Vick and Vine. Oh, please, Pappa!"

They had, of course, been through all the business about the dogs before. Charley, like Jesse, had been convinced no dog, regardless of how well behaved, belonged on such an extended trek as theirs. Lindsay and his beloved greyhounds, however, would not be parted. Charley was disapproving and made it plain. Charley glowered at the children, who had brought up a sore subject.

At that time Charley had not been particularly stout. He'd been a solid block of a man. She watched him set his jaw. The sweat glistened down the thick column of his neck as he turned to leave them. He said sharply, "Melinda!," his way of telling her the children were her precinct on this day, that he was tired, concerned with matters far more important than the family dog.

Tears welling, Lucy, the eldest, looked at her beseechingly. "Oh, please, Mamma, it's so hard to leave just *everything.*" Tears in her own eyes, she replied, "Your pa has said not, children. Leave him be now!" Oh, and leave me be, too, she said to herself, feeling her throat constrict, ready to heave up its cornbread and black breakfast coffee.

When they first pulled away from the two-storied log cabin that had been her home, she remembered how the orchard had looked, the cowshed, the pigs snorting noisily in their trough beside the road. Lisbon Applegate, the oldest of the Applegate brothers, was to sell all their holdings for them. It hurt her to roll right past them. Money didn't matter to her. It had hurt even more when she took her last look at the three rosebushes her mother had given her from Tennessee cuttings.

And this place on the Osage was her true home. Leaving it made no sense. The sassafras trees slid by in a dream, gray-green, their pungent odor filling her nostrils. She felt the tug of the oxen on the wagon pulling her away, tearing her from the things she knew.

Oh Soft Missouri—thickening with low green
Flickering scarlet of your Red-Bud trees
This early May!

Why? Why were they going? All the years since then—the poor ones and the bountiful ones in their new country, Oregon—she had often asked herself the same question. Why had they ever left Missouri?

Yes, there had been hard times, but by 1841 and '42, things had got better. During the bad, severe years the price of pork and every other kind of stock had fallen so low a man could not sell a thing he'd raised, much less get it to market. Nor could anyone trust the currency that was then changing hands. Her brother-in-law Jesse had actually been reduced to selling his hogs to the river boats, which used the fat for fuel because it was cheaper than wood. In the late 1830s even she had grown disgusted with Missouri. But all that passed. They were selling their produce again. The weather had been better. Money was dear, but they all had their share. They were better off than most. Why, for the first time they even had enough for boughten shoes for everyone in the family that winter.

What would their future have held if they had never known Robert Shortess? She still thought of him with bitterness: the letters and maps he sent them from Oregon. "I never hear of failures here," he'd written. Her brothers-in-law had an adventuresome streak, all right. They were family men but never happy with what they had already. However, Charley had always been prudent. He had a strong, practical nature. He'd always stayed close to what was his through hard work or so she'd thought as she watched Jesse and Lindsay act like men under whom a fire had been set. Emigrant meetings that had been farther and farther away. Lindsay had even advertised in the newspaper to find men of like mind. She remembered when she'd told Charley how foolish she thought his brothers were: the idea of traveling two thousand miles just to live in a country with less than two hundred white folks in it.

She had never really understood it. It had not seemed to matter then, any more than it did now that she did understand—as far as Charley was concerned.

And he had been even worse during the first decade or so of their marriage. It hadn't mattered that he was far from young—a full forty years old. It hadn't mattered that there had been sick spells. Oregon would cure him, he said. In the end, she supposed, it was as simple as the bond of blood; her practical husband, his streak of caution abandoned for kinship's sake. "The Fever" she had heard it called, and it was surely that. A year or so before they themselves had left for Oregon, a man had passed through the settlements with a banner pinned to his wagon that said OREGON OR THE GRAVE. Whether he ever got there they never knew.

It seemed to her that even the good sense of the family women was tainted. Going to Oregon, she told them, was not like going to St. Louis to see the sights. Could they not see the seriousness of their husbands' "talk"? They had both looked at her as if she were peculiar. Maybe Oregon wasn't such a bad idea "for some people," they said. One year later, she looked at Cynthia and Betsy and shared their sorrow. The price for their men's enthusiasm had been dear: two boys lost to the furious torrents of the Columbia. From then on she had forgotten all else save that they were sisters of her heart and women loving their little ones. And there were even more troubles and hardships to follow.

But in Missouri, on that day when they were all making their quilts together, she had felt cut to the very quick. She had never before been excluded. As the eldest and most experienced of the three women, her advice had always been sought. She had felt especially humiliated when she learned that the brothers' plans had been afoot for many more months than she had imagined. It had never been said outright, and she herself had never asked, even years later.

Nevertheless, she was certain that Betsy and Cynthia had known she was going to Oregon before she knew herself.

"Oregon, Oregon," even the littlest child whispered. By the winter the murmur had grown to a chorus, and by spring it seemed as if half the settlers in Missouri were considering packing up.

> Oh Missouri, sweet Missouri
> Where in spring the cycadas
> Disperse their yellow parasols
> In feather's spin
> Missouri swelling deep
> Heavy lowland river's place
> Farewell!

Suggested Further Reading

Applegate, Shannon. *Skookum: An Oregon Pioneer Family's History and Lore*. New York: William Morrow, 1988.

Jeffrey, Julie Roy. *Frontier Women: The Trans-Mississippi West, 1840-1880*. New York: Hill and Wang, 1979.

Schlissel, Lillian. *Women's Diaries of the Westward Journey*. New York: Schocken Books, 1982.

Harvey W. Scott
1838-1910

Harvey W. Scott was the most influential newspaper editor in the history of the Pacific Northwest. Born in Illinois, Scott crossed the Oregon Trail with his family as a teenager, fought in the Yakima War in the 1850s, and worked as a woodcutter. He became the first graduate of Pacific University in 1860.

Scott was editor of the (Portland) *Oregonian* from 1865 to 1870 and again from 1877 until 1910. His editorials expressed great pride in Oregon's past and prophesied a glorious future for the state. In spite of this optimism, however, Scott took a conservative stance on most social and political issues. One of the modern institutions that he opposed was the public high school, an establishment he attacked in the following editorial, which first appeared in the *Oregonian* on 16 April 1879.

Cure for Drones

In support of the statement so often urged through the *Oregonian*, that the public school system in many and perhaps all our states is turning out more drones than society can well support, we find an article in the *Philadelphia Record* of recent date which goes so directly to the marrow of the matter that we cannot refrain from reproducing in these columns its principal parts. As an example, the case of a family is taken in which the first boy is old enough to succeed to his father's trade and earn enough to be no longer an expense to his parents. But he is not put to work, and as there are not places to be found for all in stores or other "light and genteel employment," his parents conclude to continue him in school, since the school is free and offers good advantages for an advanced education. The next boy of the family comes up in the same way, and the next likewise. At last all have received a good education, but neither can now find employment congenial to the inclinations which his education has developed. As for employment in a workshop or store, nobody who controls such establishments wants a high-school boy, except maybe now and then as a machine bookkeeper. The parents cannot afford to send the boy to a medical college, the offices of lawyers and others are overrun with their own kinfolk or the sons of intimate friends, so the young men become drones in the household. Thus the prosperity of families is destroyed by the necessity of supporting involuntary drones, and the drag is felt by society at large. It may be asked, "Why blame the school system, when the boy of fifteen, even sixteen, even if he 'stops school,' can find no employment?" The answer is that the school system itself has created this abnormal condition of society. As idleness begets poverty, poverty disenables people from buying, and the fields of employment are contracted. The leaven of idleness is in the school system. The acquisition of book learning is, in itself, beneficial; but the opportunity offered—the temptation, it may be called—to acquire book learning which ministers only to an ambition that must necessarily be disappointed in ninety-nine cases out of a hundred at the expense of the only time accorded to youth for learning to make their hands useful in producing something which ministers to the necessities of life, is manifestly destructive of prosperity and happiness.

Look at the subject from another point of view. It is an axiom of those principles of political economy which are professed by all enlightened nations that taxation, however cunningly devised, is ultimately paid by the laboring classes. The real estate owners and the owners of taxable personal property are, after all, nothing but "middle-men" in the taxation business. The laboring classes are the real sufferers for the extravagant expenditures in the name of free education, which would otherwise seek investment in organized industries, that would afford their children employment and make their households happy. It is the laboring classes who ultimately pay the bills that enable the schoolbook rings to ring changes upon textbooks used in public schools. It is the laboring classes who ultimately pay for teaching music and foreign languages to the thousands of people who afterward become drones on society. The only republican idea in public education is to teach people enough to take care of themselves and to keep out of jail; but the cunning of those whose aim is to live without work has dazzled the bone and sinew of the country into the support of a system of public education which gives them double toll in supporting their own children as drones.

No observer can dispute the correctness of these propositions and conclusions. Discussion of the subject has become so general that there can be no doubt of the tendency of the public mind toward final comprehension of it. The conclusion is this: Give every child a good common school English education at public expense, and then stop. There have been two presidents of the United States who received less aid than this in their school education; if any want more, let those who dance pay the fiddler. This is the cure for drones. It is the way, too, to make the public schools a public blessing, instead of allowing them to develop into nurseries of imbecility and idleness.

Suggested Further Reading

Nash, Lee M. "Scott of the *Oregonian*: The Editor as Historian." *Oregon Historical Quarterly* 70 (1969): 197-232.

Scott, Harvey W. *History of the Oregon Country*. Leslie M. Scott, compiler. Cambridge: The Riverside Press, 1924.

Dorothy O. Johansen
1904-

Oregonians often speculate about what differentiates them from citizens of other states. Dorothy O. Johansen, one of Oregon's most distinguished historians, examines the state's distinctiveness from the perspective of the past in this selection from *Empire of the Columbia* (1967).

Johansen was born in Oregon, and holds degrees from Reed College and the University of Washington. Co-author with Charles M. Gates of *Empire of the Columbia*, she has also edited two volumes, and written many scholarly articles and reviews. Currently working on a history of Reed College, where she taught history and humanities from 1939 to 1969, Johansen received the C.E.S. Wood Retrospective Award of the Oregon Institute for Literary Arts in 1988 for lifetime accomplishment in letters.

The Oregon Magnet

Whether the country was the New Eden, to be occupied because it was part of the United States' natural dominion, or because it was, remotely to be sure, "the hither edge of the frontier," it appealed to some people. Missionaries and emigrants already in Oregon, finding the country good, urged families and friends to join them. Their letters were published in Midwest weekly newspapers and quoted far and wide. "I was as much opposed to coming as anyone could be," wrote one young woman after her arrival in 1846, "if I were back there and knew what I know now I should be perfectly willing to come. . . . It is an easy place to make a living."

Oregon may have invited some people because it was the gateway to the Orient; or because it was an easy place to make a living, to get free land, or to achieve freedom; but other places in one way or another also held out promises. Given alternative choices, why did a handful of people choose Oregon? It is possible that what was said about Oregon was heard only by those whose expectations could be satisfied nowhere else. Hence, what was said about Oregon was immensely important in determining who went to Oregon.

Asked in later years why they chose Oregon, men gave the answers expected of them: to save the souls of the Indians, to save Oregon from the British, to escape slave competition. But sometimes their anecdotes revealed more about their motivations than their studied answers. Oldtimers told how in gold-rush days, immigrants arriving at Pacific Springs had to choose between the road to California, marked by a heap of glittering quartz, and the northwesterly road indicated by a sign bearing the words "To Oregon." Those who could read went to Oregon. Private letters and diaries reveal motivations. Young Charles Putnam wrote home from Fort Hall that he would go to Oregon because "the Aristocracy or respectable portion" of the companies in his train would go there. A wife, having arrived with her husband in time to qualify for land in her own right, was disappointed when her husband decided to work in a town. "Now," she wrote in her diary, "I shall be dependent upon a man for the rest of my life." Thus we suggest that in this matter of determining why people chose Oregon, we add another category of possible explanations under the rubric "values."

Although in many respects emigrants to Oregon resembled those who chose other destinations, we assume characteristics that made them more responsive to Oregon's promises than to those of Texas, California, or Kansas. We suggest that settlers in Oregon found that it met their expectations and they reported it in terms—sometimes value terms—that appealed to persons like themselves. In effect, they chose their own successors. This process, repeated over the decades, built a community which, though not entirely homogeneous, was distinguished from developing communities elsewhere, just as those communities were distinguished from one another.

Suggested Further Reading

Johansen, Dorothy O., with Charles M. Gates. *Empire of the Columbia: A History of the Pacific Northwest.* 2nd edition. New York: Harper & Row, 1967.

———. *Robert Newell's Memoranda.* Portland: Champoeg Press, 1959.

Kim R. Stafford
1949-

Kim R. Stafford was born in Oregon and grew up in
Oregon, Iowa, Indiana, California, and Alaska,
following his parents as they taught and traveled
through the West. He has taught at Lewis and Clark
College since 1979, where he directs the Northwest
Writing Institute and the Oregon Folk Arts Program.
He has received creative writing fellowships from the
National Endowment for the Arts, and his book *Having
Everything Right* (1986), from which the selection
below is taken, won a Western States Book Awards
Citation for Excellence in 1986. His poems, stories,
essays, and reviews have appeared in the *Atlantic
Monthly,* the *New York Times Book Review, Hudson
Review, Virginia Quarterly Review, American West,
Oregon English Journal,* and other periodicals.

Camp Polk, about three miles northeast of Sisters,
Oregon, was created as a base for volunteer soldiers at
the time of an Indian war in eastern Oregon. It was
named by its commander for his home, Polk County, in
western Oregon. The post was in service only
throughout the winter of 1865-66.

December Meditation at Camp Polk Cemetery

You have to listen real hard to hear anything at all: a little snow ticking down through juniper trees; the click of the chain around a family plot flexing in the cold. Wind. You hear it quite a while before it arrives. Then the eastern half of your face might just as well be stone.

Ten years ago I was here to do a formal study of the cemetery layout. As part of my folkloristic fieldwork, I made a systematic ramble of thirteen central Oregon cemeteries, stepping respectfully in the August dust of memorial plots at Grizzly, Antelope, Ashwood, Grandview, Madras, Hay Creek, Bakeoven, Warm Springs, Simnasho, Camp Polk, and three without names. I wanted to know how the adjacent communities of the living marked, surveyed, and maintained these trim little cities of stone and sage. I wanted to know how many gravemarkers listed family relations, military rank, professions, hobbies, wise proverbs, and the verse of grief or hope. I wanted to know how these stretches of sacred ground were isolated from the cattle range surrounding them: wood fence, iron gate, barbed wire, poplar square. On the main street of how many towns would there be a sign for the "Cemetery: 2 miles"? How many plots would be simple local secrets tucked away up a side canyon?

I wanted to seek and listen, to map and ponder the visible artifacts of religious belief my people hold. I did all that. The study is in the archive. The memory works on me.

But now it's dusk at Camp Polk, and I'm visiting old friends.

Here's Ray, by the champion juniper gnarl he loved to paint. His name in my mouth brings up a riff of banjo jangle I heard him play. There's a snow-swirl dancer over his place now.

I remember my discovery ten years ago, that graves everywhere planted heads to the west. This marks the Christian readiness to rise up facing Christ as He will bloom from the east on Judgment Day. And I remember how many of the thirteen cemeteries marked the end of a dead-end road: the Ashwood plot up a dirt track with no sign. The Grizzly cemetery at the ripe heart of a wheatfield with no road at all, forgotten like the town of Grizzly itself, which some prosperous corporation bought. I drove around and around that field, knowing I was close, my map fluttering from my hand in the heat, until finally I squinted my eyes past the shimmering wheat and saw the cemetery fence out there in the middle of everything.

236 Kim R. Stafford

Somewhere near the cemetery here at Camp Polk, a hundred odd years ago, the U. S. Army buried a cannon before fleeing from the Indians. Treasure hunters have sought it, as if it were a memory they owned by rights, as if that brass body might be raised up and carried away. You have to brave a series of "No Trespassing" signs to get to Camp Polk. Ten years ago there was a sign to invite visitors on toward the cemetery on its little hill beyond the most handsome of falling barns. This evening, there is no sign. You have to know.

Driving into Shaniko, on my cemetery route in 1975, I remember slowing the car to ask directions of an old-timer crumpled easily beside a shed, whittling steadily at a stub of wood. I didn't realize until too late the impertinence of my opening question:

"Excuse me, sir, could you direct me to the cemetery?"

There was a tremendous pause, as he turned slowly up from his work to unroll a vacant smile. No answer was on the way. I thanked him, and drove on to the Eat Cafe. This time, I tried to be a bit more discreet, making my request in hushed tones to the waitress as she came rollicking across the room with half a dozen steaming plates along her arms.

"Excuse me, I'm trying to find the cemetery—for research."

She lurched expertly to a stop without jostling a plate, and shouted to the long table of white-haired ladies at the far end of the room,

"Hey girls, we got a cemetery?" They vaguely shook their heads.

"Mister," she said, "we ain't got one. Try Antelope."

I explained that I had already been there, and learned what I could.

"Well," she said, "then I don't think we can help you. We don't figure to do much dying in *this* town."

If you lie on your back to watch the snow come down, you will hear little rustlings in the grass, and you seem to see a long way up into the sky. You can try to be as still as everyone else, as hopeful and content.

I remember the gravestone at Agency Plains, the one with the sheriff's badge carved deep into the marble beside one name. Neighbors told me later he had never been sheriff, but that was his life-long wish. Deputy, yes. Sheriff, never. Until then.

Religion in the desert has a lot to do with patience, and patience has a lot to to with silence. Beyond my feet where I lie at Camp Polk, there is a stone with an infant's oval ceramic photograph fixed to the pedestal. Someone sometime has used it for target practice, and the gray print of the bullet shies away low and to the left. There are so many children, and they are all so silent they are a chorus. The desert is big enough to hold it.

At Ashwood in that ten years back I heard a wind coming. All was still where I crouched, but I heard that wind. Hot. There was a permanence to every stone crumb and weed-stalk in the little enclosure of wire where I stood up. About a quarter mile away, a single tree was moving. The others were inert. I folded my map and put it away. Then the little whirlwind moved down the hill into another tree and left the first tree alone. There was a weight to the afternoon. Then all the trees were still and the wind was a slender spiral of dust coming down toward me.

Even under the snow I can see the varieties of hope at Camp Polk: the ring of stone, the chain perimeter, the lichen-shredded picket fence, concrete moat, rusted cast-iron rail around a rich man's land. In the sweep of open desert ground, the grave plot is a pouch, a box, a small fenced span of certainty. That's all. That's enough. It's nearly dark.

As I rise up, fervent and happy for every movement I make, snow shakes off my coat into my body's print on the ground. There is one thing still I must do. One of Camp Polk's oldest stones has fallen from its pedestal. Carved on the stone are the twin gates of heaven thrust wide. An orange swathe of lichen has covered the spirit's name. I can see only a submerged swirl of graceful lettering where the stone-cutter engraved a name, a year, a lamb, and a verse.

I bend to lift the stone back into place, but it is frozen to the earth. I try to kick it loose, but my toes are numb. Then I see the initials. Chipped ruggedly at the base of the stone, never intended to be seen once it had been fit forever to the pedestal, are the stonecutter's secret letters "J.A.W.O.S." What for immortality? Public proclamations are prey to time. Only the secrets survive.

Was it at Grizzly? Was it at Hay Creek: the nameless stone sunk almost gone into the earth, with its moss-word "Mother"? Or was that Warm Springs, among the gifts of favorite things, the scattered trinkets love makes us give back to a place where we believe?

Good night, Ray. Bit windy, wouldn't you say? One thing about snow, though. It don't ever last.

Suggested Further Reading

Stafford, Kim (with Gary Braasch). *Entering the Grove.* Layton, UT: Gibbs Smith Publisher, 1990.
———. *Having Everything Right: Essays of Place.* Lewiston, ID: Confluence Press, 1986.
———. *Lochsa Road: A Pilgrim in the West.* Lewiston, ID: Confluence Press, 1991.

SECTION VI
Oregon and the World

Chinook Indians

This eighteenth-century legend tells of the first meeting
of a powerful Native-American group with white
people. Although the details of the encounter are
vague, the Indians of the northern Oregon coast were
visited by American, British, and Spanish vessels in the
eighteenth century. The account that follows
foreshadows the relationship between the Indian and
white cultures which was fraught with possibilities for
good and ill. Chinook-speaking peoples comprised
many tribes living north and south of the Columbia
River mouth; along both banks of the Columbia to
Celilo; and in the lower Willamette River Valley. They
were great traders, economically advanced, and
possessed a complex social hierarchy. This legend first
was published in *Chinook Texts* (1894), and was
reprinted with editorial comments by Jarold Ramsey in
Coyote Was Going There (1977).

The First European Ship Comes to Clatsop County

The son of an old woman had died. She wailed for him for a whole year and then she stopped. Now one day she went to Seaside. There she used to stop, and she returned. She returned walking along the beach. She nearly reached Clatsop; now she saw something. She thought it was a whale.

When she came near it she saw two spruce trees standing upright on it. She thought, "Behold! it is no whale. It is a monster!" She reached the thing that lay there. Now she saw that its outer side was all covered with copper. Ropes were tied to those spruce trees, and it was full of iron. Then a bear came out of it. He stood on the thing that lay there. He looked just like a bear, but his face was that of a human being. Then she went home. She thought of her son, and cried, saying, "Oh my son is dead and the thing about which we have heard in tales is on shore!"

When she (had) nearly reached the town she continued to cry. (The people said), "Oh, a person comes crying. Perhaps somebody struck her." The people made themselves ready. They took their arrows. An old man said, "Listen!" Then the old woman said again and again, "Oh, my son is dead, and the thing about which we have heard in tales is on shore!" The people said, "What can it be?" They went running to meet her. They said, "What is it?"—"Ah, something lies there and it is thus. There are two bears on it, or maybe they are people."

Then the people ran. They reached the thing that lay there. Now the bears, or whatever they might be, held two copper kettles in their hands. The people were arriving. Now the two persons took their hands to their mouths and gave the people their kettles. They had lids. The men pointed inland and asked for water. Then [the] two people ran inland. They hid themselves behind a log. They returned again and ran down to the beach.

One man [of the people from the town] climbed up and entered the thing. He went down into the ship. He looked about in the interior; it was full of boxes. He found brass buttons in strings half a fathom long. He went out again to call his relatives, but they had already set fire to the ship. He jumped down. Those two persons had also gone down.

It burned just like fat. Then the Clatsop gathered the iron, the copper, and the brass. Then all the people learned about it. The two persons were taken to the chief of the Clatsop. Then the chief of the one town said, "I want to keep one of those men with me!" The people almost began to fight. Now one of them [sailors] was returned to one town, and the chief there was satisfied. Now the Quinault, the Chehalis, and the Willapa came. The people of all the towns came there. The Cascades, the Cowlitz, and the Klickitat came down the river. All those of the upper part of the river came down to Clatsop. The Quinault, the Chehalis, and the Willapa went. The people of all the towns went there. The Cascades, the Cowlitz, and the Klickitat came down river. . . .

Strips of copper two fingers wide and going around the arm were exchanged for one slave each. A piece of iron as long as one-half the forearm was exchanged for one slave. A piece of brass two fingers wide was exchanged for one slave. A nail was sold for a good curried deerskin. Several nails were given for long dentalia. They bought all this and the Clatsop became rich. Then iron and brass were seen for the first time. Now they kept those two persons. One was kept by each [Clatsop] chief, one was at the Clatsop town at the cape.

Suggested Further Reading

Boas, Franz, editor. *Chinook Texts.* U.S. Bureau of Ethnology Bulletin no. 20, 1894.

Ramsey, Jarold, comp. and ed. *Coyote Was Going There: Indian Literature of the Oregon Country.* Seattle and London: University of Washington Press, 1977.

Ruby, Robert H., and John A. Brown. *The Chinook Indians: Traders of the Lower Columbia River.* Norman: University of Oklahoma Press, 1976.

Frances Fuller Victor
1828-1902

Oregon's first distinguished author was Frances Fuller Victor. Born in New York, she came to San Francisco in 1863 with her husband, who was an engineer. The Victors came to Oregon in 1864. After her husband's death, Victor wrote for a living, a task that she performed well in a variety of genres: biography, poetry, history, travel accounts, and newspaper and magazine articles on numerous subjects. Her historical writings are characterized by clarity, diligent research, and objectivity. She wrote four volumes (and parts of four others) in Hubert Howe Bancroft's *History of the Pacific Coast*. Victor also committed herself to the political causes of the legal equality of women and of woman suffrage.

The account below, taken from *The River of the West* (1870), her biography of the famous Oregon mountain man, settler, and politician, Joe Meek, describes Meek's journey to Washington, D.C., to attempt to persuade President James Knox Polk to work for the creation of a territorial government in Oregon.

A Frontiersman Visits the President

While Meek was stopping at Independence, he was recognized by a sister, whom he had not seen for nineteen years; who, marrying and emigrating from Virginia, had settled on the frontier of Missouri. But he gave himself no time for family reunion and gossip. A steamboat that had been frozen up in the ice all winter, was just about starting for St. Louis and on board of this he went, with an introduction to the captain, which secured for him every privilege the boat afforded, together with the kindest attention of its officers.

When the steamer arrived in St. Louis, by one of those fortuitous circumstances so common in our hero's career, he was met at the landing by Campbell, a Rocky Mountain trader who had formerly belonged to the St. Louis Company. This meeting relieved him of any care about his night's entertainment in St. Louis, and it also had another effect—that of relieving him of any further care about the remainder of his journey; for, after hearing Meek's story of the position of affairs in Oregon and his errand to the United States, Campbell had given the same to the newspaper reporters, and Meek, like Byron, waked up next morning to find himself famous.

Having telegraphed to Washington, and received the President's order to come on, the previous evening, our hero wended his way to the levee the morning after his arrival in St. Louis. There were two steamers lying side by side, both up for Pittsburg, with runners for each, striving to outdo each other in securing passengers. A bright thought occurred to the moneyless envoy— he would earn his passage!

Walking on board one of the boats, which bore the name of *The Declaration*, himself a figure which attracted all eyes by his size and outlandish dress, he mounted to the hurricane deck and began to harrangue the crowd upon the levee, in the voice of a Stentor:

"This way, gentlemen, if you please. Come right on board *The Declaration*. I am the man from Oregon, with dispatches to the President of these United States, that you all read about in this morning's paper. Come on board, ladies and gentlemen, if you want to hear the news from Oregon. I've just come across the plains, two months from the Columbia River, where the Injuns are killing your missionaries. Those passengers who come aboard *The Declaration* shall hear all about it before they get to Pittsburg. Don't stop thar, looking at my old wolf-skin cap, but just come aboard, and hear what I've got to tell!"

The novelty of this sort of solicitation operated capitally. Many persons crowded on board *The Declaration* only to get a closer look at this picturesque personage who invited them, and many more because they were really interested to know the news from the far off young territory which had fallen into trouble. So it chanced that *The Declaration* was inconveniently crowded on this particular morning.

After the boat had got under way, the captain approached his roughest looking cabin passenger and inquired in a low tone of voice if he were really and truly the messenger from Oregon.

"Thar's what I've got to show for it," answered Meek, producing his papers.

"Well, all I have to say is, Mr. Meek, that you are the best runner this boat ever had; and you are welcome to your passage ticket, and anything you desire besides."

Finding that his bright thought had succeeded so well, Meek's spirit rose with the occasion, and the passengers had no reason to complain that he had not kept his word. Before he reached Wheeling his popularity was immense, notwithstanding the condition of his wardrobe. At Cincinnati he had time to present a letter to the celebrated Doctor, who gave him another, which proved to be an "open sesame" wherever he went thereafter.

On the morning of his arrival in Wheeling it happened that the stage which then carried passengers to Cumberland, where they took the train for Washington, had already departed. Elated by his previous good fortune our ragged hero resolved not to be delayed by so trivial a circumstance; but walking pompously into the stage office inquired, with an air which must have smacked strongly of the mock-heroic, if he "could have a stage for Cumberland?"

The nicely dressed, dignified elderly gentleman who managed the business of the office, regarded the man who proffered this modest request for a moment in motionless silence, then slowly raising the spectacles over his eyes to a position on his forehead, finished his survey with unassisted vision. Somewhat impressed by the manner in which Meek bore this scrutiny, he ended by demanding, "Who are you?"

Tickled by the absurdity of the tableau they were enacting, Meek straightened himself up to his six feet two, and replied with an air of superb self assurance—

"I am Envoy extraordinary and minister plenipotentiary from the Republic of Oregon to the Court of the United States!"

He was admitted to the Presidential mansion by a mulatto of about his own age, with whom he remembered playing when a lad, for it must be remembered that the Meeks and Polks were related, and this servant had grown up in the family. On inquiring if he could see the President, he was directed to the office of the private Secretary, Knox Walker, also a relative of Meek's on the mother's side.

On entering he found the room filled with gentlemen waiting to see the President, each when his turn to be admitted should arrive. The Secretary sat reading a paper, over the top of which he glanced but once at the newcomer, to ask him to be seated. But Meek was not in the humor for sitting. He had not traveled express for more than two months, in storm and cold, on foot and on horseback, by day and by night, with or without food, as it chanced, to sit down quietly now and wait. So he took a few turns up and down the room, and seeing that the Secretary glanced at him a little curiously, stopped and said:

"I should like to see the President immediately. Just tell him if you please that there is a gentleman from Oregon waiting to see him on very important business."

At the word *Oregon,* the Secretary sprang up, dashed his paper to the ground, and crying out "Uncle Joe!" came forward with both hands extended to greet his long lost relative.

"Take care, Knox! don't come too close," said Meek stepping back, "I'm ragged, dirty, and—lousy."

But Walker seized his cousin's hand, without seeming fear of the consequences, and for a few moments there was an animated exchange of questions and answers, which Meek at last interrupted to repeat his request to be admitted to the President without delay. Several times the Secretary turned to leave the room, but as often came back with some fresh inquiry, until Meek fairly refused to say another word, until he had delivered his dispatches.

When once the Secretary got away he soon returned with a request from the President for the appearance of the Oregon messenger, all other visitors being dismissed for that day. Polk's reception proved as cordial as Walker's had been. He seized the hand of his newly found relative, and welcomed him in his own name, as well as that of messenger from the distant, much loved, and long neglected Oregon. The interview lasted for a couple of hours. Oregon affairs and family affairs were talked over together; the President promising to do all for Oregon that he could do; at the same time he bade Meek make himself at home in the Presidential mansion, with true southern hospitality.

But Meek, although he had carried off his poverty and all his deficiencies in so brave a style hitherto, felt his assurance leaving him, when, his errand performed, he stood, in the presence of rank and elegance, a mere mountainman in ragged blankets, whose only wealth consisted of an order for five hundred dollars on the Methodist mission in New York, unavailable for present emergencies. And so he declined the hospitalities of the White House, saying he "could make himself at home in an Indian wigwam in Oregon, or among the Rocky Mountains, but in the residence of the chief magistrate of a great nation, he felt out of place, and ill at ease."

Polk, however, would listen to no refusal, and still further abashed his Oregon cousin by sending for Mrs. Polk and Mrs. Walker, to make his acquaintance. Says Meek:

"When I heard the silks rustling in the passage, I felt more frightened than if a hundred Blackfeet had whooped in my ear. A mist came over my eyes, and when Mrs. Polk spoke to me I couldn't think of anything to say in return."

But the ladies were so kind and courteous that he soon began to see a little, though not quite plainly while their visit lasted. Before the interview with the President and his family was ended, the poverty of the Oregon envoy became known, which led to the immediate supplying of all his wants. Major Polk was called in and introduced; and to him was deputed the business of seeing Meek "got up" in a style creditable to himself and his relations. Meek avers that when he had gone through the hands of the barber and tailor, and surveyed himself in a full-length mirror, he was at first rather embarrassed, being under the impression that he was being introduced to a fashionable and decidedly good-looking gentleman, before whose over-powering style he was disposed to shrink, with the old familiar feeling of being in blankets.

But Meek was not the sort of man to be long in getting used to a situation however novel or difficult. In a very short time he was *au fait* in the customs of the capital. His perfect frankness led people to laugh at his errors as eccentricities; his good looks and natural *bonhomie* procured him plenty of admirers; while his position at the White House caused him to be envied and lionized at once.

Suggested Further Reading

Bancroft, Hubert Howe. *History of Oregon, 1834-1848. The Works of Hubert Howe Bancroft.* Volume 29. San Francisco: The History Company, 1886.

———. *History of Oregon, 1848-1888. The Works of Hubert Howe Bancroft.* Volume 30. San Francisco: The History Company, 1888.

Martin, Jim. *A Bit of Blue: The Life and Works of Frances Fuller Victor.* Salem: Deep Well Publishing Co., 1992.

Victor, Frances Fuller. *The Early Indian Wars of Oregon.* Salem: F. C. Baker, 1894.

———. *The River of the West.* San Francisco: R. J. Trumbull & Co., 1870.

Ronald G. Callvert
1873-1955

Militarism and totalitarianism were on the march in the fall of 1938. Mussolini's Italy had conquered Ethiopia. Francisco Franco, the fascist, was on the eve of victory in the Spanish Civil War. In 1937 Japan had invaded China, and a year later Adolph Hitler annexed Austria. Most Americans in those ominous days rejoiced that war still seemed far from our shores and that the United States was not threatened by internal enemies.

The following editorial, which appeared in the (Portland) *Oregonian* on 2 October 1938, captured this mood of complacency and pride. This opinion piece, in conjunction with the balance of his editorial work during 1938, won the Pulitzer Prize for its author, Ronald G. Callvert. Callvert was born in Iowa in 1873. After working on other newspapers, he joined the staff of the *Oregonian* in 1909, and rose from reporter to become associate editor at the time of his retirement in 1951.

"My Country 'Tis of Thee . . ."

I
n this land of ours, this America, the man we choose as leader dons at no time uniform or insignia to denote his constitutional position as commander-in-chief of armed forces. No member of his cabinet, no civil subordinate, ever attires himself in garments significant of military power.

In this land of ours, this America, the average citizen sees so little of the army that he has not learned to distinguish between a major and a lieutenant from his shoulder straps. When the chief executive addresses his fellow countrymen they gather about him within handclasp distance. Goose-stepping regiments are not paraded before him. When he speaks to the civilian population, it is not over rank upon rank of helmeted heads.

In this land of ours, this America, there is no tramp of military boots to entertain the visiting statesman. There is no effort to affright him with display of mobile cannon or of facility for mass production of aerial bombers.

In this land of ours, this America, there is no fortification along the several thousand miles of the northern border. In the great fresh water seas that partly separate it from another dominion no naval craft plies the waters. Along its southern border there are no forts, no show of martial strength.

In this land of ours, this America, no youth is conscripted to labor on devices of defense; military training he may take or leave at option. There is no armed force consistent with a policy of aggression. The navy is built against no menace from the western hemisphere, but wholly for defense against that which may threaten from Europe or Asia.

In this land of ours, this America, one-third of the population is foreign born, or native born of foreign or mixed parentage. Our more numerous "minorities" come from fourteen nations. The native born, whatever his descent, has all political and other rights possessed by him who traces his ancestry to the founding fathers. The foreign born of races that are assimilable are admitted to all these privileges if they want them. We have "minorities" but no minority problem.

In this land of ours, this America, the common citizen may criticize without restraint the policies of government or the aims of the chief executive. He may vote as his judgment or his conscience advises and not as a ruler dictates.

In this land of ours, this America, our songs are dedicated to love and romance, the blue of the night, sails in the sunset, and not to might or to a martyrdom to political cause. Our national anthem has martial words; difficult air. But if you want to hear the organ roll give the people its companion—"America . . . of thee I sing." In lighter patriotism we are nationally cosmopolitan. Unitedly we sing of Dixie or of Ioway, where the tall corn grows, of springtime in the Rockies, or of California, here I come.

In this land of ours, this America, there is not a bomb-proof shelter, and a gas mask is a curiosity. It is not needed that we teach our children where to run when death-hawks darken our sky.

In this land of ours, this America, our troubles present or prospective come from within—come from our own mistakes, and injure us alone. Our pledges of peace toward our neighbors are stronger than ruler's promise of written treaty. We guarantee them by devoting our resources, greater than the resources of any other nations, to upbuilding the industries of peace. We strut no armed might that could be ours. We cause no nation in our half of the world to fear us. None does fear us, nor arm against us.

In this land of ours, this America, we have illuminated the true road to permanent peace. But that is not the sole moral sought herein to be drawn. Rather it is the blessings of liberty and equality and peace that have been herein recounted are possessed nowhere in the same measure in Europe or Asia and wane or disappear as one nears or enters a land of dictatorship of whatever brand. This liberty, this equality, this peace, are imbedded in the American form of government. We shall ever retain them if foreign isms that would dig them out and destroy them are barred from our shores. If you cherish this liberty, this equality, this peace that is peace material and peace spiritual—then defend with all your might the American ideal of government.

Suggested Further Reading

(Portland) *Oregonian*, 2 May 1939, pp. 1, 3. Biographical information about Callvert is contained in the *Oregonian* of 15 February 1955, p. 15.

Wayne L. Morse
1900-1974

One of Oregon's most famous political figures, Wayne L. Morse was born in Wisconsin and educated at the universities of Wisconsin and Minnesota, and Columbia University Law School. He came to Oregon in 1929 as professor of law at the University of Oregon. His courage, intelligence, and integrity first came to national attention when President Franklin Roosevelt appointed him to the War Labor Board in 1942. Morse was elected to the United States Senate in 1944 and 1950 as a Republican, became an independent in 1952, and then joined the Democratic Party in 1955. He was again elected to the Senate in 1956 and 1960. As a senator, Morse worked for civil rights, education, and labor legislation.

Although an internationalist in foreign affairs, and an opponent of Soviet expansionism, Morse was an early opponent of United States participation in the Vietnam War. He was one of two senators who spoke and voted against the Gulf of Tonkin Resolution, which authorized President Lyndon B. Johnson to escalate American participation in the war. A portion of that speech, delivered in the Senate on 5 August 1964 (and taken from the *Congressional Record* of that date), is given below.

Speech Against the Gulf of Tonkin Resolution

Mr. President, I rise to speak in opposition to the joint resolution. I do so with a very sad heart. But I consider the resolution, as I considered the resolution of 1955, known as the Formosa Resolution, and the subsequent resolution, known as the Middle East Resolution, to be naught but a resolution which embodies a predated declaration of war.

Article I, section 8, of our Constitution does not permit the President to make war at his discretion. Therefore I stand on this issue as I have stood before in the Senate, perfectly willing to take the judgment of history as to the merits of my cause. I note in passing that the warnings which the Senator from New York, Mr. Lehman, and the senior Senator from Oregon uttered in 1955 in opposition to the Formosa Resolution have been proved to be correct by history. I am satisfied that history will render a final verdict in opposition to the joint resolution introduced today.

The senior Senator from Oregon has no illusions as to the reactions which will be aroused in some quarters in this Republic. However, I make the speech because it represents the convictions of my conscience and because I consider it essential to make it in keeping the sworn trust that I undertook when I came into this body on four different occasions and was sworn in as a Senator from the State of Oregon, pledging myself to uphold the Constitution.

I have one other remark by way of preface, not contained in the manuscript. I yield to no other Senator, or to anyone else in this country in my opposition to communism and all that communism stands for.

In our time a great struggle, which may very well be a deathlock struggle, is going on in the world between freedom on the one hand and the totalitarianism of communism on the other.

However, I am satisfied that that struggle can never be settled by war. I am satisfied that if the hope of anyone is that the struggle between freedom and communism can be settled by war, and that course is followed, both freedom and communism will lose, for there will be no victory in that war.

Because of our own deep interest in the struggle against communism, we in the United States are inclined to overlook some of the other struggles which are occupying others. We try to force every issue into the context of freedom versus communism. That is one of our great mistakes in Asia. There is much communism there, and much totalitarianism in other forms. We say we are

253

opposing communism there, but that does not mean we are advancing freedom, because we are not.

Senators will note as I proceed in the presentation of my case in opposition to the resolution that I believe the only hope for the establishment of a permanent peace in the world is to practice our oft-repeated American professing that we believe in the substitution of the rule of law for the jungle law of military force as a means of settling disputes which threaten the peace of the world.

The difficulty with that professing or preaching by the United States is that the United States, like some Communist nations, does not practice it.

Hope for Peace Lies with Other Members of United Nations

The stark reality is that North and South Vietnam, China, and the United States are in this hour endangering the peace of the world. We have said we will make charges against North Vietnam before the United Nations Security Council.

Why in the world we did not make those charges against North Vietnam several years ago, I shall never understand. We are going to make charges now because we are in open conflict with North Vietnam. But we have had evidence for years that North Vietnam was undoubtedly a violator of the Geneva Accord of 1954. But instead of taking our charges and our proof to the United Nations, we sent 15,000 military personnel to South Vietnam to engage in unilateral military action in South Vietnam, in violation of three articles of the Geneva Accord that I have already cited in this speech, and have violated, time and time again, article after article of the United Nations Charter. That is our sorry record.

What about the infiltration of North Vietnamese into South Vietnam to advise the Vietcong?

What about the 21,000 American troops in South Vietnam advising the Government?

What about the American air attack on North Vietnam naval bases?

What about the shelling of the islands in Tonkin Bay by South Vietnamese vessels? These were all clear acts of war.

Why is not Ambassador Stevenson going to lay these incidents, too, before the Security Council?

The best hope for peace would seem to be that the noncombatant members of the United Nations will see to it that all of the provocative activities in the Indochina Peninsula are brought before the Security Council or the General Assembly of the United Nations, in accordance with the procedures of the

Charter. They should invoke all—I repeat—all applicable provisions of the United Nations Charter irrespective of which country initiates charges or must be called to account.

They should call upon South Vietnam, North Vietnam, Laos, Cambodia, China, and the United States to stop their fighting and proceed to the conference table, where there can be applied the rules of reason rather than the fortunes of war for the settlement of the conflict.

These U. N. members not involved in this conflict must face up to one of the great challenges in all history. If they do not, they will see the United Nations Charter consumed as a casualty in the war flames of the struggle. They must enforce the Charter against all who are fighting in Asia. That is the issue—the issue of peace or war—that is facing them as well as us.

I close by pleading that my country, and its people, not forsake the moral principles and values which cry out to be saved in this hour. I plead with them not to commit themselves to a unilateral war in Asia for purposes which many of their own political leaders were ill advised in the first place. There is still no answer to the Biblical injunction:

> He shall judge among many people and rebuke strong nations afar off; and they shall beat their swords into plowshares, and their spears into pruning hooks.

The United States has everything to gain and little to lose by seeking to implement that teaching at an international conference table.

The United States has much to lose and little to gain by continuing our unilateral military action in southeast Asia, unsanctioned by the United Nations and unaccompanied by allies.

No nation in history has had such a great opportunity as this one now has to strike a blow for peace at an international conference table.

I shall not support any substitute which takes the form of a predated declaration of war. In my judgment, that is what the pending joint resolution is.

I shall not support any delegation of the duty of Congress—of Congress, not the President—to determine an issue of war or peace.

I shall not support any substitute which takes the form of military action to expand the war or that encourages our puppets in Saigon to expand the war.

Adherence to the United Nations Charter is the only policy that affords the hope of leading the American people out of this jam without a war. I shall continue to plead for such a policy as long as time remains.

Suggested Further Reading

Abell, Ron. "On the Tiger's Anniversary: He Gave Politics a Good Name." *Oregon Magazine* (October 1980): 44-46.

Smith, A. Robert. *The Tiger in the Senate: The Biography of Wayne Morse.* Garden City, NY: Doubleday, 1962.

James DePreist
1936-

Oregon has long had its share of distinguished figures in the arts. Names such as Ursula Le Guin, Pietro Belluschi, and Manuel Izquierdo are recognized both in the United States and abroad. One of the most eminent of Oregon's cultural figures is James DePreist. DePreist was born in Philadelphia, where he took undergraduate and advanced degrees at the University of Pennsylvania. He studied at the Philadelphia Conservatory and won first prize in the Dimitri Mitropoulos International Conducting Competition in 1964. He has conducted many distinguished orchestras throughout the world, has written two books of poetry, and has been awarded eleven honorary doctoral degrees.

Since 1980 DePreist has been music director and conductor of the Oregon Symphony Orchestra. The selection below is his testimony on 19 March 1985 before the United States House of Representatives Appropriations Subcommittee on the Department of the Interior, in which he makes his case for appropriations for the National Endowment for the Arts. The speech appeared in *Symphony Magazine* (June-July 1985).

Missiles and Mozart

Two aspects of my personal history came rushing back to me this morning as I sat looking at those photographs behind you of the Lincoln Memorial under construction and listening to the testimony of Mr. Lou Harris.

I am familiar with the Lincoln Memorial and particularly the image of Marian Anderson singing before it in 1939, years before there was an NEA. Marian Anderson happens to be my aunt, an accident for which I unfortunately can take no credit, but seeing that photograph reminded me of how long my family has had a meaningful connection with the Department of the Interior.

Listening to Mr. Harris, I understood for the first time the relevance and beauty of the statistics courses I took while earning my bachelor of science degree in economics at the Wharton School. I found his testimony most persuasive in indicating that the data are there to support our cause. It seems to some of us in the arts that one way to avoid a cut in the NEA budget would be to have it attached as a rider to the defense bill. Equal amounts of cynicism, pragmatism, and idealism are at the heart of so bizarre-sounding a notion.

The arts, erroneously deemed by some as superfluous, and defense, considered by others sacrosanct, would appear to be the most antithetical of bedfellows. It is true that the former tends to be a tad more "user friendly" than the latter, but basically missiles and Mozart share a remarkable commonality: protection.

One can make a persuasive case for our national security requiring an adequate defense, but we are deluding ourselves if our concept of defense is limited to the restrictively narrow category of military armaments.

What provides our defense against insensitivity? What provides protection against dehumanization? The arts. And much more: essential protection for a civilized society that leaves both buildings and people intact while elevating the spirit.

By informing our lives with a beauty of artistic expression that ignites the senses, the arts reveal to us a universe as wondrous as our imaginations—at once subtle, splendid, spectacular. The arts are society's most eloquent defense against becoming immune to the beautiful.

The arts celebrate human creativity and thus the human spirit. The unique vision and insight of the artist expose and magnify the spectrum of life on this planet by lifting us out of this world. Yet, miraculously, from the perspective of the audience, for all of us, the stage becomes a mirror of our better selves.

   The arts experience is an active participatory experience with listeners who actually hear and viewers who do indeed see—audiences aware and eager to comprehend a message that technology cannot teach—the concrete, very real power of the intangible.

   A government of the people should be a representative extension of the national will, ensuring the highest quality of life for its citizens. And that quality of life is, in reality, the ultimate yardstick by which we measure a civilized society. The arts are not the frosting on that cake. They constitute the core of what we're about as people, and they help define us as a nation to others and to ourselves. The arts serve the people, and we, the people—artists and audience alike—urge your support.

Suggested Further Reading

DePreist, James. *This Precipice Garden*. Portland: University of Portland Press, 1987.

David Johnson
1945-

World War II caught up many American citizens whose religious or philosophical convictions would not permit them to fight in it. Among these conscientious objectors were men interned at Camp Waldport on the Pacific Ocean in southwestern Oregon. Some of these internees used the years of destruction for works of creativity, works that not only pleased themselves during the war, but contributed to an American literary and artistic renaissance after its conclusion.

In the following essay, which first appeared in *What's Happening* (23 August 1990), David Johnson assesses that contribution. Johnson was born and raised in Eugene. He has worked as a journalist for several newspapers, published numerous free-lance articles, designed and produced literary magazines, and written books of natural history and poetry.

The Shadow of Camp Waldport

"These are the years of destruction; we offer against them the creative act."
—The Untide Press
Camp Angel, Waldport, Oregon

During World War II, men conscientiously opposed to participating in the war effort were interned in camps throughout the country, where they performed work of "national importance" under civilian supervision.

Of the three internment sites in Oregon—Cascade Locks, Elkton, and Waldport—the last location played a unique role in our cultural history as the conscientious objector program's "fine arts camp." At Waldport's Camp Angel, poets, writers, artists, actors, and musicians who also were conscientious objectors printed books of poetry, edited literary magazines, staged plays and produced concerts in a burst of collaborative energy that contributed significantly to the San Francisco Renaissance of the '50s and '60s.

Until now, those creative times on the Oregon Coast were an obscure footnote to a turbulent era.

On September 16, 1940, Congress approved the Selective Training and Service Act establishing the first peacetime military conscription program. Based primarily on the poor treatment of COs during World War I, the legislators decided that "no individual who by reason of religious training and belief is conscientiously opposed to participating in the war in any form, would be subject to military service."

The program, referred to as Civilian Public Service, was administered for the Selective Service by the Mennonites, Church of the Brethren, and the Society of Friends or Quakers. These "historic peace churches" provided camp supervisors, funds, and support services, and the U. S. Government added additional funding and in most cases the use of Civilian Conservation Corps camps left over from the '30s.

CPS activities included serving as orderlies in mental hospitals, guinea pigs at university medical schools, and firefighters, road-builders and treeplanters in rural locations. To give the interns the same level of hardship as military draftees, they were assigned to camps at least 200 miles from their homes.

Camp 56, also known as Camp Angel and Camp Waldport, was established in October 1942 as a base for general forest service work. The main task of

COs at Camp Angel was the reforestation and repair of the Blodgett Burn, a spruce forest harvested during World War I for lumber used to make plane fuselages. The loggers were soldiers, who weren't required to burn the slash left over after their cuts. The resultant wild fires that rampaged through these woods left a wasteland of snags and fallen logs. It was the task of the CO "campers" to clean up the mess.

During the day, the men risked their necks in highly dangerous work for which they were ill-equipped and undertrained. According to [poet and printer William] Everson, four of their number died from accidents in the woods during the three-year history of Camp Waldport.

In the evenings and on weekends, the campers were allowed to pursue their own creative interests. Not all the interns were writers and artists—a few were fundamentalist farm boys from the Midwest—but many were what was then known as "free thinkers." The government didn't object to their fine arts activities, but they didn't shell out any bucks either. As James Fox [Rare Books Librarian, Knight Library, University of Oregon] wryly points out, there wasn't a National Endowment for the Arts at the time.

On the other hand, there didn't seem to be any censorship from the feds or the peace churches, with the exception of the Spring 1943 issue of *The Illiterati,* an irreverent literary magazine first published at Cascade Locks and later at Camp Waldport. Copies of the issue, which contained some nude cartoons harmless by today's standards, were confiscated and destroyed by the Cascade Locks Post Office as unfit to go through the mails.

As well as *The Illiterati,* the COs cranked out a bounty of mimeographed publications both official and unofficial. Cascade Locks published *The Columbian* and *The Compass,* Elkton and its satellite camps produced *Taproot, Scrivener, Potpourri, Elkton Newsletter, Big Creek Reporter,* and *The Rebel Clarion;* and Waldport printed *The Tide.* Everson cheerfully recounted that the latter, a sedate, conventional newsletter, had an "evil twin" called *The Untide,* also produced on the camp mimeograph machine, but printed after hours by underground journalists who remained nominally anonymous. Their motto was "What is not Tide is Untide."

Ironically, *The Untide* became famous among COs, completely overshadowing *The Tide.* According to Everson, the notoriety of the underground sheet contributed significantly to Waldport's reputation as the fine arts camp.

As an adjunct to the newsletter, Everson and other printer/poets started the Untide Press, which published books of poetry as well as posters for camp theater projects. In retrospect, this modest publishing effort was a precursor of the West Coast literary revolution that culminated in the Beat Movement.

Along with Everson, contributing campers were: Adrian Wilson, author of *The Design of Books,* one of the most influential texts on book design published in this century; Kemper Nomland, who went on to become a prominent Los Angeles architect; Kermit Sheets, founder of Interplayers, a well-known San Francisco theater group; and Glenn Coffield, poet and arguably the first hippy.

A photo of Coffield presents the startling image of a white Rastafarian with long, tangled locks, a full beard and intense eyes. Originally a Missouri school-teacher, Coffield was the activities coordinator at Camp Waldport. His book of poems, *The Horned Moon,* was handprinted on the camp's 5x8" Kelsey press. After the war, Coffield started the Grundtvig Folk School, "a Humanist school in the woods," on the Columbia Gorge near Eagle Creek.

The most well-known CO on the West Coast, Oregon's "Poet Laureate" William Stafford, was interned at the Santa Barbara, California, camp but did contribute poems to Untide Press publications.

Other contributors to Waldport fine arts projects were: Kenneth Patchen, a poet and novelist whose book of poetry, *An Astonished Eye Looks Out of the Air,* was published by the press; Henry Miller, who contributed "The Soul of Anaesthesia," a portion of his *Air Conditioned Nightmare;* prominent poets Kenneth Rexroth and Kenneth O. Hanson; and Oregon painter Morris Graves, who spent six weeks at the camp.

The most significant participant, however, was Everson himself, a Californian born in 1912, who attended the University of California at Fresno. During his stay at Waldport, Everson published four volumes of verse, including the influential *X War Elegies.* After the war, he entered the Dominican Order as a lay brother, changing his name to Brother Antoninus. During that time he was awarded a Guggenheim (1949) and published *The Crooked Lines of God,* a stunning collection of spiritual poetry. In the '60s and '70s, Everson combined his interests in fine printing and poetry as a teacher at UC Santa Cruz.

Rexroth paid tribute to Everson's literary legacy in a 1957 issue of *Evergreen Review,* a literary magazine based in San Francisco. He wrote that "during the war he (Everson) was instrumental in starting an arts program, out of which have come many still-active people, projects, and forces which help give SF culture its intensely libertarian character."

Everson corroborates the notion that he and the other Waldport campers helped to foment the San Francisco Movement. Interviewer Guido Palandri asked him, "Is it legitimate to consider the Waldport Fine Arts Group as a forerunner of the Bay Area poets and the Beat Generation?"

Everson answered, "It was. Definitely. That whole SF Renaissance had in some way a powerful inception in Waldport."

University of Oregon English teacher Paul Dresman confirms that the writings of COs during World War II greatly influenced the work of Robert Duncan, Jack Spicer, and many of the other Beat poets. Also, he suggests that there is a direct lineage between the public pacifism of the war-era COs and the origin of Pacifica Radio and today's National Public Radio.

So that's a brief history of a short moment in time when a bunch of young guys who fiercely believed in the sanctity of life planted trees during the day and radical thought at night. Little did they know that their anarchistic collaboration would impact our culture by sowing the seeds of a philosophical/spiritual/cultural tradition still going strong in the coffeehouses, classrooms, and lofts of a new generation.

Suggested Further Reading

Johnson, David. *The Tufted Puffins.* Bandon, OR: Bandon Historical Society, 1979.

William A. Hilliard
1927-

Martin Luther King, Jr. (1929-68) was one of the most influential Americans of the twentieth century. His name and achievements were known to millions around the world. One of those whose life he changed was William A. Hilliard, the editor of the (Portland) *Oregonian*. Born in Chicago, Hilliard graduated from Pacific University, and joined the *Oregonian* as a copy aide in 1952. He rose to become editor of the largest newspaper in the Pacific Northwest in 1986. Hilliard has served six times as a Pulitzer Prize juror, and was chosen president of the American Society of Newspaper Editors in 1993. His assessment of the significance of Martin Luther King's life originally appeared in the *Oregonian* on 19 January 1992.

King Pierced the Armor

When I was a youngster living in Southeast Portland, I had a dream. I dreamed that one day I would become a newspaper reporter and then an editor.

Of course, it was just a dream because the only people I saw working for newspapers were white.

Blacks were different. Most black women worked as domestics in the homes of white women. Most black men were janitors, waiters, Pullman car porters, redcaps, boot-blacks, handymen or chauffeurs for white folks.

There were no role models of color to inspire me to become anything other than a menial laborer. Black men could not be firemen, policemen, bus or streetcar operators, clerks in grocery or department stores, postmen, school-teachers or elected officials.

I lived in a white world that gave me little reason to believe that I could use my talents to pursue a career of my choice.

It was a world dominated by white males, a world with a white-male network—father to son, friend to friend—that made it possible for white men to move into areas of responsibility and decision-making.

For instance, most whites take for granted membership in social and athletic clubs—both public and private. The only barrier is economics. Race never has been a factor in membership qualifications.

Race has not been an obstacle for them to gain acceptance or a goal in life, nor has race robbed them of their dignity or self-respect.

But to blacks in America, race is a constant factor in their lives.

Growing up in a racially discriminatory environment forced me to look at the world differently than my white schoolmates, but it also stiffened my resolve to achieve in spite of the racial barriers.

The only work I could find in high school was busing dishes in hotel restaurants downtown.

I worked my way through college as a dining car waiter on the Union Pacific's City of Portland between here and Chicago and as a redcap at Union Station, carrying luggage.

I began work on the *Oregonian* in 1952 as a copyboy, and at the time never dreamed that I would become an editor. Nor did I dream I would live to see blacks as sheriff of Multnomah County, director of the Oregon Symphony

Orchestra, superintendent of the Portland Public Schools or as elected officials in city and state government.

All of these advances happened because of Dr. Martin Luther King Jr. American society was irretrievably changed by Dr. Martin Luther King Jr.

It was King who pierced the armor that protected the conscience of white America. He called on Americans to practice equality on the job, in the streets, in public places of accommodation, in the home and in their social life. He wanted white Americans especially to speak out when racially discriminatory voices were heard.

Few whites have thought of what it means to be black and to be asked to identify with an American hero who is black. That is one of the important aspects of the King holiday.

By making King's birthday anniversary a state and national holiday to be observed by all Americans, we make King a national hero, and it is just as important for white youngsters to see and recognize a hero who is black as it is for a black youngster to identify with that hero. Then all of them will see King as a hero who believed in all this country stands for.

Despite the advances we have made, we still live in a racially divided society. It is important that blacks and other minorities believe that they can achieve the goals they set for themselves as youngsters. And role models can certainly help shape the young minds.

I did not have black role models when I was young. Star black athletes in professional basketball, football and baseball were not around yet.

I remain frustrated with what so many Americans take for granted and what they see as a "color blind" society. And, too, I am frustrated by the insensitivity of so many of those who have benefited from a white-male-dominated network. It is among this latter group that I find those with no understanding of the psychological damage caused by a history of racial discrimination and separation in this country.

And I am frightened by—but not afraid of—the rise of racial hatred in America again, because it threatens democracy and my belief in a multicultural society.

America is a beautiful country because of its diversity, but it can become more beautiful for all of us if we take advantage of that diversity. No other country in the world gives to its people the opportunity to achieve that this country does. What we need desperately is a discipline to preserve it.

The events in my life—the personal achievements, the professional successes, the disappointments and the frustrations—have taught me to cherish and protect freedom. They also have taught me to see all Americans as human beings and to be fair in my judgment of them.

I could identify with King because I saw in him a fierce belief of basic human rights for all Americans. King, who was committed to an integrated America, practiced what he preached.

You don't have to give up your racial, ethnic, or cultural heritage to be a part of a multicultural society. King did not speak just for black Americans, he spoke for all Americans.

I want the freedom to choose my friends, to live in a neighborhood of my choice and to go to a school of my choice.

King saw the civil-rights movement as "a revolution to 'get in' rather than to overthrow"—a movement that would ensure that all Americans shared in the nation's economy, housing market, educational system, and social structure.

Yes, I had a boyhood dream, but it was not until King came along that I thought it could possibly come true. And even now, years after his death, I still am moved when I hear his "I Have a Dream" speech, so deeply do I feel for this country and for all for which it stands.

King's dream was "deeply rooted in the American dream that one day this nation will rise up and live out the true meaning of its creed—we hold these truths to be self-evident, that all men are created equal."

I feel good today because my country had a Dr. Martin Luther King Jr. I can identify more fully with my country because I have a stake in it.

The final words of King's "I Have a Dream" speech ought to be memorized and remembered by everyone:

> And when we allow freedom to ring, when we let it ring from every village and hamlet, from every state and city, we will be able to speed up that day when all of God's children—black men and white men, Jews and gentiles, Catholics and Protestants—will be able to join hands and to sing in the words of the old Negro spiritual, "Free at last, free at last; thank God Almighty, we are free at last."

I have been colored, and I have been a Negro. I have been black and now there are those who want me to be African-American. These words do not change the color of my skin.

Suggested Further Reading

McLagan, Elizabeth. *A Peculiar Paradise: A History of Blacks in Oregon, 1788-1940.* Portland: The Georgian Press, 1980.

SECTION VII
Individuals and Individualism

Asahel Bush
1824-1913

Pioneer newspaper editors wrote with verve and venom. So vicious were their personal attacks against rival editors and public figures, so partisan were their politics, that their manner of writing became nationally notorious as the "Oregon style." A classic example of this vindictive prose is the following editorial written by Asahel Bush in his *Oregon Statesman* on 1 April 1851.

Bush was born in Massachusetts, and moved to Oregon in 1851, where he not only founded a newspaper in Oregon City but also became one of the founders of the Democratic Party in Oregon Territory. The victim of Bush's assault in this essay was Thomas Dryer (1808-79), editor of the rival Portland newspaper, the *Weekly Oregonian*, which Dryer began publishing in 1850. Born in New York State, Dryer was a founder of the Whig Party in Oregon and later became one of the first Republicans in the Territory.

Grovelling Scurrility, Falsehood, and Ribald Blackguardism: The Oregon Style

The *Oregonian*, after announcing that the contents of the *Statesman is* a curiosity, and that "it had made war against the *Spectator, Star, Oregonian*, Secretary Hamilton and Gov. Gaines, and all others "who *has* said aught against the acts of the late Legislative Assembly, or *has* not joined, &c.," devotes about a half column to a blustering lecture on personalities, and a whining complaint of having been attacked in that manner by the *Statesman*.

Complaints of this kind come with a special grace from a paper devoted from its first to its last number almost exclusively to the grossest personal abuse, the most foul-mouthed slander, grovelling scurrility, falsehood and ribald blackguardism; insomuch that it has long since ceased to sustain any but a pot-house reputation, or to receive the countenance and respect of any party or community. Nothing that incurred the editor's displeasure has escaped. Business concerns, personal difficulties, public and private matters, have all alike been drawn through the slime and slander of his columns. And now he complains, and without reason too, of our employment of personalities, and whines over the matter like a whipped spaniel. He should learn to take blows before he ventures to give them. After showering his personal abuse and fish-market slang about him without stint, for months, he flies into a passion about a little newspaper squib, and makes an exhibition of himself that few men would be unashamed of. If the gentleman is not himself chagrined at his conduct, his friends are sorely so for him.

But the gentleman's shrewdness should have taught him better than to have made such a public display of his weakness, for people are apt to suspect a fluttering bird of being wounded. He would do well to study the following Quaker maxim, and govern his conduct by it in the future: "Be not affronted at a jest. If one throws salt at thee thou wilt receive no harm, unless thou hast sore places."

We are truly sorry to see this exhibition of ill temper and over sensitiveness on the part of the *Oregonian* editor, for, occupying his present post, he must be always in nettles. We knew he was a highly excitable gentleman, and liable in his anger to commit almost any indiscretion; but we were not prepared to see him make so perfect a "judy" of himself as he has.

But, assuming a belligerent aspect, the editor wants us "to *distinctly under-stand* (the italics are his own) that we cannot be permitted to assail his private character with impunity," and threatens us in genuine Bombastes Furioso style generally. He blazes away about his "reserved rights," his "determination to *protect* (his own italics, again) himself," "to *defend* himself to the *last*, regardless of consequences," &c., &c., in a manner most ridiculous to himself and mortifying to his friends. If the gentleman means by all this display of paper bravery and ruffianism merely to gratify his propensity for swaggering and braggartism, we are not disposed to deprive him of the harmless amusement; although he makes himself, as in this instance, the laughing stock of the public. But if he intends by it to intimidate or frighten us, and expects to deter us from the utterance of one syllable we are disposed to utter, we assure him, most emphatically, that he has mistaken his man. We are not to be affected, nor our course or conduct influenced by threats of personal violence. And we want this gentleman to "distinctly understand" this, (to use his own threatening bombast) for threats are a favorite weapon of his, and he may be inclined to use them again. They may have succeeded with the other papers here, but they cannot with us.

And we have lived long enough to see the frequent verification of the homely adage that "a barking cur never bites," and to learn that a man who carries his sword constantly in his mouth never wields one with his hands. If the editor would have us believe that he is possessed of rare courage, he should boast of it less loudly and less frequently.

And it is likewise unnecessary for him to defend his reputation so valiantly and vauntingly. If it is a spotless one, the public will find it out without a weekly proclamation of it. And innuendoes or insinuations will not have the power to injure it, or disturb the tranquillity of his mind. If it is not devoid of blemish, protestations will not make it so, but only direct attention to its defects. The shameless bawd may boast of her immaculate virtue, but it will not establish confidence in her purity, or blot out the record of her infamy. If the gentleman's reputation is unblemished, as he asserts, it needs no defense from his injudicious pen; if it is not, it will suffer from being thus defended before it is attacked. In any event, silence is the part of wisdom.

Suggested Further Reading

Turnbull, George S. *History of Oregon Newspapers.* Portland: Binford & Mort, 1939.

Abigail Scott Duniway
1834-1915

Abigail Jane (Scott) Duniway was a migrant to Oregon in the wagon trains of 1852. She became a teacher and a farmer's wife and, after an injury to her husband, the main financial support of her family. The pioneer values of independence, hard work, and equality that she had inherited from her frontier ancestors first manifested themselves publicly in her interest in woman suffrage. She became the best-known advocate of this cause in the Pacific Northwest until Oregon women obtained the vote in 1912. She was a tireless lecturer and prolific writer for other causes as well, including monetary reform, distribution of land to the landless, immigration restriction, and improved family life.

Duniway's principal outlet for her ideas was the *New Northwest*, a newspaper that she founded in 1871 in order to counterbalance the *Oregonian*, edited by her brother, Harvey W. Scott, which refused to cover women's issues and news. The selection that follows is her first editorial in that paper, published 5 May 1871.

About Ourself

In coming before the reading public in the capacity of editor and proprietor of a newspaper, and presuming to occupy ground which has heretofore been *monopolized by gentlemen*, we feel the responsibility of our position, and realize the necessity of making our work come up practically to the high standard which alone should satisfy the gleaners after truth. As our work belongs to the public, we feel that the public has a right to know something about us; so we will indulge our readers in the following account of our stewardship.

The first nine years of our married life were spent upon a farm where, surrounded by a growing family, we unhesitatingly performed prodigies of labor, doing anything and everything that came in our way, until health was destroyed and constitution broken. We are naturally acquisitive, calculating and fond of active business life; and though on the farm we had work enough to do, yet every farmer's wife knows that her work is considered wholly unremunerative so far as herself is concerned. We are not complaining, just simply stating facts. Before marriage we had learned some of the sweets of pecuniary independence, for we had taught school and followed dress-making and millinery. Desiring to please our good husband, we struggled to be contented and remain upon the farm. To relieve our active brain we began to scribble. It always was our forte, and if we had been a man, we'd have had an editor's position and a handsome salary at twenty-one. Sketches for newspapers, with occasional poems and letters, occupied us for a while, but health entirely failing, we were compelled to spend hours of each day in a reclining position, surrounded, in a lonely farm house, with the prattle of happy children, and occupied with our own intense thoughts. We had reached the advanced age of twenty-two years, the age at which most boys enter college, and there we were, a wife and mother, but a broken-down, yet hopeful, spirited child; nothing more, nothing less. When tired out with household cares and no longer able to sit up, we would recline upon the lounge and scribble. We wrote a book. We published. It failed. Any body might have known it would who had one particle of public experience. The thing never had a stronger censor than ourself. It was full of ideal nothings and a good deal of good sense, but it contained many imperfections of our own and the publisher's and we both lost money. We deserved to lose it.

Misfortunes following us, we left the farm and engaged in teaching school. Here commenced our real battle with public life. Strong men, who might have been better employed in making rails, opposed our work, but we struggled on and succeeded. We taught school for four years, having had under our care during that time some thirteen hundred children. Health failed again and we tried a millinery and dress-making business. We succeeded again, and active business in a new direction again restored our health.

We served a regular apprenticeship at working—washing, scrubbing, patching, darning, ironing, plain sewing, raising babies, milking, churning and poultry raising. We have kept boarders, taught school, taught music, wrote for the newspapers, made speeches and carried on an extensive millinery and dress-making business. We can prove by the public that this work has long been *well* done. Now, having reached the age of thirty-six, and having brought up a family of boys to set type and a daughter to run the millinery store, we propose to edit and publish a newspaper; and we intend to establish it as one of the permanent institutions of the country.

We started out in business with strong prejudices against "strong-minded women." Experience and common sense have conquered those prejudices. We see, under the existing customs of society, one half of the women over-taxed and underpaid; hopeless, yet struggling toilers in the world's drudgery; while the other half are frivolous, idle, and expensive. Both of these conditions of society are wrong. Both have resulted from woman's lack of political and consequent pecuniary and moral responsibility. To prove this, and to elevate woman, that thereby herself and son and brother man may be benefitted and the world made better, purer, and happier, is the aim of this publication. We ask no favors of a "generous public." We shall give value received for every dollar we obtain. Half that we have planned to do we cannot now enumerate; but we shall prove to you if you will sustain our paper that we are not only in earnest, but that we know just what we are about.

Suggested Further Reading

Duniway, Abigail Scott. *Captain Gray's Company, or Crossing the Plains and Living in Oregon.* Portland: S. J. McCormick, 1859.

———. *From the West to the West: Across the Plains to Oregon.* Chicago: A. C. McClurg, 1905.

———. *Path Breaking: An Autobiographical History of the Equal Suffrage Movement in Pacific Coast States.* 2nd ed. Portland: James, Kerns & Abbott, 1914. Reprint. New York: Schocken Books, 1971.

Moynihan, Ruth Barnes. *Rebel for Rights: Abigail Scott Duniway.* New Haven and London: Yale University Press, 1983.

Nancy Wilson Ross
1910-1986

Dr. Bethenia Owens-Adair (1840-1926) was one of
Oregon's first female physicians. She was also a social
crusader, active in the woman suffrage, prohibition, and
eugenics movements of the Progressive Era. Nancy
Wilson Ross here describes a pivotal moment in Owens-
Adair's career. Ross was born in Olympia, Washington,
and had a long career as author, journalist, novelist,
lecturer, and war correspondent. She was an authority
on Asian religions, about which she wrote several books.
This selection is taken from *Westward the Women*
(1944).

The Rebel

In the 1870s the town of Roseburg, Oregon, had been afflicted for some time with a public charge, an old pauper with a complication of diseases. This derelict had visited in turn every medical man of the community, and upon his death the doctors decided to get together and hold an autopsy to determine the sources of his singular ailments.

Although in the past, in small Western communities, an autopsy was often a semi-public event, a sort of ghoulish striptease—for men only—this particular autopsy would, in all likelihood, have passed unmarked in local history had it not been for the unseemly and scandalous role played in it by Bethenia Owens. Bethenia was a former milliner who not long before had shocked everyone she knew, alienated her friends, and embarrassed her family by traipsing off across country to the Philadelphia Eclectic College to get a medical degree at the only institution that would admit women to such unwomanly pursuits.

Her return from the East coincided with the performing of the autopsy on Roseburg's leading pauper. As the six doctors gathered in the shed on the outskirts of town to perform the operation before an audience of some fifty men and boys, one of them was seized suddenly with the brilliant idea of sending a mock invitation to the "Philadelphia doctor."

When Bethenia received the note, there is little doubt that she understood the intention behind it, and all the consequences that acceptance on her part would entail. But she did not hesitate for a moment. "Give the doctors my compliments," she said formally to the boy who delivered the invitation, "and say that I will be there in a few moments."

She reached the shed on the heels of the derisive laughter with which her answer was received. Opening the door with perfect dramatic timing, she walked straight up to the nearest physician and extended her hand. Out of the abrupt and shocked silence that greeted her appearance the doctor to whom she first addressed herself managed to mumble something in a low voice. Was Bethenia aware that this particular operation involved the genitalia? She was not, replied Bethenia, standing her ground, five feet four and every inch imperious. But, said she, looking in turn into their shifting eyes, to a doctor one part of the human body is as impersonal and as sacred as another.

In the fresh silence one of the outraged men—a doctor whom Bethenia had once put in his place because of his clumsy handling of a sick child—announced flatly that he objected to the presence of a woman at a male autopsy. If she were allowed to remain he would certainly leave.

Bethenia replied promptly. "I came here," she said as coolly as she could manage, "by formal invitation, and I will leave it to a vote whether I go or stay. But first I would like to ask Dr. Palmer what is the difference between the attendance of a woman at a male autopsy, and the attendance of a man at a female autopsy."

No one, including Dr. Palmer, had a ready reply, and the doctor with whom she had first shaken hands on entering the shed finally remarked that since he had suggested that she be invited he would vote for her to remain. Four other doctors reluctantly agreed. In the end Dr. Palmer alone angrily retired.

The assembled company then turned their attention to the corpse. The pauper was lying on boards supported by sawbucks, covered with an old worn gray blanket. As one of the doctors opened a medicine case containing the instruments for the operation, the interest of the fifty men and boys in the audience picked up. To Bethenia's shocked dismay, the doctor with the medicine case handed it across to her without a word. She had hardly bargained for this, and for a moment she was too stunned to speak. When she did, it was only to ask faintly: "You don't want me to do the work, do you?"

"Oh yes, yes," he said with feigned indifference. "Go ahead!"

There was absolute silence in the close-packed shed while the men waited, watching her. Bethenia did not hesitate long. She resolutely took the instruments from him and began the operation.

As she operated, the word flew up and down the streets of the little town about what was happening in the old shed on the outskirts. If Bethenia believed that the men who were present secretly applauded her pluck and skill, she could hardly have been prepared for the reception she was to get when she emerged. She left the shed pale, shaken, but inwardly triumphant. She found the streets outside full of women and children who had come to laugh and catcall, to point their fingers, and titter behind their hands. Blinds were drawn, doors were slammed as there walked past them an ex-milliner who had dared to officiate at so disgusting a spectacle.

The whole town rocked with the incident. Had it nor been for the well-known and respected trigger eye of Dr. Bethenia's brothers, Flem and Josiah—who, though shamed to the quick by their sister's act, would allow no indignities to be visited upon her—she might have had a very bad time of it. Perhaps Flem remembered the day in childhood when he had knocked off a piece of her front tooth while wrestling with her over who should go to the barn for a bundle of oats. Perhaps he remembered how he had run off crying bitterly. Whatever the reason for the loyalty, Bethenia, writing her memoirs many years later, was willing to concede that her family name and pioneer connections in the Umpqua River countryside undoubtedly saved her from being tarred and feathered and run out of town. She knew that only a short time before, women medical students leaving a hospital in more advanced Philadelphia had been publicly rotten-egged by their male fellow students.

Suggested Further Reading

Ross, Nancy Wilson. *Three Ways of Ancient Wisdom: Hinduism, Buddhism, Zen, and Their Significance for the West.* New York: Simon & Schuster, 1966.
———. *Westward the Women.* New York: Alfred A. Knopf, 1944.

Anita Helle
1948-

Anita Plath Helle was born in Minnesota, but she has
lived most of her adult life in Seattle and Portland. She
was educated at the University of Puget Sound and at
the University of Oregon, where she received a Ph.D. in
English in 1986. She began her literary career as a poet,
winning the *Mademoiselle* Poetry Prize in 1970. Her
poetry has been published by a number of small presses,
including *West Coast Review, Epoch, Poet and Critic,*
and Prescott Street Press. Since 1986 she has taught
writing and literature at a number of universities and has
published scholarly essays, reviews, and interviews on
several modern and contemporary women writers. This
essay is a slight revision of a version that appeared in *An
Anthology of Northwest Writing* (1981).

The Odysseys of Mary Barnard

Mary Barnard is an important poet, not only because of the quality of her verse, but because of her associations with some of this century's most prominent American writers. If she was among the first Northwest poets to gain a national reputation it is, as she has put it, because "I have a lot of resolution." In one way, she is part of this place: most of her life has been spent and much of her writing has been done in Vancouver, Washington. But she has also been apart from it. Her friends were leaders of the modernist movement in poetry, and her early poems were published in vanguard "little magazines" such as *Furioso* and *New Westminster,* now collectors' items. National honors came early; at twenty-six she won *Poetry* magazine's Levinson Prize, and at thirty her first book, *Cool Country,* was published in a volume which included first books by John Berryman and Randall Jarrell. Since then her artistic scope has broadened: the 1958 translation of Sappho's poems *(Sappho: A New Translation)* and *The Mythmakers,* a systematic inquiry into the nature and origin of myths, earned her a scholarly reputation. Other poems and short stories have appeared in publications such as *The New Yorker*, *Saturday Review*, the *Kenyon Review* and the *Hudson Review*. A California composer, David Ward-Steinman, has based a musical suite on her fragments from Sappho; Tibor Serly's "The Pleiades," a choral composition (1978), uses lyrics from one of her poems about the constellation of star-women who legendarily dance across the sky.

Images of exile and return, isolation and reintegration link Barnard's life and work. Born in Vancouver, Washington, in 1909, she got acquainted with Oregon backroads as a child, when she traveled to lumber mills with her father, a timber wholesaler. She began writing poems in grade school, but her first contact with the avant-garde of the 1920s came at Reed College. A classics major, she had taken creative writing from Lloyd Reynolds, now best-known as a calligrapher. One day Reynolds wrote some lines from Ezra Pound's poem, "Homage to Sextus Propertius" on the blackboard. "The man who could do that could do anything," she remembers Reynolds saying.

When she tells this story Barnard likes to emphasize that she originally regarded the platitude with a healthy skepticism ("Harumph, I thought. That's a pretty tall statement!"). But after studying Pound on her own she became an admirer. Soon after graduation she surprised her father by announcing that she'd send a packet of poems to Pound in Rapallo, Italy—maybe he'd tell her what he thought of her work. Pound's side of this exchange with the "unknown Mary Barnard" (sic) is recorded in his *Selected Letters* (New Directions, 1950):

"Age? Intentions? Intention? How MUCH intention? I mean how hard and how long are you willing to work at it? . . . Nice gal, likely to marry and give up writing or what Oh?"

"I wrote back to Pound. 'Nice girl, not likely to marry, and as for giving up writing, the only thing that would discourage me would be advice from you, but even that wouldn't stop me,'" Barnard recalls in a recent interview at her apartment in Vancouver, Washington. At sixty-nine, her tall stature is still one of her most imposing features; her way of choosing words—as if there is only one right one, even for speech—is another. She has picked a straightbacked chair nearest the window; afternoon light softens the purposefully grouped bookcases, chairs, and objets d'art.

Barnard describes her relationship with Pound, which lasted until his death, as one in which "he was the master and I was the apprentice." She also confesses that she didn't always follow his advice concerning her work. Nevertheless, Pound was her pipeline to the people and ideas who were shaping the future direction of poetry. When she visited New York for the first time in 1936, Pound's introductions led to meetings with the leading personages: Marianne

Moore ("A dizzying talker—but rather abstract!"); *Poetry* magazine editor
Harriet Monroe ("A chipper little lady"); e. e. cummings ("He laughed from
his boots"); and William Carlos Williams ("As far as criticism of my work, his
was along one line—condense!").

After several months at Yaddo writers' colony, Barnard returned to Vancouver
and took a job as a social worker, but not happily. One letter from Williams to
Barnard in Vancouver during that period (part of Barnard's gift of five Williams' first editions to the Reed College Library) suggests second-hand her
discontented feeling of cultural isolation. "It must be lonesome out there,"
Williams' letter begins, "Fight it if you can."

By 1938 Barnard was back in New York hunting for odd jobs to support her
writing. She became a research assistant for Carl Van Doren, eventually taking
a position as curator of the Poetry Collection at the Lockwood Memorial Library in Buffalo. About her decision to move East, Barnard says, "I left
Vancouver in desperation. I wanted to be a regional poet . . . but I realized that
the regions weren't going to have any culture, or I couldn't contribute to it in
isolation. I had particularly the tendency to overvalue my work—I was the
only one who was doing what I was doing. I didn't have anyone to compare
my work with here, so I swung between feeling I was better than I was, to
feeling that I wasn't worth anything. When I came back again [in the 1950s
and 60s], the region had changed, and my position in it had changed. When
Marianne Moore and W. H. Auden came to Portland I was seated next to
them. But when I was growing up in Vancouver, I knew two people who had
gone to Europe. While I was at Reed, we heard one Englishman read his poetry one night, but nobody had ever heard his name."

Barnard's first book, *Cool Country* (New Directions, 1940), contains poems
written before and after she was apprenticed to Pound. In addition to demon-
strating a sensitive ear and precise powers of observation, the poems form a
sort of novel of initiations, looking forward and backward in time for their
influences. The prosody follows the Imagist principles set down by Pound.
There are no excess adjectives, concrete words take the place of abstract ones,
and lines sound more like musical phrases than metronomic beats. The titles,
however, are mostly native—"Logging Trestle," "Shoreline," "Highway
Bridge," "Rapids." In "Provincial II," the theme of the would-be regional
poet's dilemma is confronted directly. A "European" makes his appearance,
and he shows the persona in the poem that the silk she thinks she wears is
"merely paper," her buckskin "out of date by nearly one hundred years." Collecting her wits, the poet finds an unconvincing consolation in the "large/
Plums of the provinces." The book ends on a winsome note as the poet writes
of Miranda, Shakespeare's stranded daughter in *The Tempest*: "There is a green
place in my mind/That paces my mind's conceptions."

Illness sent Barnard home to Vancouver in 1951, but her poetic odyssey continued in new directions. "I had been led from one endeavor to another," she explains. "Pound had recommended that I translate, and when I said I hated translation, I said I would try working on metrics, especially Sappho's metric. It was when somebody sent me a volume of Quasimodo's Italian translation of Sappho [in the 1950s] that I began to translate the fragments. I tried one, then another. When I got to twelve, I began to think I would finish.

"Then Sappho led me to *The Mythmakers*. I was working on what became a footnote, and I was trying to say something about Sappho's religion. Scholars were writing about her as the priestess of a religious cult that carried on its ritual in sacred groves. The more I read that the potion was merely ritual, the more I became obsessed with working it out. I felt that something was mixed in the drink, and I felt I wanted to justify my theory. I also felt that Aphrodite was a moon goddess in Sappho's poetry, and I kept finding scholars saying that Aphrodite was *not* a moon goddess, and I was trying to justify that theory, too."

Classicism and modernism are closely linked in Barnard's *Sappho: A New Translation* of 100 poems and fragments by the ancient Lesbian poet. In his foreword, scholar Dudley Fitts praises the "direct purity of diction" of "the new" version, especially as it contrasts with nineteenth-century corruptions by Swinburne and Symonds, who made Sappho over into an image of "Yellow Book neodiabolism." Barnard's Sappho is more elegant and wise: her expressions have economy. The unstintingly clear, precise diction which Barnard had restored in Sappho was exactly what Pound and other early modernist poets were after in their own verse and the Greek poets had been among their most-admired models.

The most important innovation of Barnard's "new translation," however, is its meter. Wanting to come as close as possible to the sound of the speaking voice, Barnard considered the convention of the Japanese haiku as well as strictly quantitative metrics—which some scholars felt were impossible to convey in English. Her solution was a looser adaptation, balancing the number of weighted syllables from line to line. Consequently Sappho's colloquies with friends, as well as her wedding songs and passionate soliloquies, take their formal and intimate qualities from conversational stresses:

You may forget but

Let me tell you
this: someone in
some future time
will think of us.

The Mythmakers (1966) takes Barnard's many-sided interest in literature to a practical conclusion. It addresses a number of questions. By what process does a "faraway twinkling point of light become a mythical personality?" What is the origin of myths associated with plants? Were tribal shamans also poets? Reading the book is like being on an exotic safari, led by a cheerful guide in sensible shoes who's convinced that a little common sense and clear thinking is all that's needed to penetrate the wooly underbrush. The clarity of style and logic convinces us that many myths had their origin in useful, pleasureful, and imaginative facts, not, as Jungian theory suggests, "as emanations of a pre-conscious psyche." Summing up from the text, Barnard says, "Gods grew up through impersonations—that is, in the case of the Northwest Indians, the mask preceded the god."

More than her poetry, Barnard's prose style in *The Mythmakers* reveals the wit, intellectual curiosity, tenacity, and tough-mindedness which have been her resources. These are old-fashioned words to apply to a modern poet, but not to one whose craft has kept pace with fifty years of change. When she tells me that her latest project is a metric adaptation of Homer's *Iliad* into modern English I'm not surprised. I didn't say it, but I thought it fitting that her first translation of an epic poem should feature another wanderer, whose cunning labors took him far from home, and—eventually—brought him back again.

Suggestions for Further Reading

Barnard, Mary E. *Assault on Mount Helicon: A Literary Memoir*. Berkeley, CA: University of California Press, 1984.

———. *Collected Poems*. Portland, OR: Breitenbush Books, 1979.

———. "Ezra Pound, Sappho, and My Assault on Mount Helicon," *The Malahat Review*, 66: 140-144.

Hardt, Ulrich H. "An Interview with Four Poets," *Oregon English Journal* 11B, 69-80.

Helle, Anita. "The Odysseys of Mary Barnard," in Michael Strelow, ed., *An Anthology of Northwest Writing, 1900-1950*. Eugene: Northwest Review Books, 1981.

———. "Reading Women's Autobiographies: A Map of Reconstructed Knowing," in Nel Noddings and Carol Witherell, eds., *Stories Lives Tell: Narrative and Dialogue in Education*. New York: Teacher's College Press, 1991.

Jeffrey G. Barlow
1942-

Jeffrey G. Barlow was born in Illinois and received his doctorate at the University of California (Berkeley) in 1973. He taught at the University of Oregon from 1971 to 1975, and has been on the faculty of Lewis and Clark College since 1976. He has published four books (two jointly with his wife, Christine A. Richardson) and many articles and reviews. Barlow has traveled extensively in China and is an authority on that nation's history.

Christine A.
Richardson
1947-

Christine A. Richardson was born in North Carolina. She was educated at the University of Oregon and Lewis and Clark College, specializing in Chinese history and literature, and has taught at colleges and schools in the United States, Taiwan, and China. The co-author of three books, she is currently on the faculty of Lincoln High School in Portland.

The following selection is taken from Barlow and Richardson's *China Doctor of John Day* (1979), an account of the business operations in John Day, Oregon, of two Chinese merchants who came to serve Chinese miners at the time of the Eastern Oregon gold rush in the late nineteenth century, but remained to become respected by their Caucasian customers as well.

China Doctor of John Day

The Kam Wah Chung Building operated by Lung On and Ing Hay came to be the center of the Chinese community in Eastern Oregon. The building served many purposes for both the Chinese and white communities, but the economic survival of the building depended initially upon its success as a store in which were sold bulk lots and individual items of daily-use products. Some of the clientele were whites from the area who found the store convenient and would drop in for tobacco or canned goods. The Chinese depended on the store as almost the sole importer of Chinese foods, books, clothing, gambling equipment, firecrackers, religious articles like incense and paper for ceremonial purposes, and other sundries.

The Kam Wah Chung and Co. store also served as a sort of hiring hall for Chinese labor. Although mining had faltered and by 1900 had ended almost completely (save for the solitary figures who still tramped the hills, more committed to a style of life than to a way of making a living) there was still a demand for Chinese labor. As mining waned, ranching and farming and eventually logging began. The immigrants from Toisan were fortunate in that their county had a long tradition of woodworking crafts. A rancher wanting a skilled carpenter or a cook or sheepman, or a cowboy, could go to the Kam Wah Chung, where Lung On would soon find a reliable hand. His ability to speak good English made Lung On the intermediary between the Chinese and white communities, and like Cha-li Tong in Walla Walla, he became a very important figure.

One of the functions of major importance carried on in the Kam Wah Chung was that it served as a sort of post office for the Chinese community. Most Chinese, unlike Lung On and Doc Hay, still regarded themselves as temporary sojourners who looked forward to making enough money to return to China, and they kept in close touch with their ancestral homes and families.

Lung On, as mentioned earlier, was valued for his beautiful calligraphy and elegant style, and illiterate and semi-literate Chinese would pay him a small sum to write letters home. Some of these letters, for one reason or another, were never mailed—or perhaps they are copies of letters which were mailed. Letters coming in from China were sometimes undeliverable, and these letters also remained in the building, providing unparalleled insights into the men who lived there and into conditions in their homeland.*

* See Oregon Literature Series, volume 6, Letters and Diaries, for samples of these letters.

The Kam Wah Chung and Co. store also came to be an integral part of the religious life of the Chinese mining community. On the back wall of the room where Lung On sold dry goods and notions, there was a deep box about three feet by two feet fixed to the wall at about eye level, with the opening toward the viewer. The box had been converted to an altar and was hung with expensive brocade curtains imported from China. On another smaller box within the open outer case was a small seated image from popular Buddhist religion.

Buddhism has as many or more varieties and sects than does Christianity, ranging from deeply philosophical schools which, strictly defined, are not religious at all, to "popular" sects which teach a very colorful religion full of ghosts, demons, beneficent spirits, good-luck charms and amulets, fortune-telling, and noisy public ceremonies. The shrine in the Kam Wah Chung was of this last type. The small "Buddha" or god-figure came all the way from China and was no doubt lovingly cared for until it eventually was installed in the building and Doc Hay became its chief priest. Unfortunately the figure was stolen in the 1950s when the building stood empty, and we cannot be sure of the exact identity of the god. Since popular Buddhism has numerous gods and spirits, the figure could have represented any of dozens of common ones.

According to the many witnesses we have interviewed, Doc Hay was a very religious man. The small altar was carefully tended and daily had offerings placed before it of the "Three Precious Things"—wine, fruit and incense. It is interesting to note that several dried grapefruit were found before the altar when the building was opened prior to restoration; the Chinese introduced the culture of grapefruit to this country.

The altar served many functions for the Chinese. It was a small church in the same sense as a Christian church, where the worshippers could commune with those supernatural forces and eternal values with which the Christian's worship puts him in touch. The shrine was also a means of petitioning the god to grant favors. One can imagine that since many of Doc Hay's visitors were medical patients, the Buddha figure heard numerous petitions for good health. Doubtless other major concerns revolved around loved ones back home in China, some of whom were probably praying before a similar shrine for the support and good fortune of relatives in the gold fields of the Pacific Northwest.

The shrine also served a major purpose in divination and fortunetelling. There were a number of ways in which the petitioner or the priest, Ing Hay, could consult the Buddha figure about future events or ask its advice on personal and business problems. Before this shrine there still remain several sets of divining blocks: two pieces of wood, cut and carved from a single piece of rosewood which was originally cylindrical in shape. Cutting the piece in two, down the main axis, gave each half a flat side and a rounded side. The petitioner held the two pieces together as a cylinder before the god while he framed his question, then allowed the pieces to drop gently upon the floor in front of the altar. If both pieces landed flat side up, that was a negative answer to the question asked; if both rounded sides came up, it was a positive response; and if one of each came up, this indicated ambiguity in the god's response—a kind of "yes and no" reply.

There were also several sets of divining sticks, or "fortune sticks," as they were sometimes called. Each set had several hundred sticks, and each stick was marked with a number in Chinese. The petitioner selected a set of sticks, shook the cup gently up and down in front of the shrine until one stick fell to the floor. He would then take that stick to Ing Hay, who would look up the corresponding number in one of several books containing a verse corresponding to each number. The verses were usually quite vague and cryptic and had to be interpreted by the priest.

Another method sometimes resorted to was to cast the *I-Ching*. The *I-Ching* is a very old book of wisdom, couched also in vague and poetical terms. Using a number of yarrow stalks, or wooden sticks, the priest slowly arrives at a series of numbers which eventually lead him to the book. The book might answer a question such as that actually asked, "Should I invest in a business in Baker, Oregon?" with a response like:

> There is a want of understanding between men. Its indication is unfavorable to the firm and correct course of the superior man. We see in it the great gone and the little come.

Again, with much discussion between the inquirer and the priest, perhaps aided by the advice of bystanders, the answer would be interpreted in light of the question.

Ing Hay also had available more esoteric methods of fortunetelling. Many petitioners preferred a more direct way of communing with the gods, and for them, Ing Hay would set out on a table a number of printed sheets containing characters arranged at random in columns. He would then hold a long writing brush—or sometimes a wooden piece not unlike that used in the ouija board of western tradition—and the god's hand would guide his as the brush rose and fell, seemingly at random. Sometimes the message would be impossibly garbled; other times it would be clear and concise, giving obviously relevant responses. Hundreds of such sheets were found in the store, still bearing the original message from the Chinese gods.

To the western mind, with its more anthropomorphic and rational gods, the Chinese religions practiced in the Kam Wah Chung and its fortune-telling

Ing Hay

Lung On

aspects seem mere superstition. We must remember, however, that there are aspects of our own religious practices which seem strange and incomprehensible to the outsider, and that Christian spiritualism is itself a very long and popular tradition. The Chinese who petitioned their god were also in a sense asking for the advice of the entire community, and in asking a question like "Should I invest in a business in Baker, Oregon?" the Chinese were also paying Ing Hay and Lung On a small sum for their own opinions. As they were two of the leaders of the Chinese community, their opinions were obviously valuable and in Lung On's case, with his great business acumen and wide circle of friends, probably very valuable indeed.

It is clear that the shrine in the Kam Wah Chung and Co. store served a number of very practical functions for the two men who ran it. As each petitioner paid about fifty cents for advice, it was a nice source of revenue. The entire community joined together in raising funds for the annual refurbishment of the shrine and for special festivals and ceremonies. The occasion also brought many people into the store who might not otherwise have come there. The constant questions asked of the god probably also gave Lung On and Ing

Hay a real insight into the problems and state of affairs in the Chinese community, knowledge essential to their positions as community leaders. It is certain, however, that the main purpose of the shrine was religious and not political or economic. Long after most of the Chinese had died or returned home, Ing Hay, aged and blind, continued to worship before the shrine and to place daily the "Three Precious Things" before his god.

Perhaps the most important function of the building was its use as a social center. Chinese could come into the building, drink the tea recently imported from their homeland, consume an expensive delicacy, talk of the political situation back home, arrange loans or complicated business transactions, or if they were of a simpler turn of mind, drink and gamble.

Until American drug laws forbade it, the building was also a sort of opium den. Ing Hay and Lung On imported opium quite legally. The laborer could purchase a pipe of it, light up and "mount the dragon" in a drug-induced dream, and be temporarily wafted to his homeland. Whatever sounds filtered through to his ears would be the soft, lilting dialect of Toisan County and the smells would be those familiar from childhood: incense, soy, and cooking oils. If he occasionally opened his eyes, he would see a calendar from a Chinese bank, a moral maxim written in Lung On's strong hand, or other immigrants playing cards or sitting quietly beside the warmth of the stove.

Suggested Further Reading

Barlow, Jeffrey G., and Christine A. Richardson. *China Doctor of John Day.* Portland: Binford & Mort, 1979.

———. *Gum San: Land of the Gold Mountain.* Bend, OR: The High Desert Museum, 1991.

Don Berry
1932-

Don Berry has both numerous interests and the talents
to indulge them. Born in Minnesota, Berry attended
Reed College, and first became known as a novelist,
then as a historian. His trilogy of historical novels
dealing with the Oregon Country in the 1840s and
1850s—*Trask* (1960), *Moontrap* (1962), and *To Build a
Ship* (1963)—examines the encounters between
Caucasians and Native Americans, their respective
relationships with the natural environment, and the
transition from the world of the fur trade to that of
agriculture. His history of the Rocky Mountain Fur
Company is accurate, informative, and interesting. Berry
later turned to film making, electronic music, computer
research, and bronze sculpture. This essay first appeared
in the (Portland) *Sunday Oregonian*'s *Northwest
Magazine* (1984).

Snapshots of My Daughter, Turning

I was looking at my daughter's back the other day, strong-muscled, well-formed, with a cascade of blond hair almost to her waist. Thinking of a bronze, the way the light would take when it was polished. She turned her head over her shoulder and said something. . . .

Time collapsed suddenly, as it is said to do for someone drowning. I saw flashing before me a garland of images, visions of my daughter's back, her head turning to me over her shoulder. Like an album of brilliantly clear still photographs, or short clips from a film that has lasted three decades.

Bonny is 6. In a bend of the Willamette River called Peach Cove, I am struggling with my first novel. I'm hard to coax away from the typewriter, even on a beautiful afternoon. Bon is skipping ahead of me, hand-in-hand with her little brother, down a sun-spattered corridor between rows of holly trees. We are all heading for the river beach.

She is a gloriously sunny child, and when she turns, her face is radiant with innocence and delight, like the blooming of a flower.

"Come on, Daddy! Come on!"

Bonny is 12. We are on the Oregon Coast. Times are hard. My wife, a gourmet cook by nature, is reduced to a single menu: "Oatmeal for breakfast, tomatoes for lunch and whatever you can catch for dinner."

But catching is good, after all, for an outlaw family. David is 15, a superb hunter who brings waterfowl. Duncan is 9 and a skillful fisherman. Bonny gathers wild strawberries from the beach dunes. And all of them are out in the pre-dawn ocean chill digging clams while old Dad slumbers.

On this particular day I have taken a black bear in a deep canyon. I lash him to my back and fight my way out of the brushy depths, his great, dark head bouncing and rolling on my shoulder. It takes many hours. He weighs more than I, and I wish desperately that our encounter had been somewhere near a road.

I reach our little house on the dunes well after dark. Once again, it is Bonny's back I see.

The knives for butchering are neatly laid out. On the floor are buckets of cold water for my bloody clothes. Racks for making jerky are ready by the stove, and rolls of paper for wrapping stand at the end of the counter. Every-thing is prepared perfectly.

When Bonny turns, she is at first terrified by this man-bear, this two-headed creature that stands exhausted and bloody at the door. She catches her breath, but then she gestures to the immaculate preparations with a powerful pride.

"We're ready, Daddy."

Bonny is 15. We are at 5,000 feet over the Tualatin Valley in Oregon. This time I see her ahead of me in the front seat of a Supercub. I am flying that aircraft from the rear seat so that she can have an unobstructed view of the exquisite summer sky of stately cumulus towers. It is a time when I am doing a lot of bush-flying in Oregon, but on this rare day, we are flying just for the joy of it.

If you force a plane into a climb, then push over the top strongly, you can create a zero-G condition for a few moments. Everything loose in the cockpit floats. It is a kind of super roller-coaster sensation of weightlessness. Today was a zero-G day for Bon.

It always has been my private fancy that Bon was destined for a planet less weighty than this one, a place where all weight is lightness, where all bondage is freedom, where the spirit of joy is never impaired by the gravity of matter. I have never mentioned this to her, of course, but on this day her ecstasy in weightlessness confirms my fancy.

Her face is golden with sunlight as we go over the top into zero-G, and her eyes are like living sapphires as she turns back to me.

"Do it again, Daddy! Do it again!"

Bonny is 18. She sits ahead of me in a two-man cruising kayak, and we are in serious trouble. We are in the middle of the Imperial Eagle Channel on the west coast of Vancouver Island. We have been three weeks in this boat, explor-ing the islands of Barkley Sound, and now we are caught far from shore in a sudden, explosive gale that sweeps great rollers in from the North Pacific. Around us the surface of the sea is churned white, crashing and breaking over us.

Bonny's back is bent with effort. She puts every ounce of strength into each stroke. She is crying, I know, though I cannot see her face. Suddenly a huge wave looms ahead of us, and the kayak's bow plunges into it. Ahead of me, Bonny disappears under the tons of green water that thunder down on us.

Then we rise through it, up through white water into spray and we are finally on the surface again. Bonny turns to me for the first time, tears mingled with the sea.

"I can do it, Daddy."

Bonny is 20. We are in the tropics, the Lesser Antilles, anchored in a harbor called the Anse Mitan on the island of Martinique. The unthinkable is happening. The family is being destroyed.

We have left the land world, selling everything, leaving everything to make this 55-foot ketch our only home. And now there is a slow explosion that none of us understands, an explosion that is tearing us apart and wounding us all so deeply that, for the first time, we have lost our faith that the clan will survive anything.

Bon's to-be husband Bruce has already left the boat in anguish; Duncan will soon depart, painfully, on a tiny boat with two German sailors, to face machine guns and prison and escape in the Dominican Republic. My wife is so ill with tropical fevers that it will take a decade for her to recover.

On this morning Bonny has announced that she is shipping out on the *Atlanta* as cook. Right now. She takes little or nothing with her. I see her back, standing at the rail. The *Atlanta* already is pulling forward on her anchor nearby. Bonny dives overboard, cutting the warm, clear Caribbean waters like a spear. Just before she dives, she turns over her shoulder, her golden hair swinging, her face distorted with regret and sorrow.

"Good bye, Daddy."

Bonny is 26. We are on Vashon Island in Puget Sound. Bon is in the middle of seven years of excruciating pain, unexplained pain that racks her whole body with intolerable agony. All joy is gone from her life, even the joy of her own new daughter.

During the pregnancy, the pain disappeared for a while, but now it has returned relentlessly, crushing her spirit, twisting and mutilating her body. Her flesh is rocklike and stiff, and she moves like a woman of 80. Her mind is muddy and unremembering, and terror is always present. She cannot communicate with us; words are more torture.

Her back is bent with the pain and hopelessness, and as she leaves the little house in Quartermaster Harbor, she turns.

"I'm not making it, Daddy."

Bonny is 31. We are on a film set in Seattle. Over Bonny's back I see the camera, the director. In her lap is a large loose-leaf binder in which she keeps track of every shot, and whether Ben had his right leg crossed or otherwise.

I wrote the script for this film, and Bonny is script supervisor. Her ex-husband Bruce is the director. The clan is together, living near, working together when we can. When she turns back to me this time, her face is neutral, professional.

"In shot Nine Dog Three the actor changed his line, Daddy. Is that OK?"

Bonny, I guess it's OK. Actors are always changing their lines. There are some lines in our script, my beloved, that I would change if I had the chance to rewrite. Some harsh words I would soften, some misunderstandings to be resolved by the second reel.

I would write your part entirely around the vision of the exquisite, golden child, with her perfect world of exuberance and beauty. Delete pain. Delete anguish. Delete fear.

Something on the order of a fairy princess would be just about right, I think. Living in a magical world of crystalline beauty, where lightness and freedom are everything, and the only measure of a day is the joy it holds.

But then, I suppose that is the way all fathers feel.

Suggested Further Reading

Berry, Don. *A Majority of Scoundrels: An Informal History of the Rocky Mountain Fur Company.* New York: Harper, 1961.
———. "Snapshots of My Daughter, Turning," (Portland) *Sunday Oregonian, Northwest Magazine,* 10 June, 1984: 4-33.
Love, Glen A. *Don Berry.* Boise: Boise State University, 1978.

Ken Kesey
1935-

Ken Kesey was born in Colorado, graduated from the University of Oregon in 1957, and then studied creative writing at Stanford University. His first novel, *One Flew Over the Cuckoo's Nest*, brought him national acclaim; his second, *Sometimes a Great Notion*, was an authentic Oregon novel. Although the themes of this work are universal, the state's natural environment and small-town setting are integral to the story.

The following excerpt is Kesey's account (through the persona of the narrator, "Devlin Deboree") of his encounter with two figures of the counterculture on their way to San Francisco after the Woodstock Festival, who attempt to capitalize on his affiliation with a movement he has abandoned. The excerpt is taken from his widely published essay on the death of Neal Cassady, "The Day After Superman Died," as it appeared in *Demon Box* (1986), a prose collection. It provides an insight into one of the radical individualist movements of the 1960s and one who was individualist enough to leave it for new directions.

The Day After Superman Died

He rubbed until the sockets filled with sparks; then he lowered his fists and held both arms tight against his sides in an attempt to calm himself, standing straight and breathing steady. His chest was still choked with adrenaline. Those California goddamned clowns, both smelling of patchouli oil, and cheap sweet wine, and an angry, festering vindictiveness. Of threat, really. They reeked of threat. The older of the two, the blackbeard, had stopped the barking of M'kehla's pair of Great Danes with only a word. "Shut!" he had hissed, the sound slicing out from the side of his mouth. The dogs had immediately turned tail back to their bus.

Deboree hadn't wanted to interface with the pair from the moment he saw them come sauntering in, all long hair and dust and multipatched Levi's, but Betsy was away with the kids up Fall Creek and it was either go down and meet them in the yard or let them saunter right on into the house. They had called him *brother* when he came down to greet them—an endearment that always made him watch out for his wallet—and the younger one had lit a stick of incense to wave around while they told their tale. They were brothers of the sun. They were on their way back to the Haight, coming from the big doings in Woodstock, and had decided they'd meet the famous Devlin Deboree before going on south.

"Rest a little, rap a little, maybe riff a little. Y'know what I'm saying, bro?"

As Deboree listened, nodding, Stewart had trotted up carrying the broken bean pole.

"Don't go for Stewart's stick, by the way." He addressed the younger of the pair, a blond-bearded boy with a gleaming milk-fed smile and new motorcycle boots. "Stewart's like an old drunk with his stick. The more you throw it, the more lushed out he gets."

The dog dropped the stick between the new boots and looked eagerly into the boy's face.

"For years I tried to break him of the habit. But he just can't help it when he sees certain strangers. I finally realized it was easier training the stick throwers than the stick chasers. So just ignore it, okay? Tell him no dice. Pretty soon he goes away."

"Whatever," the boy had answered, smiling. "You heard the man, Stewart: no dice."

The boy had kicked the stick away, but the dog had snagged it from the air and planted himself again before the boots. The boy did try to ignore it. He continued his description of the great scene at Woodstock, telling dreamily what a groove it had been, how high, how happy, how everybody there had been looking for Devlin Deboree.

"You shoulda made it, man. A stone primo groove. . . ."

The dog grew impatient and picked up his stick and carried it to the other man, who was squatting in the grass on one lean haunch.

"Just tell him no dice," Deboree said to the side of the man's head. "Beat it, Stewart. Don't pester the tourists."

The other man smiled down at the dog without speaking. His beard was long and black and extremely thick, with the salt of age beginning to sprinkle around the mouth and ears. As his profile smiled, Deboree watched two long incisors grow from the black bramble of his mouth. The teeth were as yellow and broken as the boy's were perfect. This dude, Deboree remembered, had kept his face averted while they were shaking hands. He wondered if this was because he was self-conscious about his breath like a lot of people with bad teeth.

"Well, anyway, what's happening, man? What's doing? All this?" Blondboy was beaming about at his surroundings. "'Boss' place you got here, this garden and trees and shit. I can see you are into the land. That's good, that's good. We're getting it together to get a little place outside of Petaluma soon as Bob here's old lady dies. Be good for the soul. Lot of work, though, right? Watering and feeding and taking care of all this shit?"

"It keeps you occupied," Deboree had allowed.

"Just the same," the boy rambled on, "you shoulda made it back there to Woodstock. Primo, that's the only word. Acres and acres of bare titty and good weed and outa sight vibes, you get me?"

"So I've heard," Deboree answered, nodding pleasantly at the boy. But he couldn't take his mind off the other hitchhiker. Blackbeard shifted his weight to the other haunch, the movement deliberate and restrained, careful not to disturb the dust that covered him. His face was deeply tanned and his hair tied back so the leathery cords in his neck could be seen working as he followed the dog's imploring little tosses of the stick. He was without clothes from the waist up but not unadorned. He wore a string of eucalyptus berries around his neck and tooled leather wristbands on each long arm. A jail tattoo—made, Deboree recognized, by two sewing needles lashed parallel at the end of a matchstick and dipped in india ink—covered his left hand: it was a blue-black spider with legs extending down all five fingers to their ragged nails. At his hip he carried a bone-handled skinning knife in a beaded sheath, and across his knotted belly a long scar ran diagonally down out of sight into his Levi's. Grinning, the man watched Stewart prance up and down with the three-foot length of broken bean stake dripping in his mouth.

"Back off, Stewart," Deboree commanded. "Leave this guy alone!"

"Stewart don't bother me," the man said, his voice soft from the side of his mouth. "Everything gotta have its own trip."

Encouraged by the soft voice, Stewart sank to his rump before the man. This pair of motorcycle boots were old and scuffed. Unlike his partner's, these boots had tromped many a bike to life. Even now, dusty and still, they itched to kick. That itch hung in the air like the peacock's unsounded cry.

Blondboy had become aware of the tenseness of the situation at last. He smiled and broke his incense and threw the smoking half into the quince bush. "Anyhow, you shoulda dug it," he said. "Half a million freaks in the mud and the music." He was beaming impishly from one participant to the other, from Deboree to his partner, to the prancing dog, as he picked at his wide grin with the dyed end of the incense stick. "Half a million *beautiful* people . . . ."

They had all sensed it coming. Deboree had tried once more to avert it. "Don't pay him any mind, man. Just an old stick junkie—" but it had been a halfhearted try, and Stewart was already dropping the stick. It had barely touched the dusty boot before the squatting man scooped it up and in the same motion sidearmed it into the grape arbor. Stewart bounded after it.

"Come on, man," Deboree had pleaded. "Don't throw it for him. He goes through wire and thorns and gets all cut up."

"Whatever you say," Blackbeard had replied, his face averted as he watched Stewart trotting back with the retrieved stake held high. "Whatever's right." Then had thrown it again as soon as Stewart dropped it, catching and slinging it all in one motion so fast and smooth that Deboree wondered if he hadn't been a professional athlete at a younger time, baseball or maybe boxing.

This time the stick landed in the pigpen. Stewart flew between the top two strands of barbed wire and had the stick before it stopped cartwheeling. It was too long for him to jump back through the wire with. He circled the pigs lying in the shade of their shelter and jumped the wooden gate at the far end of the pen.

"But, I mean, everything has got to have its trip, don't you agree?"

Deboree had not responded. He was already feeling the adrenaline burn in his throat. Besides, there was no more to say. Blackbeard stood up. Blondboy stepped close to his companion and whispered something at the hairy ear. All Devlin could make out was "Be cool, Bob. Remember what happened in Boise, Bob. . . ."

"Everything gotta live," Blackbeard had answered. "And everything gotta give."

Stewart skidded to a halt in the gravel. Blackbeard grabbed one end of the stick before the dog could release it, wrenching it viciously from the animal's teeth. This time Deboree, moving with all the speed the adrenaline could wring from his weary limbs, had stepped in front of the hitchhiker and grabbed the other end of the stick before it could be thrown.

"I *said* don't throw it."

This time there was no averting the grin; the man looked straight at him. And Deboree had guessed right about the breath; it hissed out of the jagged mouth like a rotten wind.

"I heard what you *said*, fagbutt."

Then they had looked at each other, over the stick grasped at each end between them. Deboree forced himself to match the other man's grinning glare with his own steady smile but he knew it was only a temporary steadiness. He wasn't in shape for encounters of this caliber. There was a seething accusation burning from the man's eyes, unspecified, undirected, but so furious that Deboree felt his will withering before it. Through the bean stake he felt the fury assail his very cells. It was like holding a high-voltage terminal.

"Everything gotta try," the man had said through his ragged grin, shuffling to get a better grip on his end of the stake with both leathery hands. "And everything gotta—" He didn't finish. Deboree had brought his free fist down, sudden and hard, and had chopped the stake in twain. Then, before the man could react, Deboree had turned abruptly away from him and swatted Stewart on the rump. The dog had yelped in surpirse and run beneath the barn.

It had been a dramatic and successful maneuver. Both hitchhikers were impressed. Before they could recover, Deboree had pointed across the yard with the jaggged end of his piece and told them, "There's the trail to Haight-Ashbury, guys. Vibe central."

"Come on, Bob," Blondboy had said, sneering at Deboree. "Let's hit it. Forget him. He's gangrened. Like Leary and Lennon. All those high-rolling creeps. Gangrened. A power tripper."

Blackbeard had looked at his end. It had broken off some inches shorter than Deboree's. He finally muttered, "Whatever's shakin'," and turned on his heel.

As he sauntered back the way he had come into the yard, he drew his knife. The blond boy hurried to take up his saunter beside his partner, already murmuring and giggling up to him. Blackbeard stripped a long curving sliver of wood from his end of the stick with the blade of his knife as he walked. Another sliver followed, fluttering, like a feather.

Devlin had stood, hands on his hips, watching the chips fall from the broken stick. He had glared after them with raw eyes until they were well off the property. That was when he hurried back up to his office to resume the search for his sunglasses.

Suggested Further Reading

Kesey, Ken. *Demon Box.* New York: Viking Press, 1986.
———. *Kesey's Garage Sale.* New York: Viking Press, 1973.
———. *One Flew Over the Cuckoo's Nest.* New York: Viking Press, 1962.
———. *Sometimes a Great Notion: A Novel.* New York: Viking Press, 1964.
Tanner, Stephen L. *Ken Kesey.* Boston: Twayne Publishers, 1983.

Epilogue

Terence O'Donnell
1924-

Terence O'Donnell was born in Oregon and educated at the University of Chicago. He lived many years in Iran, and wrote an eloquent account of his experiences in that country, *Garden of the Brave in War*. O'Donnell was also a member of the staff of the Oregon Historical Society, prepared the inscriptions on the Oregon Vietnam Memorial, and helped plan Portland's Pioneer Courthouse Square. In 1992 O'Donnell won the C.E.S. Wood Award of the Oregon Institute of Literary Arts for a distinguished career in letters.

He has written three books on Oregon history. *Portland: An Informal History and Guide* (written with Thomas Vaughan) is a brief history that includes directions for tours of the city. *An Arrow in the Earth: General Joel Palmer and the Indians of Oregon* is an account of the early Indian wars of Oregon. *That Balance So Rare: The Story of Oregon* (1988), from which the following selection is taken, is a compact, informative, and graceful account of the state's history.

A Time-Deep Land

As with any object held too close, the recent past is difficult to see, events in postwar Oregon still too near to be perceived with true perspective. Still, from the present vantage point, there are certain events and trends that would appear to be of permanent significance.

Oregon's economy continues to depend heavily on lumber and agriculture. o new industries, however, have broadened the economic base: electronics and tourism. Oregon is an ideal location for the former because the electronics industry is not dependent upon raw materials or close proximity to markets but, on the other hand, does require the skilled labor force Oregon can provide. Tourism, only recently thought of as an industry, has vastly increased since the war and is now the state's third largest source of revenue. Both electronics and tourism are fortunate new directions for the state's economy since neither threaten Oregon's most important resource after its people—the land on which they live.

Another departure is the state's new political complexion. For the first time in nearly a century, the Democrats came to be the majority party, though important offices continue to be held by Republicans. In part, this Democratic majority is due to the numbers of war workers who remained on to settle. It can also be attributed to the predominantly Democratic affiliation of the large influx of easterners from the 1950s through the 1970s. At the state level, political activity has been greatly concerned with environmental legislation, though with bipartisan support. As at the beginning of the century, when Oregon led the nation with the Oregon System of legislative reform, so in the area of environmental protection it has taken the lead with such citizen-supported measures as the Scenic Rivers Act, the Land Conservation and Development Commission (LCDC), and the Bottle Bill. The first settlers believed Oregon to be an Eden. Now, a century and a half later, their descendants appear determined to see that it remains so.

Driving down the roads of Oregon today, whether in the Valley, the interior, or the coast, and looking at the landscape and all the things so recently put upon it, it is easy to forget it all began more than ten thousand years ago when the land came to rest and humans arrived to live from it. Cruising the freeway hardly brings to mind those first one hundred centuries of native life, only in detail different from our own, at bottom the same: shelter, food, some ornament and myth, birth, growing, and decay. History, it is said, is a pageant,

a procession that never pauses, both the figures and the backdrops always changing. Thus, with the long, slow centuries of native life did the pageant of Oregon
begin.

Processions, though they never pause, do proceed at different rates—the
rate in history determined by the rate of change—and so it is that the pageant
of Oregon's history begins to quicken with the first appearance off the coast of
those great black-bodied birds, the ships of the explorers. Hezeta retiring,
disappointed, from the mouth of the Columbia; Gray, triumphant, crashing
through the breakers at the bar; Lewis and Clark, waterborne as well, celebrating Christmas with "Spoiled Pounded fish and a fiew roots."

The backdrop changes to Fort Vancouver and Dr. McLoughlin belaboring
his cane on someone's back or holding up that goblet of port to the sunlight,
while thirty miles along the Willamette the French Canadian trappers with
their Indian mates are sowing wheat and children. Enter the grave, dedicated
missionaries, their faces finally cast with bafflement and failure; followed by the
immigrants, "lank, lean and tough." They are best backdropped by the falls at
Oregon City where most of them arrived, or searching for claims in the mud of
the Oregon winter. Next, there is a confusion of gold and blood, Indian wars
and miners, and at the same time, someone burns down the statehouse, and
both Whigs and Democrats are hanged in effigy. Meanwhile, the general background of all of this—the long, green valley with its meander of river—is filling
up with houses, barns, churches, schoolhouses, taverns, shops, and here and
there a huddle of them, the largest huddle of all at the last bend of the
Willamette.

No sooner has one begun to take in all of this than the backdrop begins to
broaden. At the top appears a scene half plain, half sky, vast herds of cattle
moving through it, soon to dwindle as the green of grazing passes to the gold
of wheat, while at the bottom, little lighthouses go up at the ends of the head-
lands, and the natives lose their land and die.

For some time it has been a noisy pageant—laughter, gunfire, war whoops,
the intoning of sermons, a politician's blast, the cries of love and pain, ironshod
wheels on cobblestones—all in all a terrible racket. But now there comes a
sound that splits the air like the bugles of perdition, except it is a whistle. The
railroad has arrived.

From now on, the speed of the procession is such that one can hardly keep
up with it. Wheat pours down on Portland. New towns are built. A horde of
immigrants descends. The people capture the statehouse. Women get the vote.
The automobile appears. And before we know it, we are flying down the freeway, gazing out across this time-deep land where, as we sometimes forget, so
much has happened.

Suggested Further Reading

O'Donnell, Terence. *An Arrow in the Earth: General Joel Palmer and the Indians of Oregon.* Portland: Oregon Historical Society, 1991.

————. *That Balance So Rare: The Story of Oregon.* Portland: Oregon Historical Society Press, 1988.

————, and Thomas Vaughan. *Portland: A Historical Sketch and Guide.* Portland: Oregon Historical Society, 1976.

Bibliography

This bibliography is intended both to include and ω supplement the works in the "Suggested Further Reading" sections following each selection in this anthology. Because of the scope of the material in the volume, touching as it does upon almost every subject that has been treated in Oregon prose, no attempt has been made to be comprehensive. What is provided is simply a way to begin further explorations of various dimensions of the Oregon experience.

Cultural Life

Applegate, Shannon. *Skookum: An Oregon Pioneer Family's History and Lore*. New York: William Morrow, 1988.

Beckham, Stephen Dow. *Hathaway Jones: Tall Tales from Rogue River*. Bloomington: Indiana University Press, 1974. Reprinted as *Tall Tales from Rogue River: The Yarns of Hathaway Jones* by Oregon State University Press, 1991.

Bingham, Edwin R. *Charles Erskine Scott Wood*. Boise: Boise State University, 1990.

———. "Oregon's Romantic Rebels: John Reed and Charles Erskine Scott Wood," *Pacific Northwest Quarterly* 50:3 (July 1959).

———, and Glen A. Love, editors. *Northwest Perspectives: Essays on the Culture of the Pacific Northwest*. Seattle: University of Washington Press, 1979.

Bird, Gloria. *Full Moon on the Reservation*. New York: Greenfield Review Press Book, 1993.

Bolle, Sonja. "Katherine Dunn," *Publishers Weekly* (10 March 1989): 66-67.

Booth, Brian, editor. *Wildmen, Wobblies & Whistle Punks: Stewart Holbrook's Lowbrow Northwest*. Corvallis, OR: Oregon State University Press, 1992.

Bosker, Gideon, and Lena Lencek. *Frozen Music: A History of Portland Architecture*. Portland: Oregon Historical Society, 1985.

Bryant, Paul T. *H.L. Davis*. Boston: Twayne Publishers, 1978.

Case, Victoria. *A Finger in Every Pie*. Garden City, NY: Doubleday, 1963.

———. *Applesauce Needs Sugar*. Garden City, NY: Doubleday, 1960.

Chittick, Victor L.O., editor. *Northwest Harvest, A Regional Stocktaking*. New York: Macmillan Co., 1948.

Danielson, Linda. "Oregon Fiddling: The Missouri Connection," *Missouri Folklore Journal* (forthcoming).

Davis, H.L. *Beulah Land*. New York: William Morrow & Co., 1949.

———. *Kettle of Fire*. New York: William Morrow & Co., 1959.

———. *Team Bells Woke Me and Other Stories*. New York: William Morrow & Co., 1953.

DePreist, James. *This Precipice Garden*. Portland: University of Portland Press, 1987.

Dunn, Katherine. *Attic*. New York: Harper & Row, 1970.

———. *Geek Love*. New York: Alfred A. Knopf, 1989.

———. *Truck*. New York: Harper & Row, 1971.

Edwards, G. Thomas, and Carlos A. Schwantes, editors. *Experiences in a Promised Land: Essays in Pacific Northwest History*. Seattle: University of Washington Press, 1986.

Frost, O.W. *Joaquin Miller*. New York: Twayne Publishers, 1967.

Garson, Barbara. *Macbird!* Berkeley and New York: Grassy Knoll Press, 1966.

———. *The Dinosaur Door*, first produced off-Broadway at the Theatre for the New City, June 1976.

Helle, Anita. "Reading Women's Autobiographies: A Map of Reconstructed Knowing," in Nel Noddings and Carol Witherell, editors, *Stories Lives Tell: Narrative and Dialogue in Education*. New York: Teacher's College Press, 1991.

———. "The Odysseys of Mary Barnard," in Michael Strelow, editor, *An Anthology of Northwest Writing, 1900-1950*. Eugene: Northwest Review Books, 1981.

Jackson, Carlton. *Zane Grey*. Rev. ed. Boston: Twayne Publishers, 1989.

Jones, Suzi. *Oregon Folklore*. Eugene: University of Oregon Press, 1977.

Jones, Nard. *Oregon Detour*. New York: Payson & Clarke, 1930. Reprinted by Oregon State University Press, 1990.

Josephy, Alvin M., Jr. *The Patriot Chiefs: A Chronicle of American Indian Leadership*. New York: Viking Press, 1961.

Karbo, Karen. *The Diamond Lane*. New York: G.P. Putnam's Sons, 1991.

———. *Trespassers Welcome Here*. New York: G.P. Putnam's Sons, 1989.

Kesey, Ken. *Demon Box*. New York: Viking Press, 1986.

———. *Kesey's Garage Sale*. New York: Viking Press, 1973.

———. *One Flew Over the Cuckoo's Nest*. New York: Viking Press, 1962.

———. *Sometimes a Great Notion: A Novel*. New York: Viking Press, 1964.

Lampman, Ben Hur. *At the End of the Car Line*. Portland: Binfords & Mort, 1942.

———. *How Could I Be Forgetting?* Portland: W.W.R. May, 1926.

———. *The Coming of the Pond Fishes*. Portland: Binfords & Mort, 1946.

———. *"Where Would You Go?" Exploring the Seasons with Ben Hur Lampman*. Boise: R.O. Beatty and Associates, 1975.

Le Guin, Ursula K. *Dancing at the Edge of the World: Thoughts on Words, Women, Places*. New York: Grove Press, 1989.

Love, Glen A. *Don Berry*. Boise: Boise State University, 1978.

Lucia, Ellis, editor. *This Land Around Us: A Treasury of Pacific Northwest Writing*. Garden City: Doubleday & Co.,1969.

Martin, Jim. *A Bit of Blue: The Life and Works of Frances Fuller Victor*. Salem: Deep Well Publishing Co., 1992.

Miller, Joaquin. *Songs of the Sierras*. London: Longman, Green, Reader, & Dyer, 1871.

———. *True Bear Stories*. Chicago and New York: Rand, McNally & Co., 1900.

Monroe, Anne Shannon. *Happy Valley: A Story of Oregon*. Chicago: A.C. McClurg & Co., 1916. Reprinted by Oregon State University Press, 1991.

———. *Sparks from Home Fires*. New York: Doubleday, Doran & Co., 1940.

Nash, Lee M. "Scott of the *Oregonian*: The Editor as Historian," *Oregon Historical Quarterly* 70 (1969): 197-232.

Peterson, Martin S. *Joaquin Miller, Literary Frontiersman*. Palo Alto: Stanford University Press, 1937.

Robbins, William G., Robert J. Frank, and Richard E. Ross, editors. *Regionalism and the Pacific Northwest*. Corvallis: Oregon State University Press, 1983.

Ross, Nancy Wilson. *Three Ways of Ancient Wisdom: Hinduism, Buddhism, Zen, and Their Significance for the West*. New York: Simon & Schuster, 1966.

———. *Westward the Women*. New York: Alfred A. Knopf, 1944.

Scott, Harvey W. *History of the Oregon Country*. Leslie M. Scott, compiler. Cambridge: The Riverside Press, 1924.

Stanley, Susan. "How Three Families Live Together," in J. Savells and L.J. Cross, editors, *The Changing Family*. New York: Holt, Rinehart & Winston, 1987.

Stevens, James. *Paul Bunyan*. New York: A.A. Knopf, 1948. (Originally published 1925.)

———. *Timber! The Way of Life in the Lumber Camps*. Evanston: Row Peterson & Co., 1942.

————, and H.L. Davis. *Status Rerum: A Manifesto, upon the Present Condition of Northwestern Literature: Containing Several Near-Libelous Utterances, upon Persons in the Public Eye*. The Dalles: private printing, 1927.

Swanson, Kimberly. "Eva Emery Dye and the Romance of Oregon History," *Pacific Historian* 29 (1985): 59-68.

Tanner, Stephen L. *Ken Kesey*. Boston: Twayne Publishers, 1983.

Venn, George. *Marking the Magic Circle: Poetry, Fiction and Essays*. Corvallis: Oregon State University Press, 1987.

————. *Off the Main Road: Poems by George Venn*. Portland: Prescott Street Press, 1978.

Williams, Vivian. *169 Brand New Old Time Fiddle Tunes*. Vol. 3. Seattle: Voyager Publications, 1990.

Wood, C.E.S. *Heavenly Discourse*. New York: Vanguard, 1927.

————. *The Poet in the Desert*. Portland: F.W. Baltes, 1915. Reprinted by Vanguard, New York, 1929.

Woody, Elizabeth. *Hand into Stone*. New York: Contact II Publications, 1988.

Economic Life

Berry, Don. *A Majority of Scoundrels: An Informal History of the Rocky Mountain Fur Company*. New York: Harper, 1961.

Corning, Howard McKinley. *Willamette Landings: Ghost Towns of the River*. 2nd ed. Portland: Oregon Historical Society, 1973.

Cox, Thomas R. *Mills and Markets: A History of the Pacific Coast Lumber Industry to 1900*. Seattle: University of Washington Press, 1974.

Davidson, Gordon. *The North West Company*. New York: Russell & Russell, 1967.

Dodds, Gordon B. *The Salmon King of Oregon: R.D. Hume and the Pacific Fisheries*. Chapel Hill: University of North Carolina Press, 1959.

————, and Craig E. Wollner. *The Silicon Forest: High Tech in the Portland Area, 1975-1986*. Portland: Oregon Historical Society, 1990.

French, Giles. *Cattle Country of Peter French*. Portland: Binfords & Mort, 1964.

Garson, Barbara. *All the Livelong Day: The Meaning and Demeaning of Routine Work*. Garden City, NY: Doubleday & Co.,1975.

Holbrook, Stewart. *Holy Old Mackinaw: A Natural History of the American Lumberjack*. New York: MacMillan Co., 1946. Reprinted by Comstock Editions, Sausalito, 1979.

Johansen, Dorothy O., editor. *Robert Newell's Memoranda*. Portland: Champoeg Press, 1959.

Kesselman, Amy. *Fleeting Opportunities: Women Shipyard Workers in Portland and Vancouver during World War II and Reconversion*. Albany: State University of New York Press, 1990.

Lee, Marshall M. *Winning with People: The First Forty Years of Tektronix*. Beaverton, OR: Tektronix, 1986.

Lucia, Ellis. *Head Rig: Story of the West Coast Lumber Industry*. Portland: Overland West Press, 1965.

Martin, Albro. *James J. Hill and the Opening of the Northwest*. New York: Oxford University Press, 1976.

Monroe, Anne Shannon. *Feelin' Fine! Bill Hanley's Book*. Garden City, NY: Doubleday, Doran & Co., 1930.

Oliphant, James Orin. *On the Cattle Ranges of the Oregon Country*. Seattle: University of Washington Press, 1968.

Pratt, Alice Day. *A Homesteader's Portfolio*. New York: MacMillan Co., 1922. Reprinted by Oregon State University Press, 1993.

Rich, Edwin Ernest. *The History of the Hudson's Bay Company, 1670-1870*. 3 vols. London: Hudson's Bay Record Society, 1958-59.

Robbins, William G. *Hard Times in Paradise: Coos Bay, Oregon, 1850-1986*. Seattle: University of Washington Press, 1988.

———. *Lumberjacks and Legislators: Political Economy of the U.S. Lumber Industry, 1890-1941*. College Station, TX: Texas A & M University Press, 1982.

Ronda, James P. *Astoria and Empire*. Lincoln: University of Nebraska Press, 1990.

Stevens, James. *Timber! The Way of Life in the Lumber Camps*. Evanston: Row Peterson & Co., 1942.

Throckmorton, Arthur L. *Oregon Argonauts: Merchant Adventurers on the Western Frontier*. Portland: Oregon Historical Society, 1961.

Tuhy, John E. *Sam Hill: The Prince of Castle Nowhere*. Portland: Timber Press, 1983.

Tyler, Robert L. *Rebels of the Woods: The IWW in the Pacific Northwest*. Eugene: University of Oregon Books, 1967.

Victor, Frances Fuller. *The River of the West*. San Francisco: R.J. Trumbull & Co., 1870.

Winther, Oscar O. *The Old Oregon Country: A History of Frontier Trade, Transportation, and Travel*. Palo Alto: Stanford University Press, 1950.

Wollner, Craig E. *Electrifying Eden: Portland General Electric, 1889-1965*. Portland: Oregon Historical Society, 1990.

———. *The City Builders: One Hundred Years of Union Carpentry in Portland, Oregon, 1883-1983*. Portland: Oregon Historical Society, 1990.

Exploration

Anderson, Bern. *Surveyor of the Sea: The Life and Voyages of Captain George Vancouver*. Seattle: University of Washington Press, 1960.

Beaglehole, J.C. *The Life of Captain James Cook*. Stanford: Stanford University Press, 1974.

Beals, Herbert K., editor. *Juan Perez on the Northwest Coast: Six Documents of His Expedition in 1774*. Portland: Oregon Historical Society, 1989.

Campbell, Marjorie W. *The North West Company*. Toronto: MacMillan of Canada, 1957.

Cook, Warren L. *Flood Tide of Empire: Spain and the Pacific Northwest, 1543-1819*. New Haven: Yale University Press, 1973.

Dye, Eva Emery. *The Conquest: The True Story of Lewis and Clark*. Garden City, NY: Doubleday, 1902.

Howay, F.W., editor. *Voyages of the "Columbia" to the Northwest Coast, 1787-1790 and 1790-1793*. Boston: Massachusetts Historical Society, 1941.

Moulton, Gary E., editor. *The Journals of the Lewis and Clark Expedition*. 8 vols. to date. Lincoln: University of Nebraska Press, 1983- .

General Histories of Oregon and the Pacific Northwest

Bancroft, Hubert Howe. *History of Oregon, 1834-1848. The Works of Hubert Howe Bancroft*. Vol. 29. San Francisco: The History Company, 1886.

———. *History of Oregon, 1848-1888. The Works of Hubert Howe Bancroft*. Vol. 30. San Francisco: The History Company, 1888.

Clark, Malcolm, Jr. *Eden Seekers: The Settlement of Oregon, 1818-1862*. Boston: Houghton Mifflin Co., 1981.

Dodds, Gordon B. *Oregon: A Bicentennial History*. New York and Nashville: W.W. Norton & Co., and American Association for State and Local History, 1977.

Dye, Eva Emery. *Stories of Oregon*. San Francisco: The Whitaker & Ray Co., 1900.

Holbrook, Stewart. *Far Corner, A Personal View of the Pacific Northwest*. New York: MacMillan Co., 1952. Reprinted by Comstock Editions, Sausalito, 1987.

———. *The Columbia*. New York: Rinehart & Co., 1956. Reprinted by Comstock Editions, Sausalito, 1991.

Johansen, Dorothy O. *Empire of the Columbia: A History of the Pacific Northwest.* (With Charles M. Gates.) 2nd ed. New York: Harper & Row, 1967.

Lavender, David S. *Land of Giants: The Drive to the Pacific Northwest, 1750-1950.* Garden City, NY: Doubleday, 1958.

O'Donnell, Terence. *That Balance So Rare: The Story of Oregon.* Portland: Oregon Historical Society, 1988.

Pomeroy, Earl S. *The Pacific Slope: A History of California, Oregon, Washington, Idaho, Utah, and Nevada.* New York: Alfred A. Knopf, 1965.

Tisdale, Sallie. *Stepping Westward: The Long Search for Home in the Pacific Northwest.* New York: Henry Holt & Co., 1991.

Geography

Bowen, William A. *The Willamette Valley: Migration and Settlement on the Oregon Frontier.* Seattle: University of Washington Press, 1978.

Dicken, Emily F., and Samuel Newton Dicken. *Two Centuries of Oregon Geography.* 2 vols. Portland: Oregon Historical Society, 1979-82.

Meinig, Donald W. *The Great Columbia Plain: A Historical Geography, 1805-1910.* Seattle: University of Washington Press, 1968.

Guide Books

Federal Writers' Project. *Oregon, End of the Trail. American Guide Series.* Portland: Binford & Mort, 1951.

Historical Novels

Berry, Don. *Trask.* New York: Viking, 1960.

Case, Victoria. *The Quiet Life of Mrs. General Lane.* Garden City, NY: Doubleday, 1952.

Davis, H.L. *Honey in the Horn.* New York: Harper & Brothers, 1935.

Duniway, Abigail Scott. *Captain Gray's Company, or Crossing the Plains and Living in Oregon.* Portland: S.J. McCormick, 1859.

————. *From the West to the West: Across the Plains to Oregon.* Chicago: A.C. McClurg, 1905.

Dye, Eva Emery. *McLoughlin and Old Oregon: A Chronicle.* Chicago: A.C. McClurg, 1900.

————. *Stories of Oregon.* San Francisco: The Whitaker & Ray Co., 1900.

————. *The Conquest: The True Story of Lewis and Clark.* Garden City, NY: Doubleday, 1902.

Le Guin, Ursula K. *Searoad: Chronicles of Klatsand.* New York: HarperCollins, 1991.

————. *The Lathe of Heaven.* New York: Avon, 1973.

Missionaries and Religion

Brosnan, Cornelius James. *Jason Lee, Prophet of the New Oregon.* New York: Macmillan Co., 1932.

Jeffrey, Julie. *Converting the West: A Biography of Narcissa Whitman.* Norman: University of Oklahoma Press, 1991.

Loewenberg, Robert J. *Equality on the Oregon Frontier: Jason Lee and the Methodist Mission, 1834-1843.* Seattle: University of Washington Press, 1976.

Schoenberg, Wilfred P. *A History of the Catholic Church in the Pacific Northwest, 1743-1983.* Washington, DC: The Pastoral Press, 1987.

Nature

Douglas, William O. *My Wilderness: The Pacific Northwest.* New York: Doubleday & Co., 1960. Reprinted by Comstock Editions, Sausalito, 1989.

Drake, Barbara. *Bees in Wet Weather*. Traverse City, MI: Canoe Press, 1992.

———. *Love at the Egyptian Theatre*. East Lansing, MI: Red Cedar Press, 1978.

———. *What We Say to Strangers*. Portland: Breitenbush Books, 1986.

Grey, Zane. *Tales of Fresh Water Fishing*. New York: Harper, 1928.

Haig-Brown, Roderick. *A River Never Sleeps*. New York: Morrow, 1946.

———. *Return to the River: The Story of the Chinook Run*. New York: Morrow, 1941.

———. *The Western Angler: An Account of Pacific Salmon and Western Trout*. 2 vols. New York: Derrydale Press, 1939.

Hyde, Dayton O. *Yamsi*. New York: The Dial Press, 1971.

Johnson, David. *The Tufted Puffins*. Bandon: Bandon Historical Society, 1979.

Kittredge, William. *Owning It All*. St. Paul: Graywolf Press, 1987.

Leonard, Larry. *Far Walker*. Portland: Breitenbush Books, 1988.

———. *Sturgeon Fishing*. Portland: Frank Amato, 1986.

———. *The Meanest Fish on Earth*. Portland: Frank Amato, 1984.

Lopez, Barry. *Arctic Dreams: Imagination and Desire in a Northern Landscape*. New York: Scribner, 1986.

———. *Desert Notes: Reflections in the Eye of a Raven*. Kansas City, KS: Sheed, Andrews & McNeel, 1976.

———. *Of Wolves and Men*. New York: Scribner, 1978.

Stafford, Kim. (with Gary Braasch) *Entering the Grove*. Layton, UT: Gibbs Smith Publisher, 1990.

———. *Having Everything Right: Essays of Place*. Lewiston, ID: Confluence Press, 1986.

———. *Lochsa Road: A Pilgrim in the West*. Lewiston, ID: Confluence Press, 1991.

Sullivan, William L. *Looking for Coyote*. New York: Henry Holt & Co., 1988.

Wallace, David Rains. *The Klamath Knot: Explorations of Myth and Evolution*. San Francisco: Sierra Club Books, 1983.

Oregon Trail

Faragher, John Mack. *Women and Men on the Overland Trail*. New Haven: Yale University Press, 1979.

Unruh, John D. *The Plains Across: The Overland Emigrants and the Trans-Mississippi West*. Urbana: University of Illinois Press, 1979.

Peoples of Oregon

Barlow, Jeffrey G., and Christine A. Richardson. *China Doctor of John Day*. Portland: Binford & Mort, 1979.

———. *Gum San: Land of the Gold Mountain*. Bend, OR: The High Desert Museum, 1991.

Beal, Merrill D. *"I Will Fight No More Forever": Chief Joseph and the Nez Perce War*. Seattle: University of Washington Press, 1963.

Beckham, Stephen Dow. *Requiem for a People: The Rogue Indians and the Frontiersmen*. Norman: University of Oklahoma Press, 1971.

———. *The Indians of Western Oregon: This Land Was Theirs*. Coos Bay, OR: Arago Books, 1977.

Bogle, Kathryn Hall. "An American Negro Speaks of Color," (Portland) *Sunday Oregonian*, 14 February 1937, p. 16. Reprinted in *Oregon Historical Quarterly* 89 (Spring 1988): 70-73, 78-81.

Buan, Carolyn M., and Richard Lewis, editors. *The First Oregonians: An Illustrated Collection of Essays on Traditional Lifeways, Federal-Indian Relations, and the State's Native People Today*. Portland: Oregon Council for the Humanities, 1991.

Commission on Wartime Relocation and Internment of Civilians. *Personal Justice Denied.* Washington, DC: U.S. Government Printing Office, 1982.

Cressman, Luther S. *The Sandal and the Cave.* Portland: Champoeg Press, 1964. Reprinted by Oregon State University Press, 1981.

Daniels, Roger. *Concentration Camps USA: Japanese Americans and World War II.* Hinsdale, IL: Dryden Press, 1971.

Gamboa, Erasmo. "Braceros in the Pacific Northwest: Laborers on the Domestic Front, 1942-1947," *Pacific Historical Review* 56 (August 1987): 378-398.

———. *Mexican Labor and World War II: Braceros in the Pacific Northwest.* Austin: University of Texas Press, 1990.

———. "Mexican Mule Packers and Oregon's Second Regiment Mounted Volunteers, 1855-1856," *Oregon Historical Quarterly* 92 (Spring 1991): 41-59.

———. "Oregon's Hispanic Heritage," *Oregon Humanities* (Summer 1992): 3-7.

Harmon, Rick. "Interview: Kathryn Hall Bogle on the Writing of 'An American Negro Speaks of Color'," *Oregon Historical Quarterly* 89 (1988): 82-91.

Ho, Nelson Chia-Chi. *Portland's Chinatown: The History of an Urban Ethnic District.* Portland: Portland Bureau of Planning, 1978.

Howard, Oliver O. *Famous Indian Chiefs I Have Known.* New York: The Century Co., 1908.

———. *My Life and Experiences Among Our Hostile Indians.* Hartford: A.D. Worthington & Co., 1907.

———. *Nez Perce Joseph.* Boston: Lee and Shepard Publishers, 1881.

Ito, Kazuo. *Issei: A History of Japanese Immigrants in North America.* Seattle: Japanese Community Service, 1973.

Josephy, Alvin M., Jr., *The Nez Perce Indians and the Opening of the Northwest.* New Haven: Yale University Press, 1965.

Lerner, Andrea, editor. *Dancing on the Rim of the World: An Anthology of Contemporary Northwest Native American Writing.* Tucson: University of Arizona Press, 1990.

Lowenstein, Steven. *The Jews of Oregon, 1850-1950.* Portland: Jewish Historical Society of Oregon, 1987.

Maves, Norm, Jr. "Kathryn Bogle," (Portland) *Oregonian*, 10 September 1989, Section 6, p. 1.

McLagan, Elizabeth. *A Peculiar Paradise: A History of Blacks in Oregon, 1788-1940.* Portland: The Georgian Press, 1980.

Meacham, Alfred. *Wigwam and War-Path; or, the Royal Chief in Chains.* Boston: J.R. Dale & Co., 1875.

———. *Wi-ne-ma (the Woman Chief) and Her People.* Hartford: American Publishing Co., 1876.

Miller, Joaquin. *Life Amongst the Modocs: Unwritten History.* London: Richard Bentley & Sons, 1873.

Murray, Keith. *The Modocs and Their War.* Norman: University of Oklahoma Press, 1959.

Oregon Lung Association. *Notable Women in the History of Oregon.* Portland: n.p., 1982.

Ramsey, Jarold, compiler and editor. *Coyote Was Going There: Indian Literature of the Oregon Country.* Seattle and London: University of Washington Press, 1977.

Riddle, Jeff. *The Indian History of the Modoc War and the Causes That Led to It.* San Francisco: Marnell & Co., 1914.

Ruby, Robert H., and John A. Brown. *Indians of the Pacific Northwest: A History.* Norman: University of Oklahoma Press, 1981.

———. *The Chinook Indians: Traders of the Lower Columbia River.* Norman: University of Oklahoma Press, 1976.

Stern, Theodore. *The Klamath Tribe: A People and Their Reservation*. Seattle: University of Washington Press, 1965.

Tateishi, John, editor. *And Justice for All: An Oral History of the Japanese American Detention Camps*. New York: Random House, 1984.

Toll, William. *The Making of an Ethnic Middle Class: Portland Jewry Over Four Generations*. Albany, NY: State University of New York Press, 1982.

Wilfong, Cheryl. *Following the Nez Perce Trail: A Guide to the Nee-Me-Poo National Historic Trail with Eyewitness Accounts*. Corvallis, OR: Oregon State University Press, 1990.

Yasui, Barbara. "The Nikkei in Oregon, 1834-1940," *Oregon Historical Quarterly* 76 (1975): 225-257.

Politics

Abell, Ron. "On the Tiger's Anniversary: He Gave Politics a Good Name," *Oregon Magazine* (October 1980): 44-46.

Bone, Arthur H., editor. *Oregon Cattleman/Governor/Congressman: Memoirs and Times of Walter M. Pierce*. Portland, Oregon Historical Society, 1981.

Buan, Carolyn M., editor. *The First Duty: A History of the U.S. District Court for Oregon*. Portland: U.S. District Court of Oregon Historical Society, 1993.

Burton, Robert E. *Democrats of Oregon: The Pattern of Minority Politics, 1900-1956*. Eugene: University of Oregon Books, 1970.

Douglas, William O. *Go East, Young Man: The Early Years. The Autobiography of William O. Douglas*. New York: Random House, 1974.

———. *The Court Years: The Autobiography of William O. Douglas*. New York: Random House, 1980.

Duniway, Abigail Scott. *Path Breaking: An Autobiographical History of the Equal Suffrage Movement in Pacific Coast States*. Portland: James, Kerns & Abbott, 1914. Reprint: New York: Schocken Books, 1971.

Edwards, G. Thomas. *Sowing Good Seeds: The Northwest Suffrage Campaigns of Susan B. Anthony*. Portland: Oregon Historical Society, 1990.

Hendrickson, James E. *Joe Lane of Oregon: Machine Politics and the Sectional Crisis, 1849-1861*. New Haven: Yale University Press, 1967.

Johannsen, Robert W. *Frontier Politics and the Sectional Conflict: The Pacific Northwest on the Eve of the Civil War*. Seattle: University of Washington Press, 1955.

Johnson, David Alan. *Founding the Far West: California, Oregon, and Nevada, 1840-1890*. Berkeley and Los Angeles: University of California Press, 1992.

Moynihan, Ruth Barnes. *Rebel for Rights: Abigail Scott Duniway*. New Haven and London: Yale University Press, 1983.

Neal, Steve. *McNary of Oregon: A Political Biography*. Portland: Oregon Historical Society, 1985.

Neuberger, Richard. *Adventures in Politics: We Go to the Legislature*. New York: Oxford University Press, 1954.

———. *Our Promised Land*. New York: Macmillan Co., 1938.

———. *They Never Go Back to Pocatello: The Selected Essays of Richard Neuberger*. Steve Neal, editor. Portland: Oregon Historical Society, 1988.

O'Donnell, Terence. *An Arrow in the Earth: General Joel Palmer and the Indians of Oregon*. Portland: Oregon Historical Society, 1991.

Schafer, Joseph. "Jesse Applegate: Pioneer, Statesman, and Philosopher," *Washington Historical Quarterly* 7 (1907): 217-233.

Simon, James F. *Independent Journey: The Life of William O. Douglas*. New York: Harper & Row, 1980.

Smith, A. Robert. *The Tiger in the Senate: The Biography of Wayne Morse*. Garden City, NY: Doubleday, 1962.

Victor, Frances Fuller. *The Early Indian Wars of Oregon*. Salem: F.C. Baker, 1894.

———. *The Women's War with Whisky*. Portland: Geo. H. Himes, 1874.

Reference Works

Corning, Howard M., editor. *Dictionary of Oregon History*. Portland: Binfords & Mort, 1956.

Jackson, Philip, and A. Jon Kimerling, editors. *Atlas of the Pacific Northwest*. 8th edition. Corvallis: Oregon State University Press, 1993.

McArthur, Lewis A. *Oregon Geographic Names*. 6th edition. Portland: Oregon Historical Society, 1992.

Turnbull, George S. *History of Oregon Newspapers*. Portland: Binford & Mort, 1939.

Zucker, Jeff, Kay Hummel, and Bob Høgfoss. *Oregon Indians: Culture, History & Current Affairs: An Atlas & Introduction*. Portland: Oregon Historical Society, 1983.

Science and Medicine

Clark, Robert D. *The Odyssey of Thomas Condon: Irish Immigrant, Frontier Missionary, Oregon Geologist*. Portland: Oregon Historical Society, 1989.

Condon, Thomas. *The Two Islands and What Came of Them*. Portland: The J.K. Gill Co., 1902.

Larsell, Olof. *The Doctor in Oregon: A Medical History*. Portland: Binfords & Mort, 1947.

Stanley, Susan. *Maternity Ward: A Behind the Scenes Look at a Big City Hospital*. New York: William Morrow & Co., 1992.

Tisdale, Sallie. *Harvest Moon: Portrait of a Nursing Home*. New York: Henry Holt & Co., 1987.

———. *The Sorcerer's Apprentice: Tales of the Modern Hospital*. New York: McGraw-Hill, 1986.

Urban History

Abbott, Carl. *The Great Experiment: Portland and the Lewis and Clark Exposition*. Portland: Oregon Historical Society, 1981.

———. *Portland: Gateway to the Northwest*. Northridge, CA: Windsor Publications, 1985.

———. *Portland: Planning, Politics, and Growth in a Twentieth-Century City*. Lincoln: University of Nebraska Press, 1983.

Bailey, Barbara Ruth. *Main Street, Northeastern Oregon: The Founding and Development of Small Towns*. Portland: Oregon Historical Society, 1982.

Maben, Manly. *Vanport*. Portland: Oregon Historical Society, 1987.

MacColl, E. Kimbark. *The Shaping of a City: Business and Politics in Portland, Oregon, 1885-1915*. Portland: The Georgian Press, 1976.

———. *The Growth of a City: Portland, 1915-1950*. Portland: The Georgian Press, 1979.

———, with Harry H. Stein. *Merchants, Money, and Power: The Portland Establishment, 1843-1913*. Portland: The Georgian Press, 1988.

Snyder, Eugene. *Early Portland: Stump-Town Triumphant*. Portland: Binfords & Mort, 1970.

Vaughan, Thomas, and Terence O'Donnell. *Portland: A Historical Sketch and Guide*. Portland: Oregon Historical Society, 1976.

Copyright Acknowledgments

TEXTS

Applegate, Jesse, "A Day with the Cow Column" from *A Day with the Cow Column in 1843* by Jesse Applegate. Champoeg Press, 1952. Copyright © 1952 by Champoeg Press. Used by permission of Champoeg Press.

Applegate, Shannon, "The Marrow" from *Skookum: An Oregon Pioneer Family's History and Lore.*Copyright © 1988 by Shannon Applegate. By permission of William Morrow and Company Inc.

Barlow, Jeffrey G., and Christine A. Richardson, "China Doctor of John Day" from *China Doctor of John Day* by Jeffrey Barlow and Christine Richardson. Portland: Binford & Mort, 1979. Copyright © 1979 by Binford & Mort. Used by permission of Binford & Mort.

Beckham, Stephen Dow, "Requiem for a People" from *Requiem for a People: The Rogue Indians and the Frontiersmen* by Stephen Dow Beckham. Copyright © 1971 by the University of Oklahoma Press.

Berry, Don, "Snapshots of My Daughter Turning." Copyright © 1984 by Don Berry. Used by permission of the author.

Bogle, Kathryn Hall, "An American Negro Speaks of Color" from *Oregon Historical Quarterly* 89, Spring 1988. Copyright © 1988 by Oregon Historical Society Press. Used by permission of Oregon Historical Society Press.

Chinook Indians, "The First European Ship Comes to Clatsop County" from *Coyote Was Going There: Indian Literature of the Oregon Country*, edited by Jarold Ramsey. Seattle: University of Washington Press, 1977. Copyright © 1977 by University of Washington Press. Used by permission of University of Washington Press.

Danielson, Linda, "Fiddling." Copyright © 1977 by Linda Danielson. Used by permission of Randall V. Mills Archives of Northwest Folklore.

Davis, H.L., "Oregon" from *Kettle of Fire* by H.L. Davis. Copyright © 1959 by H.L. Davis. By permission of William Morrow and Company, Inc.

DePreist, James, "Missiles and Mozart" from *Oregon Symphony Magazine*, June-July 1985. Copyright © 1985 by James DePreist. Used by permission of the author.

Douglas, William O., "Hart Mountain" from *My Wilderness: The Pacific Northwest* by William O. Douglas. Reprinted by permission of William Morris Agency on behalf of the author. Copyright © 1960 by William O. Douglas.

Drake, Barbara, "Birth of a Lamb" from (Portland) *Sunday Oregonian, Northwest Magazine,* 6 May, 1990. Reprinted by permission of the author.

Dunn, Katherine, "Why I Live in Portland" from *Pacific Northwest Magazine*, January 1989. Copyright © 1989 by Katherine Dunn. Used by permission of the author.

Fairley, Deborah, "Glory Days" first published in *Oregon*, May-June 1988. Copyright © 1988 by Deborah Fairley. Used by permission of the author.

Gamboa, Erasmo, "Oregon's Hispanic Heritage" reprinted from *Oregon Humanities*, Summer 1992. Copyright © 1992 by Erasmo Gamboa. *Oregon Humanities* is published by the Oregon Council for the Humanities. Used by permission of the author.

"Be-bop, Portland, December 30, 1949," photograph by Al Monner, on page 113. Courtesy of the Oregon Historical Society, negative OrHi38668.

"Japanese Internment Camp, Heart Mountain, Wyoming," photographer unknown, on page 130. Courtesy of the Oregon Historical Society, negative OrHi44601.

Petroglyph cast stone document from Columbia River on page 139. Reproduced by permission of Hansen Studio.

"Carlos Martinez and Rosendo Patlan at Dayton FSA camp, Mexican Independence Day," photographer unknown, on page 148. Courtesy of the Oregon Historical Society, negative OrHi61736.

"John Day River" by Ken Paul on page 159. Screenprint, 1983. Reproduced courtesy of the Portland Art Museum, Vivian and Gordon Gilkey Collection.

"Mirror Room" by George Johanson on page 179. Relief intaglio, 1987. Reproduced courtesy of the Portland Art Museum, Vivian and Gordon Gilkey Collection.

"The Audition" by Kevin Fletcher on page 193. Woodcut. Reproduced courtesy of the Portland Art Museum, Vivian and Gordon Gilkey Collection.

"Can Filling and Sealing Room" from *Salmon of the Pacific Coast* by Robert D. Hume on page 206. Wood engraving. From the Beckham Collection, courtesy of Stephen Dow Beckham.

"William Hanley, 'the King of Eastern Oregon,' rides with his cattle on the Bell A Ranch in Harney County," photographer unknown, on page 219. Courtesy of the Oregon Historical Society, negative OrHi62367.

"Portland Directory, 1878," artist unknown on page 232. Courtesy of the Oregon Historical Society, negative OrHi89097.

"The Studio" by Jennifer Guske on page 259. Linocut, 1991. Reproduced courtesy of the Portland Art Museum, Vivian and Gordon Gilkey Collection.

"Untitled" by Molia Jensen on page 268. Dry point etching, 1989. Reproduced courtesy of the Portland Art Museum, Vivian and Gordon Gilkey Collection.

"Two Books" by Liza Jones on page 284. Etching, 1983. Reproduced courtesy of the Portland Art Museum, Vivian and Gordon Gilkey Collection.

"Ing Hay" and "Lung On," photographer unknown, on page 297. Courtesy of the Oregon Historical Society, negatives OrHi26468 and OrHi53840.

"Cumulus, Still Life, Bread" by James McGarrell on page 308. Lithograph. Reproduced courtesy of the Portland Art Museum, Vivian and Gordon Gilkey Collection.

AUTHOR PHOTOGRAPHS

The Oregon Council of Teachers of English and the Oregon State University Press would like to thank the following for providing photographs of authors and for permission to reproduce them: Linda Danielson, photograph © Cliff Coles 1993; Katherine Dunn, photograph by Skip Williams; William Kittredge, photograph by Mel Buffington; Ursula K. Le Guin, 1990, photograph by Marian Wood Kolisch; Barry Lopez, photograph by Richard Feldman; Don Berry, photograph by Peter Fromm; Ken Kesey, photograph by Mel Buffington; Minoru Yasui, photograph courtesy of Holly Yasui; Erasmo Gamboa, © 1992 Erasmo Gamboa, University of Washington; Alice Day Pratt, credit to Bowman Museum, Crook County Historical Society; Roderick Haig-Brown, photograph courtesy Valerie Haig-Brown; George Venn photograph by Jan Boles.

The following photographs of authors were provided courtesy of the Oregon Historical Society: Eva Emery Dye, negative CN021678; portrait of Chief Joseph taken during Spokane Industrial Exposition, October 1899, negative OrHi26126; portrait of C.E.S. Wood by William E. Dassonville, 1920, negative CN 021696; Jeff Riddle, negative OrHi89093; James

Stevens, negative OrHi27739; H.L. Davis, negative OrHi27399; Beatrice Cannady, photograph by Portland Studio, 1929, negative CN011493; Richard Neuberger, 1938, negative CN009748; Thomas Condon, photograph by Joseph Buchtel, negative OrHi55652; William O. Douglas, negative CN005261; Anne Shannon Monroe, negative OrHi88284; Ben Hur Lampman, negative Oregonian 5393; Jesse Applegate, negative OrHi044; Harvey W. Scott, negative CN003452; Asahel Bush, negative CN000420; Abigail Scott Duniway, negative OrHi37312; Frances Fuller Victor, negative OrHi5463; Dorothy O. Johansen, negative CN011378; Ronald G. Callvert, negative CN001256; Wayne Morse, negative CN013763; Terence O'Donnell, negative OrHi83078.

The following photographs were provided by the authors: Stephen Dow Beckham, Barbara Drake, Shannon Applegate, Kim Stafford, James DePreist, David Johnson, William Hilliard, Deborah Fairley

Thanks to John Turley for the drawing of H. L. Davis.

Index